REDISCOVERED DUNDEE

REDISCOVERED DUNDEE

Brian King

Copyright © 2020 Brian King

The moral right of the author has been asserted.

Apart from any fair dealing for the purposes of research or private study, or criticism or review, as permitted under the Copyright, Designs and Patents Act 1988, this publication may only be reproduced, stored or transmitted, in any form or by any means, with the prior permission in writing of the publishers, or in the case of reprographic reproduction in accordance with the terms of licences issued by the Copyright Licensing Agency. Enquiries concerning reproduction outside those terms should be sent to the publishers.

Matador
9 Priory Business Park,
Wistow Road, Kibworth Beauchamp,
Leicestershire. LE8 0RX
Tel: 0116 279 2299
Email: books@troubador.co.uk
Web: www.troubador.co.uk/matador
Twitter: @matadorbooks

ISBN 978 183859 192 2

British Library Cataloguing in Publication Data.
A catalogue record for this book is available from the British Library.

Printed and bound by CPI Group (UK) Ltd, Croydon, CR0 4YY
Typeset in 11pt Adobe Garamond Pro by Troubador Publishing Ltd, Leicester, UK

Matador is an imprint of Troubador Publishing Ltd

For my sister Maureen and all
my family in Dundee

Contents

	Introduction	ix
1	Arrival	1
2	Music Hall Days	28
3	Relics	55
4	The Passing Show	79
5	Modern Myths	102
6	Our American Cousins	130
7	The Sporting Life	160
8	Ordinary Dundonians?	190

Introduction

In September 1844, Queen Victoria and her consort, Prince Albert, arrived at Dundee docks. A temporary wooden arch was erected for the occasion and in commemoration of their visit a permanent decorative stone arch was constructed a few years later. It might have been thought that this structure would, in common with the triumphal arches that have been constructed around the world since Roman times, become a treasured monument and immune to developments around it – but after standing for more than a century, Dundee's Royal Arch was demolished.

Whatever differing views might have been taken of its architectural merit, or whatever criticism might have been made (as with all such structures) of its lack of any real practical function, when it was removed the Royal Arch became symbolic of what happened to Dundee from the 1960s onwards. The destruction of a part of the city's history with no apparent serious consideration of alternatives or thought for the consequences was reflected in other demolitions across the city. Also, as the gateway to Dundee's central docks, the arch's removal was part of the process that saw these docks filled in and the city centre separated from the River Tay by a no-man's land of roads, raised pedestrian walkways and the approaches to the Tay Road Bridge.

It is perhaps fitting then, that the symbol of the redevelopment of this area and the rediscovery of the relationship of the city to the river – the V & A Museum of Design – should commemorate the names of Victoria and Albert. The V & A sits at the heart of a waterfront development that has adopted a long-term view of the city's future while respecting its past and taking advantage of its unique setting. In many ways the views that prevail in Dundee today are the antithesis of the mindset that saw the Royal Arch reduced to rubble.

If Dundee can be confident of its future, then, it can also be sure that there is an interesting past just waiting to be rediscovered. *Rediscovered Dundee* is an anthology of stories from that past. Many will be unfamiliar, it is hoped, having been uncovered during the research for this book, which returned to original documents and contemporary reports in an effort to uncover some of the city's less well-known people and events. Even in the case of the more familiar stories that have been included, it is hoped that at least some information has been added that is new to most readers.

The story of any city is the story of its people, and this book features accounts of the lives of some Dundonians whose names have been long absent from the history books. Their adventures – which sometimes took them far from the city – might have been well known by their contemporaries but have been forgotten over time. Their names might not be commemorated in plaques or statues or street names but at least their stories can be rediscovered.

One person whose name is commemorated in Dundee is the missionary Mary Slessor, after whom Slessor Gardens, part of the waterfront redevelopment, is named. When work was being undertaken to lay out the gardens, the foundations of the Royal Arch were rediscovered, and the arch's site is now marked on the ground. There are other places in the city where physical relics of the past are still visible, but sometimes the stories of how they came to be there have been forgotten. This book also seeks to rediscover those stories.

Sometimes, of course, stories are all we have and local myths have grown up and have been passed on down the years. Here, of course, what we are trying to rediscover, if possible, is the truth.

Just as a hidden history is waiting to be rediscovered, so Dundee itself is being rediscovered by people from elsewhere as tourists, drawn by the V&A find that the city has much more to offer. For a long time, it seemed that many thought there was no real reason to visit Dundee. Tourists from all over the world, it appeared, would visit the home of golf in St Andrews without bothering to make the short journey north to the city. This was not always the case, however, and part of this book looks at the visits of various people through the years. For some, such as many of the music hall artists or other travelling performers discussed, Dundee would have been just another stop on the road, someplace that perhaps they would not even remember having been. In cases such as these, the interest is in the impact that their visit had on the city at the time, or indeed, with the passage of time, in uncovering the fact that they ever set foot there. In other cases, a visit to Dundee would be the setting for an important or memorable episode in their lives.

There have been calls from some to rebuild the Royal Arch as a symbol of Dundee's renewal and as, in some way, a reclamation of the city's lost inheritance. While its destruction might be seen by some as regrettable and a rebuilt arch would be an interesting curiosity, it would also incur much expense and, having lost the context of the docks, would be completely bereft of any purpose it once had. Dundee has a new symbol in the V & A museum and one which, while it curates the past, is itself the symbol of the city's future. The past cannot be brought back – but it can be rediscovered.

I

Arrival

One day, early in the second decade of the twenty-first century, your train pulls into Dundee station. You step onto the platform. There is nothing remarkable to see. You are standing in a Victorian railway station of a type found throughout the country. Arrivals and departures go on as they have done for more than a century.

You walk along Platform One towards the exit and look along the track, but all you can see is the entrance to a dark tunnel. You enter the brightly lit main concourse, which is enclosed in a modern structure of glass and metal. On passing through the automatic ticket barrier you are confronted with a steep staircase. You walk up the stairs. Twenty-first-century health and safety concerns are reflected in signs with the words "Do not run" on the risers of some of the steps. A disembodied voice reminds you to hold the handrail at all times.

Emerging from the station, you find yourself in a nondescript car park. You look around. You see the *RRS Discovery* berthed in the Tay at the quay which bears its name, but it is perhaps the only thing of interest in the vicinity. The other things that catch your eye are mainly uninspiring buildings such as the Olympia Leisure Centre. The multi-storey office block Tayside House dominates the skyline and creates a sun-starved passageway between itself and the back of the Caird Hall. Elsewhere, you notice that there seem to be a lot of roadworks in progress. Welcome to Dundee.

The most mundane of settings, though, can conceal a hidden history. You pause for a moment to consider some of the events that have occurred in the railway station that you have just passed through – the numerous tearful separations and joyful reunions that have taken place there, the chance meetings, the new beginnings, the excited departures and weary homecomings; the thousands of ordinary (and, no doubt, extraordinary) stories that are lost to history.

Not every story is lost, though. The station – originally known as Tay Bridge Station – was the setting or the starting point for other stories too, which are recorded. Some of these remain well known to this day, while others have slipped out of the general consciousness.

Another day, a few years later, and your train pulls into Dundee station once more. This time you make your walk to the exit mindful of the station's history – beginning with the most dramatic night in that history, and many would argue, in the history of Dundee itself.

"You step onto the platform…"

SUNDAY 28 DECEMBER 1879

Broken glass crunches under James Smith's foot as he steps onto the platform. Part of the station's glass roof has collapsed. The stationmaster should not be working this evening, but such is the severity of the storm that locomotive foreman James Moyes came to his house to fetch him. Loaded goods wagons were being moved about by the force of the gale.

Smith has not experienced a storm as bad as this one in his twenty-five years with the North British Railway Company. He has been stationmaster of Tay Bridge Station since it opened in June the previous year. He orders the South Union Street exit to be closed, fearing that the whole roof at this part of the station might fall. Passengers can still come and go via the stairs in the centre of the station, as Smith judges that this is less dangerous. He asks that the train that is due to leave for Newport be brought to the foot of these stairs rather than leaving from one of the docks at the west end of the station.

Stationmaster Smith's attention turns to the train he is expecting from Edinburgh. He discovers that the signals indicate that the train must have passed the signal box at the south end of the bridge. It should be here any minute. Ten minutes go by. Smith becomes increasingly worried. He asks for someone who can work the telegraph, and the guard from the last train over the bridge, Robert Shand, volunteers himself. Shand attempts to send a message to the signalman on the south side of the river asking if the Edinburgh train has crossed the bridge, but none of the instruments work.

Emerging from the telegraph office, Smith and Shand run into two men – James Lawson and George Clark – who live nearby. Each was watching the bridge this evening and each believes that he saw the train fall into the river. They excitedly tell the stationmaster their stories of seeing the train enter onto the south side of the bridge and of fire falling from the top of the bridge to the river and how they supposed it to be the train. Smith tells them to say nothing of this to anybody. Perhaps he is not wholly convinced of the truth of their accounts, but he is clearly deeply concerned, though, as he orders the entire station closed.

Smith makes his way to the engine sheds where he meets James Roberts, the locomotive foreman. Roberts should have finished work for the evening but has stayed behind to help barricade the doors of the engine shed which he fears might be blown off their hinges by the gale. The two men make their way to the north signal box where they talk to the signalman Henry Somerville. He tells of how he had received a telegraph message to say that the train was on the bridge at 7.14 pm but has heard nothing since. All his attempts to contact the south side of the bridge have failed.

Smith and Roberts decide that they have no option but to venture out onto the bridge to see for themselves what has happened. It is a brave decision. The storm is still raging and the wind soon forces them to their knees. After a while, Smith can go no further. He has become giddy, Roberts supposes. The locomotive foreman carries on alone, inching his way through the darkness to the end of the bridge's "low girders" some half a mile from the shore. Ahead of him should be the cage-like structure of the central section of the bridge – the "high girders" – but instead there is nothing but blackness. Roberts ventures to within eight or nine yards of what he now realises is a gap in the bridge. He sees the broken rails. They are not twisted but bent downwards. A water pipe runs across the bridge to Newport and a jet of water is now gushing from its severed end. There is no doubt what has happened. The bridge is down…

All seventy-five passengers and crew died when the central section of the Tay Bridge collapsed that stormy night in 1879. Designed by Thomas Bouch, and only opened in the previous year, it had briefly been regarded as a triumph of Victorian engineering. Bouch's reputation never recovered and he died less than a year later.

The bridge after the accident. James Roberts crawled out to within eight or nine yards of this point on the night of the disaster.

On 5 January 1880, the body of off duty railway guard David Johnston was recovered from the Tay. His North British Railway watch was found in his pocket. It had stopped at 7.16 pm – shortly after the time that the ill-fated train had boarded the bridge.

"Arrivals..."

FRIDAY 10 JULY 1914

The station is brightly decorated today. The sound of a large naval gun echoes from the river but there is no cause for alarm. This comes from *HMS Vulcan*, stationed on the Tay, and is both a salute and a signal that *the* train has crossed the bridge. On the platform stands a welcoming party which includes Dundee's Lord Provost Sir James Urquhart, Sheriff Ferguson, the Sheriff of Forfarshire and the county's Lord Lieutenant the Earl of Strathmore, all resplendent in their official dress.

The train arrives and a footman emerges to open the carriage door. His Majesty King George V steps out of the carriage and in doing so sets foot in Dundee, becoming the first reigning monarch to visit Dundee since his grandmother Queen Victoria, and the first reigning King since James VI and I to visit the city.[1] The King is accompanied by Queen Mary and their daughter Princess Mary.

A large crowd has gathered in Union Street to greet the royal party. Indeed, so great is the number attending and so intense the heat that some people faint. The King is the first of the party to emerge from the station into the summer sunshine. With his top hat in his hand, he acknowledges the salute of the Territorials and the cheers of the crowd. He ushers the Queen and the princess into an open coach before joining them and setting off on a tour of the city.

Every conceivable vantage point is taken as the procession travels up Union Street, along the Nethergate and the High Street and up Reform Street. In Reform Street a mounted policeman is thrown from his horse but gets up unharmed and remounts, earning a loud cheer from the crowds.

---

1   Royalists would perhaps add that Charles II was, in fact, the rightful king on the three occasions he was in Dundee during what was known as the interregnum. Indeed, by the time of his last visit he had been crowned King of Scots at Scone. Jacobites might also contend that the last reigning king before George V to visit Dundee was James VIII and III (known to Hanoverians as the "Old Pretender") in 1716.

The royal party in Albert Square.

Albert Square has been crowded all morning. The guard of honour, in the shape of the 4th (City of Dundee) Battalion of the Black Watch, waits patiently outside the bunting-bedecked Courier building. Regimental bands are positioned outside the High School. When the royal visitors finally arrive, the square erupts in a frenzy of cheering and flag waving. The King gets out to inspect the guard of honour. He waves his hat to acknowledge the crowd. The royal party climbs the staircase at the front of the Albert Institute.[2] Inside, there are formal speeches and presentations in the presence of an assembly of some 200 of the great and the good including local MP Winston Churchill and his wife Clementine.

The royal party leaves the Albert Institute. As their carriage completes its circuit of Albert Square, it pauses at the brightly decorated factory of Messrs James Keiller and Son, part of which has been transformed into a mock orange grove for the occasion. The workers are assembled at the front of the factory. Miss Nellie Gairns, a forewoman in the chocolate department who won a ballot among the employees, presents the Queen with a box of chocolates, while a Miss Allen presents Princess Mary with a silk bag of sweets. Like that

---

2   The press will later report that Queen Mary looked down into the square at this stage and pointed out to her husband the statue of his grandmother Queen Victoria, but retracing the royal party's steps today, the statue is not visible from the staircase.

of her colleague, Miss Allan's interaction with the royal family takes the form of a carefully rehearsed, stilted sentence: "May it please your Royal Highness to accept this bag of caramels, made at Messrs Keillers." The princess's gracious thanks are equally formal. The managing director of the factory, William Boyd, is presented by the Lord Provost and the King regrets that their itinerary does not allow for a full tour of the factory. The Queen remarks on the "splendid" decorations and the "pretty girls".

Instead, the party heads back down to the esplanade to be greeted by some 20,000 school children and members of the Scouts and the Boys' Brigade. At Magdalen Green they stop off at the Institute for the Blind before making their way to Ashton Works, the premises of Messrs Caird in Blackness Road from where they will remotely effect the laying of the foundation stones of the new hall that Sir James Key Caird has donated to the city.

At the Greenmarket, a large crowd has gathered to watch the foundation stones being laid.[3] A grandstand has been erected and is occupied by local councillors and dignitaries. City Architect James Thomson places a casket in the cavity beneath where the stone is to be placed. It contains a minute of the council meeting at which the Caird gift was announced, copies of local newspapers, a Dundee directory, a Corporation diary and all the coins currently in circulation from a farthing to a sovereign.

Back at Ashton Works, the King presses an emerald button and a sign appears stating that the stone had been laid. The Queen presses a button made of jade and a similar notice appears. At the Greenmarket, a click is heard as the stones drop into place. Bailie Paton makes a speech about "a new Dundee yet to be" and how the "royal touch" had well and truly laid the first stone in a great city improvement scheme about which the city's old men had seen visions and young men had dreamed dreams. There are three cheers for Mr. Caird and a further three for the King and Queen before the national anthem is played.

The royal visitors leave Ashton Works and head towards their final destination in the city. The King's frock coat now sports a thin layer of jute mill "stour". The procession travels down Hawkhill and into the Perth Road, along the Nethergate and High Street and into Commercial Street.

Among those hoping to catch a glimpse of the King today is a woman in her late twenties named Olive Walton. Olive has no interest in frivolous

---

3   The stones are still visible today at the corner of Crichton Street and Shore Terrace.

clothes but today leaves her house in Wellington Street wearing a bright green outfit covered with a green knitted jacket. She is also sporting a wide brimmed hat as she heads down the Hilltown.

The royal coach leaves Commercial Street and proceeds up Meadowside, heading towards Victoria Road. Olive Walton has secured herself a good vantage point at the foot of the Hilltown. She is near the front of the crowd with only some children standing in front of her. The carriage rounds the bend. When it reaches the point where Olive is standing, she pushes past the children and rushes into the road towards the vehicle. The King is on the other side of the coach and does not appear to notice anything untoward but the Queen raises her hand to shield her face and Princess Mary shrinks back in her seat as Olive produces something from under her jacket and hurls it towards the coach.

The royal party emerged unscathed from this incident to continue its tour of the city. The missile – some papers attached to a rubber ball – simply bounced off the side of the coach. Olive Walton was quickly arrested by Police Constable George Smith and led away to the central police station to the accompaniment of jeers and boos from the crowd. She had provided no real threat to the royal family but her intention had been deadly serious. Attached to the ball was a plea to the King to stop the enforced feeding of suffragettes. This was something that Olive Walton had known from personal experience. As an active campaigner in the struggle for women's right to vote, she had been imprisoned for her part in a window-smashing campaign in 1912 and forcibly fed while in prison.

Born in 1886, Olive Walton was the daughter of a retired wine merchant from Tunbridge Wells. Her activities in the suffrage movement were seen as an embarrassment by her well-to-do family – particularly when she was sent to prison. At first a member of the moderate National Union of Women's Suffrage Societies, she had later joined the Women's Social and Political Union (WSPU), the leading militant organisation, under the leadership of Mrs. Emmeline Pankhurst and her daughters. Olive became an organiser for the WSPU at first in Turnbridge Wells and then, in November 1913, in Dundee.

It has been reported that Queen Mary herself sent word to the police station that no charges should be brought against Olive Walton and that she was duly released as a consequence. If this was, in fact, the case and Her Majesty expected gratitude or an end to campaigning from Olive, however, she was to be disappointed. Two days later, the suffragette tried exactly the same thing again as the royal family were on their way from a church service at St

The arrest of Olive Walton
© Museum of London

Giles Cathedral in Edinburgh. This time the ball landed in Queen Mary's lap but she simply brushed it aside.

The struggle for women's suffrage would eventually be won but events were unfolding in Europe that were to put the campaign to achieve it on hold in the meantime. While Olive Walton was trying to attract the attention of the royal family with her protest in Dundee, the outbreak of a world war was only weeks away. When war was eventually declared, she left Dundee and, of all things, joined the police, becoming one of the first Women Police Volunteers.

Olive Walton's attempt to throw something into the King's carriage was just one of many actions undertaken by suffragettes in Dundee in this period, and as a relatively minor incident, it has largely been forgotten. Viewed from the distance of a century later and seen in its historic context, though, it is the lax nature of the security surrounding the King and his family that stands out. Given that the train of events that led to the outbreak of the First World War had already started with the assassination in Sarajevo of the Archduke Franz

Ferdinand, it is astonishing to think that a mere twelve days later, a young woman was able to get so close to the royal carriage twice in the space of three days. Had Olive Walton been carrying a bomb rather than a rubber ball that sunny July day in Dundee, then the course of world history might have been altered forever at the foot of the Hilltown.

"...and departures..."

FRIDAY 30 OCTOBER 1914

A few short months after the King's visit and the Union Flag again adorns Tay Bridge Station. Patriotism is in the air once more but this time it is no mere joyful flag-waving sentiment but something that is helping to fuel the bloodiest conflict that the world has yet seen – the "Great War" as a Canadian magazine has this month called it.

This morning the 5th (Angus and Dundee) Battalion of the Black Watch is leaving the city to take up active service. Trains are bringing men from Broughty Ferry and Stannergate. Men who are housed in the city's Western Barracks in the Liff and Benvie Poorhouse (or "grubber" as it is known locally) on Blackness Road will march to the station. Despite heavy rain, many people – mainly women – have spent the night outside the barracks. At 7.20 am, the troops leave to the sound of the bagpipes and cheers from the crowd. Indeed, they are followed and cheered all along the route as they make their way down Blackness Road to the West Port, down Tay Street and along the Nethergate, before approaching the station via Union Street. All the way, they excitedly chat and respond to the crowd. They sing a parody of a popular song with lyrics written by one Lance Corporal Leonard. They sing it so often that the people following pick up the words and are able to join in:

> It's a long way to Berlin City
> It's a long way to go
> On the Kaiser we'll have no pity
> When we get there, what ho!
> Goodbye to the "grubber"
> Murraygate and Albert Square
> It's a long, long way to Berlin City
> But we're going there

When the troops finally arrive at the station, the public is not permitted to follow them inside, but people soon circumvent this rule by heading round to Riverside where they can look over the wall and down onto the platform. The men face a longer than expected delay as some carriages bringing their comrades from the Stannergate have been derailed. The pipers keep the crowd entertained while the soldiers dance reels. Spirits are high and cheerful comments are passed. One man plays "La Marseillaise" on the piccolo to the amusement of all. When the troop train finally leaves it is to the jaunty accompaniment of "Sing us a Song of Bonnie Scotland".

So it was that young men from Dundee began to leave to take part in the "war to end all wars". There would be many such journeys to the station over the next four years and many such departures, but the patriotic enthusiasm must surely have declined as the wounded returned and, more particularly, as the fallen did not. Perhaps, though, among the jingoistic throng there was always an element that knew the true price of war. The journalist William Linton Andrews in his war memoir *Haunting Years* recalled his own chaotic journey to Tay Bridge Station a few short months later. It had been impossible, he said, to keep military formation, so enthusiastic were the crowds. One group, though had a different reaction:

> "a few of the women from mean streets were sobbing. Useless for us to tell them that we were only to guard lines of communications. The women in the mean streets know by tradition what war is. And perhaps their own men were dead already."[4]

"You walk along Platform One..."

WEDNESDAY 25 APRIL 1928

An innovation is reported in the *Courier* today. A new system of dealing with passenger traffic has been inaugurated at Tay Bridge Station: "The platforms have been numbered consecutively. Number one is the 'down' platform, numbers two and three are the 'docks' and number four is the 'up' platform. The numbers

---

4 Andrews, William Linton, Haunting Years (1930), London: Hutchison & Co (Publishers) Ltd, page 31.

are painted in white on black boards suspended from the iron girders of the roof of the station. A train indicator has been erected facing the Union Street entrance and another on the wall in the booking hall. The indicators are divided into four sections. Each section corresponds to a section or dock and will bear the time of the train followed by a list of stations at which it will call."

"...all you can see is a dark tunnel..."

22 SEPTEMBER 1896

A policeman stands at the Tay Bridge Station end of the Dock Street tunnel, this afternoon, as a precaution. For anyone to make their way through to this side, though, they would already have had to pass an equivalent sentry at the other end. It is only one of many security measures that have been undertaken. All approaches to the station have been closed and lines of policemen guard the doors.

Crowds mill around outside in the drizzle hoping to catch a glimpse of what is going on. The weather has ensured that the numbers are not as large as they might have been, but this may also be due to the fact that there will be very little to see. Even within the station itself, seven-foot-high boards shield the northbound platform. People have gathered in the vicinity of the Esplanade Station, hoping to see the train as it crosses the bridge, but when it eventually does there is little to be seen as it speeds past.

It seems that the people of Dundee are going to see nothing out of the ordinary and certainly nothing of the train's illustrious passengers for whom flags are flying from the city's public buildings. When the train arrives in the station, there is a rush of people to the wall at South Union Street but they can only see the tops of the carriages.

Meanwhile, the South Union Street entrance has already seen the arrival of Dundee's civic dignitaries and others lucky enough to have an invitation. They gather on the platform where at 3.53 pm precisely, the train arrives. The band of the City Rifles strikes up – playing two national anthems. The second of these is represented only by a few bars. This is the British national anthem – played in recognition that on this train is the Prince of Wales, heir to the throne and the man who will one day be King Edward VII. He is very much a secondary attraction on this particular occasion, though, and the rendition of another national anthem takes precedence. This is the Russian national anthem and it is being played to commemorate that today, for a few minutes at least,

Nikolai Aleksandrovich Romanov, Emperor and Autocrat of all the Russias – Tsar Nicholas II – will be in Dundee.

The train has stopped precisely at the point where the dignitaries have gathered. After a few moments, the Tsar and Tsarina come to the door of their carriage and stand with the Prince of Wales to their right. The Tsar wears a military uniform while the prince is dressed as an admiral. The speeches are kept to a minimum. The town clerk, Sir Thomas Thornton, addresses the Tsar: "May it please your Imperial Majesty, I have the great honour and pleasure of submitting for your Majesty's gracious acceptance this address from the citizens of Dundee." Acting Chief Magistrate Ferrier adds: "May I be permitted to wish your Majesty a safe and happy journey." Thornton hands Ferrier a silver casket containing a formal address to the Tsar, which Ferrier passes to him. It bears the inscription:

To
His Imperial Majesty
The Emperor of Russia
From
The City of Dundee
22nd September 1896

After some words of thanks from the Tsar, the royal party return to the carriage for tea. There are cheers from those assembled on the platform for the Tsar and his wife and for the Prince and Princess of Wales. The train heads into the blackness of the Dock Street tunnel. The entire stop has lasted around ten minutes.

At the other end of the tunnel people have gathered at East Dock Street to see the train. This part of the track is probably the best area for people to stand any chance of seeing the royal party as the train speeds past. Within a few moments though, it has passed, heading northwards and out of Dundee. Tsar Nicholas II's fleeting visit to the city is over.

It is clear that the Tsar's brief stop off at Dundee in 1896 on the way to Balmoral to visit Queen Victoria attracted much less public interest than that of his cousin King George V some eighteen years later. Conversely, the security measures employed for Nicholas II were far greater than those employed for the later visit. The relative lack of interest can probably be put down to the twin factors of the poor weather and the fact that there was little for the public to see given that the Tsar did not emerge from the railway station to make a public appearance. A contemporary report in the *Courier* vividly illustrates the lack of a public spectacle:

> "As the carriages swept on handkerchiefs, hats and umbrellas were waved, and a slight cheer was raised, but when the last carriage disappeared behind the station buildings many of the spectators gave vent to peals of laughter. One old lady quoted the passage relating to John the Baptist: 'What went ye out to see, a reed shaken with the wind? – a train crossing the Tay Bridge. You may see that any hour of the day.'"

The tight security was due to numerous real threats to the Tsar's safety from various political groupings. Nicholas had been present when his grandfather Alexander II had been assassinated and wanted to make sure that he did not suffer the same fate. History was not to grant him his wish, however, and in July 1918 he was shot along with his family in Yekaterinburg following the Bolshevik Revolution of the previous year. The bodies of the royal family were crudely disposed of and buried in a pit but decades later were recovered and laid to rest in SS Peter and Paul Cathedral in St Petersburg. In 2000, more than a century after the Tsar's brief stop in Dundee, the Romanovs were controversially declared to be saints by the Russian Orthodox Church.

Boarding or alighting from a train in Dundee's busy railway station today, it is difficult to imagine that the northbound platform might once have been visited by a saint but perhaps no more so than imagining that it might once have played host, however fleetingly, to the last tsar and emperor of Russia and the man whose overthrow was one of the great turning points of twentieth-century history.

"You are confronted with a steep staircase…"

SATURDAY, 6 JULY 1889

Tay Bridge Station can be a noisy place, but there is something about the nature of the strange sounds that he hears this evening that causes the signalman positioned at the South Union Street entrance to investigate their origin. Together with two members of the public he traces the source of the noise to a small wicker hamper that has been left under the stairs. The hamper is covered with a lid and has a label attached which reads: "Miss Stirling, Mrs. Murray, 12 Hatton Place, Grange, Edinburgh - with care; this side up."

When the basket is opened it is found to contain a child of about one month old. The baby girl is well dressed and her head is resting on a pillow and protected by a hood. There are spare clothes and a blanket neatly folded in the hamper. The teat of a still-warm bottle of milk is in the child's mouth. The signalman and his friends contact the authorities and the baby is sent in a cab to be examined by Doctor Templeman, the Dundee police surgeon, before being sent to the East Poor House.

The initial police investigations into the child's identity and how she came to be left in the station bring little in the way of results. A telegram is sent to the address on the luggage label and it transpires from this that the Miss Stirling mentioned on the label is the matron of an institution for "waifs" in Edinburgh, but she is currently in Nova Scotia. There are reports of a woman seen buying a hamper at a local shop about half an hour before the child was discovered. The identity of whoever left the basket at the station, however, remains elusive.

The "Dundee Child Mystery", as it was known by the press, caused a minor sensation in the summer of 1889. Within a fortnight of the child's discovery, however, an arrest had been made. Lieutenant Lamb and Detective Campbell of the Dundee Police travelled to Tuttienook in the parish of Carmyllie, where they took in to custody one Janet Phillip, a domestic servant.

At the subsequent trial it emerged that the child abandoned at Tay Bridge Station was not the first illegitimate child that Janet Phillip had borne, having given birth to another some three years earlier. Both were children of the same father – a man named James Tait whom she had first met when he was a ploughman at Balmossie Farm. In the intervening years, Tait had often promised to marry Janet but had never actually done so – nor had he paid the money that he had promised for the child's upkeep.

When Janet Phillip found herself pregnant again, she was unemployed and desperate. After the birth of her first child, she had been too ashamed to visit her father for eight months. The old man had eventually taken that child to live with him, but now she felt that she could not ask him for help or to take in another. When she asked James Tait for assistance, he refused to give the child a home and said that he would deny paternity altogether if she did not take the child away again. He offered to pay money towards the upkeep of his daughter, but Janet found herself unable to put any faith in his promises. She knew of the reputation of Miss Stirling in Edinburgh as a charitable woman and decided to take drastic action.

The birth of a child in nineteenth-century Dundee was not always a cause for celebration. For some women, like Janet Philip, it was the scandal of illegitimacy that was the cause of their distress, while for others it was the fact that – whether born within marriage or not – the child was another mouth that they could not afford to feed. This was certainly not the first instance of a child being abandoned by its mother in the locality. The Reverend William Cumming Skinner in his 1927 book *The Baronie of Hilltowne Dundee* quotes a case referred to in a Kirk Session book for 1776 about a child found in the Hilltown:

> "The Session being informed that there had been a child laid down in the Hill; that search had been made for the mother but she could not be found that no nurse can be got for the child until such time as it be baptised, the Session were therefore of the opinion that said child should be baptised and that they should stand sponsors for it, which being accordingly done it was named – John Hilltown; the Session also ordered clothes for the child and fifteen pounds Scots to be paid quarterly with it."[5]

It is not known what became of John Hilltown but at least he was given a good start in life – some unfortunate children paid the ultimate price for desperate situations in which their mothers found themselves. Two Dundee mothers were condemned to death for infanticide: Catherine Symon in 1841 and Bridget Kiernan in 1860, though the sentence was not carried out in either case. There were other recorded instances of child killing in the city that did not end in the death sentence and there may have been many more that remained undetected. The problem of overlaying, where a young child was suffocated as a result of sharing a bed with an adult or adults, was of particular concern in Dundee. In 1896, Doctor Templeman, the man who had been called to collect Janet Phillip's baby, told a meeting of the sanitary committee of the council that prosecution was difficult in these cases for various reasons – the only witnesses were often the parents themselves; there was always the possibility that the deaths of such young children were accidental and there was little external medical evidence. In the ten years to 1891, Doctor Templeman examined 258

---

5   Skinner, Reverend William Cumming, The Baronie of Hilltowne Dundee (1927), Dundee: David Winter and Son, page 183.

cases of overlaying in the city. There was no doubt that some of these deaths could have been accidental – the result of overcrowding where several people were sharing one bed – but suspicion remained in many cases.

Against this background, Janet Phillip's actions in abandoning her child do not, perhaps, seem so bad and this was recognised at her trial. While Sheriff Campbell Smith acknowledged that she had pleaded guilty to the crime of deserting her child, and placing its life in danger, he accepted that she had meant the child no harm. He contrasted the course she had taken with the hypothetical case of a woman who abandoned her child in a wood or on a moor – a place where nobody was likely to be. Instead, Miss Phillip had left the child at a railway station, "within hearing of people moving about – one of the most public places in the country, and one where the child was very likely soon to be discovered and rescued". She had nonetheless committed an offence and had not fully considered the possible dangers to the child.

It was the child's father, James Tait, who came in for the most criticism from the Sheriff, who said that he bore the "moral blame" and was really "the principal criminal". However, while he acknowledged Tait's failings and condemned them, Sheriff Campbell Smith added that human law had placed responsibility on Janet Phillip and that she must bear the "social responsibility of being disgraced on account of being the mother of two illegitimate children having got them both to a man who has no good moral principle to marry you after he has promised to do it". It was quite right, he concluded, that the responsibility should rest on her, because she had been guilty of the offence with which she was charged – disobeying the most imperative instinct of Nature, which provides for the preservation of life on the earth – sinking herself "below the level of the beasts of prey" in neglecting the duty of a mother to cherish and protect a child.

Sheriff Campbell Smith concluded, nonetheless, that Janet Phillip had "suffered enormously already" and that it was not necessary he should aggravate her sufferings. He could not fail to punish her but promised to make her punishment as light as he possibly could. She was therefore sentenced to fourteen days in prison. Perhaps it was as well that Campbell Smith was lenient by the standards of the time, because fate had one more cruel punishment in store for Janet Phillip. On 1 August, while she was serving her sentence, her daughter, Janet Philip junior, the child at the centre of the mystery, died in the East Poor House.

"You walk up the stairs…"

FRIDAY, 12 OCTOBER 1923

A flurry of scarlet gowns brightens up the station as a group of students arrives to meet a lunchtime train. When the train pulls in, an unremarkable looking 57-year-old man with a moustache and round framed glasses emerges onto the platform and is immediately hoisted onto the shoulders of the students.

Dundee does not have its own university at this point – these students belong to University College, Dundee, which is part of the University of St Andrews. The man they are carrying aloft is the rector of that institution. Later, he will use a speech to the great and the good of Dundee to appeal for funds for the university. He will particularly ask those who have lost sons in the Great War to make a donation so that their names might live on. This is not mere opportunism on his part. His own 18-year-old son, like a large number of Dundonians, died at the Battle of Loos in 1915.

The excited group makes its way towards the station's South Union Street exit. Although his elevated position seems precarious at times, the rector continues to take it all in good humour. The students reach the stairs and begin the tricky business of climbing them while still carrying their passenger at shoulder height. As they reach the top of the stairs, however, the narrowing angle and decreasing headroom defeat them. Despite what is happening around him, their passenger manages to keep his head and he is brought down to earth in a somewhat undignified manner. His name is Rudyard Kipling.

"…health and safety concerns…"

1 JANUARY 1902

It is just after eight o'clock in the morning on the first day of the year, and for some in Dundee the New Year celebrations are still going on. For railway workers Alan Bain and Owen McLuskie, however, it is just another working day. They are walking through the Dock Street tunnel from the station side, swinging their lamps as they go. About sixty yards from the tunnel entrance they hear a moaning sound and go to investigate. The sight that greets their eyes when they reach the source of the noise is horrific. The tracks are covered in blood and a man lies face down at the side of the rails. His leg has been completely severed and lies a few feet from his body. Bain and McLuskie turn the man over to reveal he also has severe facial injuries.

One of the men runs back to the station to raise the alarm, and a stretcher is brought into the tunnel. With some difficulty, the man is raised onto it and is brought to the platform. A porter recognises the victim from his clothing as a man that he ordered out of the station an hour or two earlier. The man had been wandering about the platform in a dangerous manner and the porter had warned him that he might fall onto the rails and suffer a terrible accident. It seems that the man paid no heed and re-entered the station at some point. He is transferred by ambulance to the Dundee Royal Infirmary. There is thought to be little or no hope that he will survive.

The victim of this horrific accident died later that same morning. At the time of his death that Wednesday morning he was still unidentified. It was not until the Saturday that his identify came to light. He was Alexander Smith, a 37-year-old warehouseman from Glasgow. He was married with five children. A tattoo with the initials A.S. on his left wrist had provided the vital clue when his description was circulated in the newspapers.

A tragic accident such as the death of Alexander Smith might be thought to be an extremely rare occurrence, but Tay Bridge Station was not always a safe place to be in its early years. The list that follows contains some, though by no means all, of the fatal accidents that happened at or near the station in its first quarter century:

1880: A washerwoman by the name of Mrs. Stevens was doing some washing for the stationmaster's wife. She was hanging out washing on a line towards the west of the station when she fell through the glass roof and onto the platform.

1882: William Jack, a railway shunter who lived in Paton's Lane, fell between two wagons while uncoupling them. The wagons ran over his legs and almost severed them. He was carried into the parcel office where a doctor attended to him but there was little that could be done. He died the next day in the Dundee Royal Infirmary.

1883: Shoemaker Robert Wilson was decapitated by a train near the station's goods shed, while walking home during the night. He had left his shop in the High Street at seven o'clock the previous evening. No one was able to account for how he came to be there, but it was assumed that he had taken a wrong turning in the dark while walking down by the Esplanade.

1884: Surfaceman Robert Johnston was hit by a passenger train in the Dock Street tunnel. He and a colleague, James Harper, had been going to carry out repair work at the east end of the tunnel. When they were about halfway through, Johnston remarked to Harper that he heard a train coming. Harper managed to get clear of the rails in time but, when the train had passed, he saw Johnston lying on the track, having been run over by the train. Harper ran for help, but Johnston was found to be dead.

1885: Mary McEwan from the Overgate was a poor woman who was in the habit of searching the docks and the railway stations for stray pieces of coal that might have fallen from one of the heavily laden carts that were often to be seen there. A large train of such carts had just passed through and she was searching the line for remnants. Unfortunately, she was out of the sight of William Coutts, the driver of an oncoming engine.

1890: William Thomson, a tailor from Kelso, arrived in Dundee on Friday, 14 February in search of work. Two days later, his horrifically mangled body was discovered lying on the rails between the goods yard and the western side of the passenger station. It was not known how he came to be there, but it was supposed that he had lost his way some time on the Saturday night or Sunday morning and ended up between some wagons. As the wagons had been shunted about, he must have been run over several times. In his pocket were discovered the tools of his trade – a bone bodkin and a thimble.

1894: James Scott, the general contracting agent of Messrs Mutter Howie and Co, railway contractors in Aberdeen, was killed by the Dundee to Edinburgh train. It is thought that he believed the train was going to Aberdeen and rushed to try to join it.

1897: Porter Alexander Laurie had just finished cleaning a saloon car at the station and jumped down from it onto the track when he was hit by the incoming train from Glasgow. Attempts were made at the station to attend to his wounds but he died the following day in the Infirmary.

1897: 48-year-old Elizabeth Macpherson from the Overgate was seeing friends off at the station. After the train had started, the guard noticed that she was still on the footboard. He tried to help her off but her shawl came away in his hands and she fell between the platform and the train. She died later in hospital.

1898: Peter Brannan was oiling points in the railway goods yard. He stepped out of the way of an approaching engine only to step into the path of another which he had not seen. The driver and fireman did not have time to bring the engine to a halt and it ran over the unfortunate man, severing both his right leg and right hand. He died forty-five minutes later. On the day of Brannan's death, two young men were killed by an express train on the Tay Bridge. Joseph Barrett and James Hume had been working on the bridge and were walking home with colleagues at the end of their shift when they were hit by the train from Edinburgh.

1902: Andrew MacBayne, a foreman surfaceman, was tightening sleepers beside the engine sheds. The driver and fireman of the approaching 4.16 pm train from Ladybank were aware that there might be people working in this area and were keeping a lookout but, tragically, did not see MacBayne. It was not until the train came to a stop at the station that they learned they had run him over. Several other workers had come to MacBayne's aid but he was unconscious and his injuries were severe. He died soon afterwards.

"Do not run..."

SATURDAY 3 MAY 1941

Three soldiers enter the station this evening but they attract little attention. In the early years of the Second World War, military uniforms are commonplace in Tay Bridge Station. What happens next, however, is far from commonplace.

One of the soldiers, Lance Corporal James Dunlop, goes to buy tickets for the train to London. His two colleagues who are left behind are equal in rank but not in status. Private John Fitzgerald of the Pioneer Corps is a prisoner, and Private Stephen Sheppard has been left guarding him while Dunlop collects the tickets. Dunlop and Sheppard have been sent to Dundee to collect Fitzgerald, who has been charged with desertion, and are escorting him back to his unit. Unusual as it may seem in the circumstances, all three men have been drinking.

The men are standing near the station's hoist. Its operator, James Stalker, sees Fitzgerald, who he later describes as being "pretty stotty", move away from Sheppard. Fitzgerald says, "I'll play the game. I'll play the game" and waves his hand. Stalker watches as Sheppard raises his rifle, puts it to his shoulder and takes aim. A shot rings out and Private Fitzgerald falls to the ground. The bullet has hit him in the chest, killing him. A post-mortem will give the cause of death as "shock and haemorrhage from a gunshot wound". Petty Officer William Peck sees Sheppard while he still has the rifle in his hand and hears him say, "He has been asking for it all day." Andrew Smith, a porter at the station, hears Sheppard say to Lance Corporal Dunlop, "I told him I would do it and I have done it."

Private Sheppard was charged with the murder of John Fitzgerald, but when the case came to trial before Lord Robertson on 10 June, the charge was reduced to one of culpable homicide. During the course of the trial, the full story of the events leading up to the shooting emerged. Lance Corporal Dunlop told the court that he and Sheppard had gone to the police station about midday to collect Fitzgerald. The police had wanted to keep him in custody until nearer the time of departure of their train that evening, but Dunlop admitted that he had insisted on taking him out. He then went on to tell the court of how they had accompanied Fitzgerald on visits to his home and to relatives, to a football match – the final of the Forfarshire Cup between Forfar Celtic and United Juniors at Beechwood Park – and to three public houses where they each had a total of six drinks over the course of the day. He denied being drunk. Dunlop stated that Sheppard had told him after the shooting that he had shouted a warning to the prisoner when he tried to escape but that this had been ignored.

Three witnesses from the railway station, Petty Officer William Peck, porter Andrew Smith and James Stalker, the hoist operator, gave the court their accounts of the shooting. Stalker told of how he had seen Fitzgerald fall as the shot was fired, hitting a barrow with his hands before turning on his back.

Stalker added that he honestly thought that he could have been recaptured without having to be shot.

Captain Turner, the second in command of Sheppard's regiment, gave evidence for the defence. He said that at the time of the incident there were no instructions given to escorts. This was only done on 3 May. He gave Sheppard, who had served in France prior to Dunkirk, a glowing reference saying that he was a man he would choose to go anywhere with him and that he was "definitely a very good soldier".

Stephen Sheppard himself then took the witness box, answering questions from his counsel, Mr McIntyre. He said that he had had no instructions about not firing when on escort duty. He had been on escort duty five times previously and had never been given any such instruction. In fact, as he had been given a rifle and ammunition, he had assumed that he could shoot to frighten or lame if the prisoner attempted to escape.

When they had gone to the police station to collect their prisoner, Sheppard testified, the lieutenant in charge had told them that if he were in their position, he would leave Fitzgerald there until 6.30 pm. He also said that he would provide a motor car to take them to the station. Fitzgerald, the lieutenant said, was a slippery customer and they would need to keep their eye on him.

In response to a question from Mr. McIntyre, Sheppard said that if he had been in command of the escort, he would not have taken Fitzgerald out in the morning nor taken him to public houses. In a Lochee pub, in the afternoon, Sheppard told Fitzgerald to "play the game" or he would be "for it". When Fitzgerald had gone outside to speak to his wife, he heard somebody in the pub say, "there's a move on". Sheppard immediately went to the door and accompanied Fitzgerald back into the pub. In another incident at a pub nearer the station, Fitzgerald had gone out of the pub while Sheppard was distracted. He had again followed him and brought him back. This time, he had been about twenty yards away, heading in the opposite direction to the station. Sheppard thought both the incident in Lochee and the later one were genuine attempts to escape. He had then loaded his rifle in Fitzgerald's presence and Lance Corporal Dunlop told the prisoner that he was "finished" and that they were going to the station. He told Fitzgerald to "play the game" and said to Sheppard, "Don't stand any nonsense from him. Fire."

On arrival at the station, when Dunlop had gone for the tickets, Sheppard had repeated to Fitzgerald Dunlop's order to "play the game" and had shaken hands with him, but the prisoner had started to walk away. Sheppard claimed that he then shouted "Halt, or I fire" but that there was no reply. He had therefore raised his rifle. Fitzgerald had turned, waved his hand and kept going further away. In response to a question from Mr McIntyre, Private Sheppard said that he believed that waving of the hand was meant to "put him off". He thought that Fitzgerald's intention was to lose himself and Dunlop, both of whom were English and strangers to Dundee, in the streets of the city once he had got outside the station. This being the case, he thought that the circumstances were such that the order he had received from Dunlop to fire should be acted upon and that it was his duty to do so. He had attempted to fire over Fitzgerald's shoulder. He had not intended to kill but did not feel that he could fire to the side of him on account of the danger of hitting a civilian in the street. The bullet from a shot over the shoulder, reckoned Sheppard, would land in the wooden partition of the station. Although he considered himself a good shot, the fact that Fitzgerald was still moving had affected matters and he had been hit. No one was more sorry than Sheppard that the shot had been fatal.

In his summing up, Lord Robertson said that the killing of Private Fitzgerald was not in dispute. The question was whether or not there was the degree of culpability to make it a crime. The jury should remember the situation in which Private Sheppard had been placed. He was a soldier on duty in charge of a deserter and under obligation to deliver him to headquarters. It would be altogether wrong to judge his actions too meticulously. The jury certainly could not be accused of being "too meticulous." They considered their verdict for all of five minutes before returning to pronounce Private Sheppard not guilty. It had been a unanimous decision.

Sheppard's acquittal, however, was not the end of the matter. In July 1941, Lance Corporal James Dunlop faced a court martial on four charges to which he pled not guilty:

1. that on 3 May he was drunk while in charge of an escort taking Private John Fitzgerald from Dundee to his unit
2. that while on active service that day he was unfit for duty owing to previous indulgence in alcohol
3. that he removed Private Fitzgerald from the custody of the civil power, improperly allowed him to visit his relatives and that he, together with Fitzgerald and Private Sheppard, drank in various public houses in Dundee,
4. that while in charge of the escort he improperly told Sheppard not to stand any nonsense from Fitzgerald and to fire if necessary.

Dunlop was found guilty of the charges relating to being unfit for duty and removing Fitzgerald from custody and taking him drinking and so on, but the other charges were dismissed. He was sentenced to 156 days detention.

There are many circumstances surrounding the shooting of John Fitzgerald that came together to end in tragedy. For one thing, there was the lack of clear guidance regarding escorts and their prisoners and the use of weapons. At both the trial of Private Sheppard and at Corporal Dunlop's court martial it was repeated that no guidelines were given regarding shooting at escaping prisoners and that most in the army believed that an escort would be allowed to fire in certain circumstances. An Army Council order about the duties of escorts was dated 30 April but was not posted at the men's camp until 3 May – the very day of the incident. They had therefore been unaware of it. Company Sergeant Major Beeson, who had ordered the men to Dundee to fetch Fitzgerald, said there had been "no fixed rules" about escorts. He said that Dunlop and Sheppard had been told to take a rifle and five rounds of ammunition "because there's a war on".

The fact that both Dunlop and Sheppard knew Fitzgerald also helped to bring about the tragic circumstances of his death. Sheppard was predisposed to be suspicious of Fitzgerald. He thought, for example, that he was only pretending to be drunk as part of an escape plan, as he had seen him drink more in both England and France without it affecting him. He described Fitzgerald as "a very plausible sort of fellow", adding that, "If you listened to him he could make you believe that the moon was made out of green cheese."

Lance Corporal Dunlop, on the other hand, considered Fitzgerald a friend. Because he thought Fitzgerald was likely to get a long sentence when they returned to their unit, he decided that it would be "nice" to let him see his wife and family before they left. The rules on the duties of an escort may not have been crystal clear, but Dunlop could surely not have thought that taking Fitzgerald to his home, his mother's house, his brother's house and a football match as well as drinking with him in pubs, was what was expected of him.

What of Private Fitzgerald? Was he the "slippery customer" that the police warned his escorts about? He was clearly guilty of desertion. He had also been convicted several times before the war by the civil authorities. A closer examination of his record in this regard, however, reveals that some of his convictions were drink-fuelled but relatively minor breaches of the peace while others were of a type not uncommon in the "Hungry Thirties" in Dundee. Fitzgerald had been unemployed and had once participated in a Hunger

March to London. It was against this background that he was charged several times with stealing coins from the gas meter in his house and on one occasion was convicted of smashing windows at the offices of the Public Assistance Department in protest at their treatment of his claim. His misdemeanours, then, were fuelled by desperation, opportunism and drink – three factors which could be said to have come together at Tay Bridge Station.

The fact remains that by the time they reached Tay Bridge Station on the fateful day all three men had been drinking and, while they were not incapable, their judgement may well have been affected. In more sober circumstances, Fitzgerald may have thought twice about walking away from a man with a loaded gun who had threatened to use it; Dunlop may have thought twice about ordering Sheppard to fire, and Sheppard himself may have thought twice about discharging the gun and might have had a more accurate aim if he did .

The likelihood remains, though, that if Dunlop had not elected to fetch Fitzgerald from custody at midday and had instead immediately taken him by car from the police station to the railway station, then the whole tragic incident would not have occurred. As it happened, a decision, born of kindness, to let a man see his wife and family before he was sentenced appears to have resulted in that wife becoming a widow and three young children losing their father.

"you find yourself in a nondescript car park..."

Standing outside the station, you look around you once more. The *RRS Discovery* is still there but now you can see that it is merely the first building block in Dundee's new waterfront development. The Olympia Leisure Centre has gone and so has Tayside House, and the area has opened up, showing Dundee's magnificent setting in a new light. The *Discovery* now nestles next to the V&A Museum of Design, which has risen on the edge of the Tay. The station building you have just exited is not the dated structure that was there on your previous visit but a modern version including a hotel. Several new hotels have opened in the city as visitor numbers have increased.

There are still roadworks in progress, but you no longer see the traffic cones, instead you see a city stretching its limbs, reaching out towards the river that gave it birth. As your walk through the station has demonstrated, though, the past is never far away if you care to look for it. Besides the presence of the

Discovery itself, the new development will contain streets bearing the names of missionary Mary Slessor, City Architect James Thomson and the regiment that has so many local connections – the Black Watch. The city is pushing into the future while maintaining one eye on its rich history. Welcome to Dundee.

2
Music Hall Days

In the early morning of Wednesday 12 October 1977, a fire broke out in a theatre in Dundee's Nethergate. Long past its heyday, the rarely used building was badly damaged in the blaze and was subsequently demolished, eventually becoming a car park. Another piece of Dundee's history had vanished and was seemingly unmourned.

The theatre had had several names during its eighty-four-year existence but most of these contained some variation of the name by which it was commonly known in Dundee – the Palace. It had opened in 1893 as a music hall known as the People's Palace – itself a replacement for earlier premises of the same name in Lochee Road. Along with the name changes, the Nethergate building had been used for several different purposes in its lifetime. For almost three decades in the early part of the twentieth century, it operated as a cinema. Even before this, it had carved out an important place in the history of cinema in Dundee when the first public showing of moving pictures in the city took place there on 8 July 1896.

In its later years the Palace was a variety theatre playing host to stars such as Jack Anthony, Alec Findlay, Harry Gordon, Robert Wilson, Johnny Victory and Dennis Clancy. In many ways, this was a return to the building's roots as many of these acts owed much to the music hall tradition of the late nineteenth and early twentieth centuries.

There were two other theatres in Dundee which could reasonably challenge any claim by the Palace to be the home of music hall in Dundee – the Gaiety, and the King's. The Gaiety was the name given to the former Royal Victoria

The interior of the King's Theatre in the music hall era

Theatre in Victoria Road when it operated as a music hall for a few years in the first decade of the twentieth century. Its time as a music hall was short-lived but coincided with a period when the form was arguably at its peak. As moving pictures began to increase in popularity the Gaiety became the Victoria Cinema – or simply "The Vic" – though it still mixed cinema with live shows until the 1930s. It continued to operate as a cinema until the 1980s and was demolished in 1990.

The King's Theatre in the Cowgate opened in 1909 and from the beginning was used to stage a variety of different types of shows including moving pictures on its "Kingscope". Nevertheless, the theatre played host to many of music hall's top stars in its early years before becoming a cinema in 1928. It was later known as the Gaumont and then the Odeon before it closed its doors in 1981. Unlike the Palace or the Gaiety, the building that housed King's Theatre is still standing. There have been campaigns for it to be restored and re-opened as a theatre. Investigations have established that, despite numerous alterations to the building over the years, enough of the original features remain intact to make this feasible. With so much of Dundee's heritage irretrievably lost, the time will surely come when the wisdom of such a restoration is grasped and the wherewithal to make it happen is found.

Like many other forms of entertainment, music hall was something that had its heyday before giving way to the next trend – in this case, cinema. Its influence, though, long outlived its existence as a living art form and can still be seen today in many aspects of popular culture such as music and comedy. This chapter, though, travels back to the time when music hall was at its height and examines what happened when some of its stars came to Dundee. Like the top billings on a music hall poster, some of their names still loom large in our consciousness today, while for others the intervening years have seen them slip down the bill into obscurity. There are also those, however, whose individual names would not even have featured on the posters at the time but whose visits to Dundee's music halls turned out to form part of an apprenticeship that led to international stardom.

Marie Lloyd

Other than those who went on to achieve Hollywood stardom, Marie Lloyd is perhaps the music hall star whose name remains best known in the twenty-first century. Born Matilda Alice Victoria Wood in London in 1870, she became known as the Queen of the Music Hall and was famous for songs such as "The Boy I Love Is Up in the Gallery" and "My Old Man (Said Follow the

Marie Lloyd

Van)." Audiences loved her cheerful humour and the double entendres which peppered her songs.

Marie Lloyd's first appearance in Dundee was in 1909 at the Gaiety Theatre. The *Courier* expressed the concern that while her songs were catchy, they were perhaps not what a Dundee audience was familiar with. In 1909 technology had not yet shrunk the world to the extent that it would in the next few decades and there was always a fear that an act might not "travel well". These concerns were not borne out, though, and the paper went on to note that "she had to respond to several encores and was presented with a magnificent bouquet."

It was to be eleven years before Marie Lloyd returned to Dundee – this time appearing at the King's Theatre. She told an *Evening Telegraph* reporter on that occasion that she had hoped to have returned to the city sooner but that circumstances had not permitted it. She said that her memories of the earlier visit were by then dim, but she did remember it as a happy stay. She went on to say that she was glad that Dundee appreciated the Cockney style of humour and that the little touches that went so well in London were quickly seized upon by the Dundee audience. At first, she had been doubtful as to whether this would be the case.

Marie Lloyd died on 7 October 1922, three days after collapsing on stage at the Empire Music Hall in Edmonton, London. Thousands attended her funeral and the cortège was said to contain twelve cars filled with flowers. The decades that followed her death proved that concerns that a Dundee audience would not appreciate Cockney songs or humour were groundless as many music hall ditties – including those popularised by Marie Lloyd herself – became part of the standard fare of singsongs and New Year parties in the city.

Charlie Chaplin

In late April 1926, huge crowds stood for hours in the pouring rain in Bank Street, Dundee, waiting to gain admission to the Kinnaird Cinema. The film they had come to see was a silent comedy which had already drawn large crowds to cinemas in Glasgow and Edinburgh as well as various places in England. Its name was *The Gold Rush* and it featured one of the most popular stars of the day, Charlie Chaplin – in his "little tramp" guise – as a hapless prospector.

There were four showings of the film daily with an additional children's matinee on Saturday. Newspaper advertisements referred to the "rush to see the Gold Rush" and noted that thousands were seen daily making their way to see the film. Despite this, it was announced at the beginning of May that there was still such a level of demand in Dundee that the film would run for another week. As the crowds who packed out the Kinnaird laughed their way through the antics of a Hollywood star at the height of his powers, there must have been those among them who recalled seeing Chaplin closer at hand, when, as a young music hall artist, he had visited Dundee.

Charlie Chaplin was only 10 years old when he first set foot in Dundee in August 1899. He appeared on that occasion at the People's Palace in the Nethergate as part of a clog dancing troupe – "The Eight Lancashire Lads". Chaplin himself was certainly not a "Lancashire lad" having been born and brought up in London. His childhood had been one marked by poverty and hardship. His parents had separated when he was very young and he had been raised by his mother. He spent time in a workhouse as a child, and in 1898 had seen his mother committed to an insane asylum.

Both of Chaplin's parents had been music hall artists and they had themselves each stopped off in Dundee at one time or another. His mother, Hannah, had appeared at the Palace of Varieties in Castle Street in 1886 under her stage name of Lily Harley. On that occasion, according to the *Courier*, she had proved herself to be "a most captivating singer" and had "gained the hearty applause of the audience". Chaplin's father, Charles Chaplin senior, appeared at the People's Palace in 1895 where his "splendid voice" had earned him a "flattering encore". Chaplin senior had played little part in his son's upbringing but nevertheless it was through his theatrical contacts that young Charlie had come to join "The Eight Lancashire Lads".

Like his parents before him, Charlie Chaplin's first appearance in Dundee earned him a favourable review from the *Courier*: "Although appearing last on the programme, the eight Lancashire lads were without doubt one of the best features in the entertainment, their clog dancing both individually and collectively being smart and neat." The review did not single Chaplin out for any particular praise but this was something that would be remedied on his next visit to Dundee.

Chaplin's fellow "Lancashire Lad", Jack Edge, later recalled their time in Dundee in an interview with the *Evening Telegraph*: "Charlie and myself were close pals. We danced together, spent our spare time together and slept together in a little combined room in the Nethergate, I believe, where an auld Scotch wife mothered us as if we were her own laddies." The two boys, Edge recalled, wandered around the town together, gazing in shop windows and admiring the smart clothes in tailors' windows. They were both ambitious, he said, and hoped someday to top the bill, though Charlie "little dreamed of the pictures".

Chaplin's first visit to the city also throws up an intriguing possibility. In his 1964 autobiography[6], he wrote of his time as a "Lancashire Lad": "When touring the provinces, we went to a school for the week in each town which did little to further my education." It is entirely possible, then, that during the week beginning 21 August 1899, Charlie Chaplin attended school in Dundee. Dundee's schools returned after the summer break that week. The log book for Tay Street School near to the People's Palace refers to a "considerable number of new pupils" but, unfortunately, no record of their names survives.

By 1903, Chaplin had given up clog dancing and turned to acting. From October that year he toured the country in Charles Frohman's production of *Sherlock Holmes*. The play reached Dundee in March 1904 where it met with some lukewarm reviews and unfavourable comparisons with a visit of the same play two years previously. Chaplin's performance, however, was universally praised. The *Courier* said: "The part of the boy Billy was sustained with more than usual skill by Charles Chaplin." The *Evening Telegraph* called Chaplin's "one of the brightest bits of acting in the play", saying that he displayed "immense activity as well as dramatic appreciation".

Four years later, Chaplin was back in Dundee – once more at the Palace. His career had taken yet another turn in the meantime. After a spell in London's West End with *Sherlock Holmes*, he had moved into comedy and was now part of a troupe of juvenile performers put together by Harry Cadle. The production was entitled *Casey's Circus* and was billed as "a street urchin's idea of producing a Circus Entertainment". "For real humour," said the *Courier*, "it is one of the best turns produced in the Palace for some time."

The show featured Chaplin doing an impression of another music hall act, Dr Walford Bodie, a hypnotist and illusionist who was known as the Electrical Wizard due to his use (or apparent use) of electricity, including an electric chair, in his act. Bodie was an extremely popular performer at this time and had himself appeared on the Dundee stage on many occasions. Chaplin's impression was said to be highly accurate and there was a strong resemblance between the pair when he donned his Bodie costume.

In Dundee the same week as *Casey's Circus* were "Fred Karno's Comedians", who appeared at the Empire Theatre in Rosebank Street and were billed as "the

---

6   Chaplin, Charlie, *My Autobiography* (1964), London: Penguin Classics; New edition (2003), page 45.

jolliest jokers on Earth". Karno was a huge star at this time and was said to have been the originator of the "custard pie in the face" gag later so beloved of so many of the makers of silent comedies. So popular was Karno that the phrase "Fred Karno's army" – meaning a chaotic group – was commonly used for decades.

It was as a member of Karno's company that Charlie Chaplin would return to Dundee in 1908. He was not the first member of the Chaplin family to become a Karno comedian, though. His older half-brother, Sydney, joined the company in 1906 and it was at Sydney's suggestion that Charlie had joined the group.

Chaplin's 1908 appearance in Dundee was at the Gaiety Theatre. The show was entitled *The Football Match* and starred Harry Weldon as Stiffy the goalkeeper. Weldon's face alone, the *Courier* assured its readers, "was sufficient to make the most serious of individuals laugh". The theatre, the paper said, had "resounded with roars of laughter throughout the piece". The Gaiety was not to resound with laughter at any of Karno's shows for the immediate future, though, as a dispute arose between the theatre's management and Karno, who claimed that he had been paid only half of the money he had been promised.

After his appearance in *The Football Match*, Dundonians would only see Charlie Chaplin on the big screen. In September 1910, he set sail for America with a company of Karno comedians. It was a journey that would eventually take him to Hollywood and ultimately into the history books. In the decades to come his name would be known worldwide and his movies would entertain millions of people. The 10-year-old clog dancer who first took to the Dundee stage in 1899 could not possibly have foreseen that his name and image would still be known throughout the world in the twenty-first century nor could he have imagined the technologies that allow him to continue to entertain audiences today.

Arthur Stanley Jefferson

In the Fred Karno company that set sail for the United States in 1910 with Charlie Chaplin was another young comedian with a great future ahead of him. Born Arthur Stanley Jefferson in Ulverston, Lancashire in 1890, he would be better known to later generations as Stan Laurel, one half of the legendary comic duo Laurel and Hardy. Stan had joined Karno's company in late 1909 after meeting Fred Karno at the Metropole Theatre in Glasgow where his father, Arthur Jefferson senior, was manager.

Charlie Chaplin may not have appeared in Dundee after 1908, but other Karno comedians certainly did. So popular was Karno's type of comedy in this period that he often had more than one troupe touring at any one time, not to mention the various other groups that based their entire acts on his. A Karno company that included the future Stan Laurel appeared at the King's Theatre in a run that began on 27 December 1909 and ended on New Year's Day 1910. He starred in what the *Evening Telegraph* described as "a couple of vivacious pieces" – one was advertised as a "screaming burlesque" and called *Early Birds*, and the other, *Mumming Birds*, was "a screaming travesty of a modern music hall".

This was not Stan Laurel's first visit to Dundee, though. In 1908, Arthur Jefferson had taken his company on tour with "an original farcical comedy sketch, in two scenes" entitled *Home from the Honeymoon*. By the time that the Jefferson company reached the Palace Theatre in Dundee on 17 August, they had been joined by young Stan. The *Courier* reviewed the sketch as "much boisterous fun" and "cleverly performed by a capable company" and said that "the audience had a hearty laugh". It is not clear if Stan himself took to the stage for *Home from the Honeymoon* in Dundee or had a behind the scenes role. The plot, written by his father, possibly with help from Stan, certainly seems to have stuck in his mind, though. It would later be reworked for the 1927 Laurel and Hardy silent comedy *Duck Soup* and again in 1930 for their talkie *Another Fine Mess*.

Even after Stan Laurel left for the United States aboard the *SS Cairnrona* in September 1910, a long hard road remained in front of him before Laurel and Hardy became household names. It would be just over a decade later that he first appeared in a film with Oliver Hardy and a further seven years before they were officially paired as a comedy team. Ultimately, though, they went on to be regarded by many as the greatest ever comedy duo and their films continue to entertain people to this day. A close look at Stan Laurel's performances in some of these films reveals the influence in the comedy grounding that he had secured on the British music hall stage.

Walford Bodie

The man that Charlie Chaplin impersonated during his 1906 visit, magician, hypnotist, illusionist, ventriloquist and "Electric Wizard" Dr. Walford Bodie, made numerous appearances in Dundee, stretching back to the earliest days of the People's Palace.

He was born Samuel Murphy Bodie in Aberdeen in 1869 (though he later managed to make three years of his age disappear: "I was born in '72," he told the *Evening Telegraph*). Despite calling himself "Doctor", he had no medical qualifications. When challenged on this by members of the medical profession, he claimed that the initials "M.D." did not denote that he was a Doctor of Medicine but rather a "Merry Devil". Nevertheless, he did claim to effect cures during the course of his stage act. In 1903, for example, a Mrs Sturrock of Wilkie's Lane, Dundee, who was said to have been paralysed for more than seven years, was reported to have "walked briskly off of the stage amidst the loud applause of the spectators" after being treated by Bodie.

Another feature of Bodie's stage show was his use of an electric chair. He would use this to quite literally shock members of the audience, though presumably with a safe level of electricity. His own turn in the chair, though, was apparently death defying with thousands of volts of electricity being passed through his body. The chair was said to have been used in Sing Sing, the notorious prison in New York State and was a gift from Bodie's friend, Harry Houdini.

A master of publicity besides his other talents, Bodie's 1896 appearance in Dundee caused a sensation in the city when he said he would put a young man in a trance for six days. A coffin was placed on the stage of the Palace in which the man was to lie during this time. Bodie said that he would be willing to explain the scientific aspects of the feat and promised to give £100 to a local charity if any medical man could prove that the patient was not in a genuine trance, artificially produced. No one appears to have successfully claimed the £100 and the invitation to "come and see the man in a trance" seems to have delivered a boost to Bodie's audiences in the city. By the time of his next visit the following year, it was reported that he was playing to packed houses in Dundee. By the turn of the century he was being advertised, with some justification, as "Dundee's favourite entertainer".

One of the most famous incidents concerning Walford Bodie in Dundee took place on Saturday, 6 August 1904. He was in town appearing at the Palace and had been out with friends on the Friday night when he got into an argument about his hypnotic powers with Andrew Philip, the proprietor of Dundee Zoo. The phrase "Dundee Zoo" might conjure up an image of some long-lost rolling parkland with animals in spacious enclosures but Philip's establishment was a double shop at the foot of Castle Street which contained among other things monkeys, wolves and hyenas as well as kestrels, hawks and owls. Philip bet

Bodie £50 that he could not hypnotise his hyenas and wolves. The "Electric Wizard" agreed to the bet and then subsequently forgot all about it.

Many years later, the *Evening Telegraph* carried Bodie's own account of what happened afterwards: "The next morning, when I was walking along the Nethergate, I met a string of sandwich men carrying boards, which stated the terms of the challenge and that the contest was to be held in the afternoon. Of course, I went to the circus [zoo] and entered the hyenas' cages. The effect was more or less instantaneous and I soon overcame the animals, and then I entered the wolves' cages and did likewise with them. I have been told that one of the hyenas was in a comatose condition for a week afterwards."

It is difficult to judge what actually happened on this occasion given that both Bodie and Philip were showmen looking for publicity and that news of the incident would benefit both of their enterprises. An advertisement for the zoo on August 10 boasted: "Wolves and Hyenas hypnotised by Dr. Walford Bodie." A cynic might speculate that the animals had been drugged. Nevertheless, Bodie was proud enough of the event to keep a newspaper cutting about it for years afterwards so perhaps his hypnotism of the animals was genuine. One theory can certainly be ruled out in any case and that is that the poor captive creatures were so naturally docile that they proved no real threat to Bodie. At the end of the same month as Bodie's appearance at the zoo, while their trainer, a man named Bardell, was trying to get the hyenas to stand up on pedestals, they began to attack each other. Bardell tried to separate them and one of the creatures turned on him. The *Evening Post* reported: "The teeth of the animal closed on his right arm, which in the struggle which ensued was terribly torn by the hyena's claws. Before he managed to free himself, Bardell had lost much blood and was greatly exhausted."

The episode with the zoo animals was not the only offstage anecdote concerning Bodie's time in Dundee. He was one of the first to drive a motor car in the city, much to the consternation of the shopkeepers in the Nethergate, who complained about the noise, earning Bodie a warning from the police.

Another story concerns one of his best friends in the city, dentist Andrew Syme, who Bodie said, was always the first to meet him when he came to the city and always waved him goodbye when he left. One day, Syme asked his friend if electricity could be used for the painless extraction of teeth. Bodie's solution did not exactly make the process pain free but rather sought to divert the patient's attention. He fitted a coil behind the hand grips on the dentist's chair. The idea was that Syme would ask the patient to hold the grips at the moment of the extraction. Bodie explained: "My idea was that the sudden shock would rob the tooth-pulling of its pain." Things did not go quite as planned, though. Bodie continued: "Well, he nearly killed his first patient and the first patient nearly killed him. Dr Syme had turned the full current on at once and the shock was too much for the patient who, when he recovered did his best to gain reprisals on the doctor." Bodie gave Syme a switch to better control the current but the dentist wisely scrapped the idea altogether.

When Bodie retired in 1929, he summed up his career and paid tribute to the Dundee audiences in particular, saying: "I have had a great time of it, and I have had great receptions, particularly in Dundee where they never seemed to have tired of my performance, no matter how often I came." This was probably just as well as, in true show business style, Bodie's retirement was very short-lived and he returned to Dundee several times in the 1930s. His last appearance in the city was at the Broadway Theatre in Arthurstone Terrace at the end of 1938. He died the following year in Blackpool at the age of 70.

Florrie Forde

Even a century or so after they were written, songs such as "Down at the Old Bull and Bush", "Has Anybody Here Seen Kelly?" and "It's A Long Way to Tipperary" are still familiar to many people. Of those who claim to know them, however, most would probably admit that their knowledge only really extends to the chorus rather than the complete song. This is not so much a reflection of knowledge being lost with the passage of time but rather of the way these songs were written and meant to be enjoyed in the first place. They were originally presented in a music hall setting with the singer relating the verses and the audience joining in on the catchy refrains. The foremost proponent of this type of entertainment was a woman named Florrie Forde.

Florrie Forde was born in Melbourne, Australia in 1875 and came to Britain in 1897 where her cheerful personality and outstanding stage presence soon endeared her to music hall audiences up and down the country. Her first visit to Dundee was in October 1908 when she appeared at the Palace Theatre to an enthusiastic reception. Her songs, according to the *Evening Telegraph,* were "of a catchy nature and the choruses were sung with great gusto. The house applauded her again and again… and she had to respond to several encores."

Less than a year later Forde was back in Dundee, playing the King's Theatre to a similar reaction – sustained applause bringing her back to the stage four times. By this time, she was already being billed as "Dundee's great favourite". A return visit to the King's in 1910 helped to cement this reputation and the *Telegraph* explained how the audience would not let her go until she (and they) had sung "Has anybody here seen Kelly?" one more time.

Forde returned to the King's Theatre in 1913. That year, she introduced a new song into her repertoire – "It's a Long Way to Tipperary". By the time of her next visit to the city in November 1914, three months after the outbreak of the Great War, the song had already been taken up by British soldiers involved in the conflict. That same month the song was recorded by the Irish tenor John McCormack and its popularity spread throughout the world.

During her 1914 visit, Florrie Forde made time to entertain wounded soldiers in the Eastern Hospital (later known as Maryfield Hospital). The visit was not an isolated incident and became an annual event. It was the kind of personal touch that only added to her immense popularity in the city. In February 1915, for example, while appearing in a pantomime at the King's Theatre, Florrie took time out to visit Tannadice Park, home of Dundee Hibernian (now Dundee United), to kick off a charity match between Balgay FC and a select eleven.

Florrie Forde's popularity was not restricted to her audiences or the general public either – she was also highly regarded by her fellow entertainers, acting as a mother figure to many of the younger performers. The comedian Bud Flanagan,[7] one half of the duo Flanagan and Allen, recalled in his autobiography, *My Crazy Life*: "She was a big woman with a heart to match and loved by everyone in and out of the profession."[8] Flanagan in particular had reason to be grateful to Florrie Forde as it was she who first teamed him up with Chesney Allen.

Having appeared in the city at least once a year from 1913 to 1921, Florrie Forde did not appear again in Dundee until 1928. Her long-awaited return saw her with Flanagan and Allen in tow as the comedy revue "Us" came to the King's Theatre. Forde herself proved as popular as ever receiving what the *Courier* called "a most enthusiastic welcome". The *Evening Telegraph* had particular praise for her new companions: "Humour of rich and abundant

---

7   Flanagan's real name was Chaim Reuben Weintrop; Florrie Forde, on the other hand, was born Flora May Augustus Flanagan.
8   Flanagan, Bud, My Crazy Life (1961), London: The New English Library Limited (1962 edition), page 84

quality is provided by Bud Flanagan, who has a capital companion in Chesney Allen. These twins of mirth present a wonderfully funny sketch – 'At the Races'." The next year the trio were back in Dundee in the revue "Flo and Co" which also earned favourable notices from the local press.

In the 1930s Flanagan and Allen went on to greater things, appearing at the London Palladium as part of the "Crazy Gang" along with two other double acts and extending into films and musical recordings. When Florrie Forde appeared in Dundee at the Victoria Theatre in 1931, however, the impression given in a report in the *Evening Telegraph* is that while she herself remained vibrant ("her wonderful personality undimmed") and popular ("the applause was deafening"), her act was one that was increasingly appealing to nostalgia. While she sang a couple of contemporary melodies ("just to show that she could sing that kind of thing if she felt like it"), it was the old favourites that held the appeal. Youngsters, the paper said, gazed in amazement at the sight of their staid elders eagerly joining in the chorus of "Antonio", a song with which they were unfamiliar. The music hall format itself was one whose best days seemed to be behind it. The bill, according to the *Telegraph*, was one "of a kind too seldom provided these days". A correspondent even went so far as to ask Florrie if she had ever considered retirement, to which she replied: "Oh no, I don't know what I would do if I wasn't working." There was still a place for music hall artistes, she said, so long as they received encouragement from the public.

The Dundee public, it seems, continued to encourage Florrie Forde. She returned to "the Vic" in 1932 and to the Broadway Theatre in 1933, 1934 and 1935, playing to packed houses and good reviews. "She is still the greatest chorus singer in the world," said the *Courier* in 1934. "Whether you are hearing Florrie singing the songs for the first time or the hundredth time they are equally enjoyable. She is an able leader too, of community singing 'a la Forde'." There were further appearances at the Broadway in 1937 and 1938, and in early 1939 a role in the pantomime *Aladdin* at the Palace Theatre. Florrie Forde took to the stage of the Palace again in September of that year – the month that saw the outbreak of the Second World War. People seemed to take comfort in hearing songs such as "It's A Long Way to Tipperary" or "Pack up your Troubles in Your Old Kit Bag", which they remembered from the previous world war. They delighted too in a new song, "We're Going to Hang out the Washing on the Siegfried Line".

The outbreak of war meant that Florrie once more took time to visit wounded servicemen. On the afternoon of 18 April 1940, while appearing at the Tivoli Theatre in Aberdeen, she performed at the Kingseat Navy Hospital to a rapturous reception. On the way back to fulfil that night's engagement, however, she collapsed. She was taken to a nursing home in Albyn Place, Aberdeen where she died a few hours later. She was 63 years old.

The Dundee press mourned her as a "generous, kindly woman" and said that she had many friends in Dundee. This was hardly surprising given that her appearances in the city had spanned more than thirty years. Indeed, she had been due back in Dundee the week after she died.

Although Florrie Forde's is not a name that would be familiar to most people in Dundee today, many of the songs she made famous seem to have entered the collective subconscious, and while the type of community singing that she once led seems, at first glance, to be something that belongs firmly to Dundee's past, a visit to any rock concert, football ground or karaoke bar proves that it is an instinct that remains alive and well in the city.

Stop Press, a Musical Burlesque

In September 1916, while Florrie Forde was enjoying a typically successful run at the King's Theatre, an interesting-sounding alternative was being advertised at the Palace Playhouse: "*Stop Press* – Musical Burlesque by Robt Hargreaves; Music by Magini".

The show consisted of five scenes, though it had little or no plot, and the acting, the *Evening Telegraph* said, went "with a merry swing". The third of these scenes, *How the Show was Rehearsed*, was said to be a particular novelty. "Such a combination of fun makers take part in it," said the *Courier*, "that constant laughter is "forced" from even the most melancholy."

The main stars of the show were a married couple named Tom and Kitty. They were each given excellent reviews for their various performances. Kitty played her three parts "to perfection", the *Telegraph* said, while Tom played five parts and, according to the paper, did justice to them all. Coming in for particular praise was his appearance as a tramp and his rendition of "When I leave the World Behind".

The couple's success in Dundee was not surprising as it was the result of many years of hard work and experience in the entertainment industry. Tom in particular had an interesting history. He was born Abraham Thomas Ball in Staffordshire in 1879, the son of a bricklayer. His family had emigrated to Pittsburgh in the United States when he was about five years old and Tom got his first taste of show business there, working in vaudeville and circuses. He returned to Britain while still in his late teens and established a successful music hall career. After his marriage to Kitty Grant, they formed a successful double act. Kitty used the name Drum, making them "Drum and Ball", and later Tom changed his name to Major to make them "Drum and Major". By the time of their 1916 visit to Dundee, they were both using the name Major.

Kitty died in the late 1920s and around the same time Tom retired from the fading music hall scene. He married his second wife, Gwen, and started a garden ornament business. In 1943, when Tom was 64 years old, the couple had a son they named John. He too was destined for fame but in a world far removed from his music hall heritage. Eighty years after his father had appeared on the Dundee stage, John Major was prime minister of the United Kingdom.

George Robey

John Major may have been British prime minister, but George Robey was the self-styled "Prime Minister of Mirth". Little remembered today, Robey was a huge star in the music hall era. His changes of costume, facial contortions and double entrendres were loved by audiences. Their laughter would be met with demands from Robey that they "Desist!", which only served to increase the effect.

Although he had not appeared in Dundee before, Robey's national fame was enough to ensure packed houses every night of the week in February 1909 when he appeared at Gaiety Theatre. Just his appearance on stage was greeted with loud and enduring cheers. The *Courier's* reviewer, for one, was impressed by Robey and his comic appearance in particular: "His style is original. Much of his success depends on his facial contortions and he is a personage who must be seen as well as heard to be fully appreciated."

Robey was a keen sportsman and took part in many charity football and cricket matches, and so it was not surprising that the Gaiety was not the only place where he made an appearance in Dundee that week. The advertisement in the *Courier* announcing his first theatrical appearance was accompanied by notice of his sporting debut in the city in a "Grand Charity Football Match" at Dens Park in aid of the unemployed.

George Robey : The Prime Minister of Mirth

The match took place on a Wednesday afternoon under the auspices of the Dundee and District Half Holiday Football Association and pitched a Dundee FC team against a select from the Wednesday League. Needless to say, it was a somewhat one-sided affair. The *Evening Telegraph* carried a match report which called the game "more of a farce than anything else". Robey captained the Dundee team and scored four goals, to say nothing, the report added, of the "certs" he missed. He was also reported to be "keen as a kitten" and "enjoying the spectacle of the Dens Park team running rings round their less experienced opponents". Some spectators may have turned up expecting a comic performance, but Robey took his football very seriously. A fifth goal was added for the home team by George Langlands, who a little over a year later would play in the side that won the Scottish Cup for Dundee. Langlands is the only Dundee player named in the report, but the team was said to comprise most of the first eleven and it can be safely supposed that the team that Robey captained largely consisted of players involved in that successful cup campaign. There is no mention of any goal scored for the other side, which comprised players from teams including Craigie, Harp and East End.

Robey's experience as Dundee captain was certainly less painful than when he fulfilled a similar role for Rangers during a run at the Glasgow Empire. On that occasion, the opposing goalkeeper, reaching for the ball, hit

Robey instead, knocked him over and left him with two broken ribs. Bravely playing on to the end of the game before going on to appear on stage that night despite the pain, Robey must surely have been less than amused that much of the crowd took the initial incident to have been a comical set piece staged for their entertainment.

In the years following his visit to Dundee, George Robey went on to even greater success. In 1916, he appeared in the revue *The Bing Boys Are Here*. The show featured a song that became a standard and Robey's theme tune: "If You Were the Only Girl (in the World)". It was certainly more memorable than the theme song he had at the beginning of his career, whose chorus included the line "They knew her by the pimple, the pimple on her nose".

In this period, Robey continued to be seen by Dundee audiences as his career had expanded into films. He was finally back in Dundee in the flesh in 1927, this time at the King's Theatre in a musical show called "Bits and Pieces". The show was a great success and the *Evening Telegraph* reviewer's only regret was that there was not more of Robey in it.

Shortly before he died in 1954, Robey accepted a knighthood for his charity work. It was the culmination of a long and varied career which had embraced theatre, recordings and films and seen him play Falstaff in Laurence Olivier's film adaptation of Shakespeare's *Henry V*. For some Dundonians, though, their fondest memory of Robey would be of that day at Dens Park when, however temporarily, he played for Dundee FC.

George Formby

By the time George Formby appeared at The King's Theatre in Dundee in November, 1915, he was one of Britain's biggest and most highly paid music hall stars. "When one has said that George Formby is coming to Dundee one has really said enough" said the *Courier*.

This was not, however, the George Formby whose name and image remain well known today – the celebrated Lancashire comedian and film star with the cheeky grin who sang and played the banjo ukulele. In 1915, he was an 11-year-old jockey, though he did, in fact, make his film debut that year in a silent film called *By the Shortest of Heads*. Instead this was his father, the now largely forgotten George Formby senior, whose fame in this period in many ways equalled that which his son would later achieve.

Neither man's name was, in fact, Formby. George Formby junior was born George Hoy Booth, and his father's name was James Booth. Booth senior's career in music hall had begun at the age of 13 as part of the Brothers Glenray – a singing duo known as the "the songbirds of the music halls". This act's time was limited, however, due to the breaking voices of its members, and Booth moved into comedy. He renamed himself Formby after the Lancashire seaside town and created John Willie – a gormless character in baggy trousers and a bowler hat.

In 1900, Formby's career was boosted when George Robey recommended him to the owner of the London Pavilion music hall. By the time he appeared at the Palace Theatre in Dundee in 1908, he had already made his first of what would turn out to be around 180 recordings. Formby's appearance in Dundee was a great success. The *Courier* said that he was "a very clever comedian" and noted that all his songs were very funny. The audience recalled him to the stage "again and again".

There was to be a long gap before Formby's next appearance in Dundee, but he was not entirely absent from the local stage. His distinctive appearance and mannerisms made him one of the most impersonated acts of the time, and so any members of the audience in 1915 who had not already seen or heard him had a reasonable idea of what to expect. They were not to be disappointed as the *Courier's* review points out: "George was in one of his most dare-devil moods, twirling his stick with amazing recklessness and dancing 'divinely' and developing excessive 'nuttiness' by parting his hair in the middle, wearing his handkerchief in his sleeve and displaying a wristlet watch." While a modern reader might marvel at what passed for recklessness and "nuttiness" at this time, there is no doubt that the 1915 audience appreciated Formby. The *Courier* reported that he got a "great reception" in Dundee. The *Evening Telegraph* said that it required a sense of humour to appreciate Formby and after the merriment that had prevailed at the King's Theatre while he was on stage, it could not be said of Scottish people – or of Dundonians at least – that they "must undergo a surgical operation before they can see a joke". The caricature of the "dour Scot", it seems, was widespread in this period – boosted in some respects by the caricatures presented by some music hall performers.

Those attending the King's Theatre were treated to all the idiosyncratic touches which had so endeared Formby to audiences throughout the country, including his habit of casually chatting to people in the stalls between musical numbers and keeping up a dialogue with the conductor of the orchestra and the musicians throughout the show. He would also deliver a humorous summary of the other acts on the bill, which some said was a particular highlight of his own act. His thoughts on the rest of the Dundee bill, such as hand-to-hand balancers the Ventoys, or novelty instrumental act Ronald George, appear to be sadly unrecorded.

Another feature of his performances had a more tragic origin and outcome. Formby suffered from chronic bronchitis and tuberculosis and was subject to violent coughing fits while on stage. He integrated these into his act with lines like "coughing better tonight" or "that was a good cough, best one I've done this year" and, most famously: "It's not the cough that carries you off – it's the coffin they carries you off in." Though some in the audience might have thought that it was all part of the act, for others in Dundee at this time, where living and working conditions had left many with chest complaints, and where tuberculosis was a feared and deadly disease, this particular brand of gallows humour would have had a deep resonance.

On Wednesday, 2 February 1921, while appearing in pantomime at Newcastle, Formby suffered a severe haemorrhage in his larynx after a particularly bad coughing fit. He returned home to Warrington where he died six days later. He left behind over £25,000 in his will and a schedule that contained solid bookings for the next five years. It was only after his death that his son George took to the stage – at first under his mother's name of Hoy and later as George Formby, going on to great success.

By the mid-1930s, when George Formby junior was one of the biggest stars in Britain, many of Dundee's music halls and variety theatres had turned into cinemas. In 1937, when George's film *Feather Your Nest* opened at the King's (then a Gaumont cinema), it is entirely possible that there were those in the audience who were able to say that they had "kent his faither" when he appeared there twenty-two years earlier.

Bob Pender's Giants

In late July 1919, the *Evening Telegraph* recommended the King's Theatre's latest variety programme as a suitable way for people to mark Dundee's traditional summer holiday. The bill-topping Kuming and Windsor were praised for their "sparkling" vocal and instrumental act which was "full of delightful comedy". There was also appreciation, however, for an act whose name could be found further down the bill: a novelty stilt-walking act called "Bob Pender's Giants". The *Telegraph* reported that the "Giants" had raised "plenty of laughter" with their act *Getting Ready for the Pantomime*. It was, the report continued, "a clever stage production, culminating in a fearsome and wonderful parade of stilted 'monsters'".

Among the "monsters" appearing on stilts with a papier-mâché head twice nightly in Dundee in 1919 was a young boy named Archie. Archie had taken advantage of a problem that had faced Bob Pender in the years after the introduction of conscription in 1916, when the young men he had recruited to his stage troupe had tended to be called up to the army as soon as they were of age. Pretending to be his own father, Archie had written to Pender enclosing a photograph and asking to join the troupe. He had neglected to say that he was not yet 14 and could not legally leave school. To the young lad's astonishment Pender wrote back and suggested to "his father" that young Archie should come to Norwich for an interview, which the boy duly did. He spent ten days practising with the troupe before his father caught up with him and took him back home.

Three days after his fourteenth birthday, Archie was back with the Pender troupe and for the next two and a half years toured the provinces learning his trade as an acrobat, comedian and stilt walker. In July 1920, he was given the opportunity to appear with Pender and seven other boys from the troupe at the Globe Theatre in New York City. He left for the United States aboard the *RMS Olympic* – sister ship of the ill-fated *Titanic* and *Britannic*. Archie could not have imagined the level of fame and success that he was to enjoy in America. He would not be remembered as a stilt walker or acrobat, though, but as an actor and movie star. Nor would history remember him as Archie either – or even by his full name of Archibald Alexander Leach – but rather he would be known to millions as Cary Grant.

Will Fyffe

If Will Fyffe's name is known at all today it is for the fact that he wrote and sang "I Belong to Glasgow", but Fyffe did not belong to Glasgow at all. He was, in fact, born in Dundee in 1885. His mother Janet was a music teacher, and his father John worked as a ship's carpenter at Gourlay's shipyard.

John Fyffe, though, had always had an ambition to be an actor, and shortly after Will was born left his job to form a touring company performing in a geggy – a portable wooden theatre which was assembled and dismantled at every venue. Will began playing parts in his father's productions from a young age and found that he enjoyed it. He would later claim to have never done a day's work in his life, as his career had always been a joy to him.

His father's decision to leave his job and go "a-journeying in theatre land" as Will later put it, meant that the family gave up their home at Ferry Road in Dundee and moved in with John Fyffe's parents in Letham, Angus. This, in turn, meant that Will was left with no childhood memories of the city at all but retained fond memories of Letham and fishing in the Vinney Burn with a home made fishing rod.

Will Fyffe returned to Dundee in 1918 in a revue at the King's Theatre. He had made the switch to variety after leaving his father's company and touring in England and Wales with other companies. In 1905, he had married an actress named Lily Wilcock. Lily met a tragic end in 1921, when the Steamer *Rowan*, onboard which she was travelling to Dublin to meet her husband, sank after a collision.

By the time Will next appeared in Dundee in 1923 he had remarried and his popularity had reached new heights. One major factor in this was "I Belong to Glasgow". How then, did someone born in Dundee and raised in Letham come to write this most Glaswegian of songs? The song, Fyffe said, was inspired by a meeting with a real drunk in Glasgow Central Station and was written at a time when he was "hard up". He had hoped to sell it to Harry Lauder, but finding himself performing as an "extra turn" at the Pavilion Theatre in Glasgow one night, had sung the song himself. It had gone down extremely well with the audience and this proved to be a turning point in his career. By the early 1920s, he was topping the bill at the London Palladium and appearing in royal command performances.

Forever associated with Glasgow, Fyffe remained fond of his native city, which he described as "a fine town to be born in". In 1931, he told the *Evening Telegraph*: "I've travelled all over the world and I've yet to see a town with a better approach. The view of Bonnie Dundee that unrolls itself before you as you cross the Tay Bridge is one of the most beautiful in the world." Echoing the words of his most famous song, he said, "I'm proud to say I belong to Dundee."

Will Fyffe enjoyed a long and highly successful career on stage and in film. In 1942, he was awarded the CBE for his work entertaining troops. His life ended in tragic circumstances, though, in December 1947, when he went to recuperate after an operation at a hotel he had bought in St Andrews. He fell from the window of his room and died in the local cottage hospital from his injuries.

Belle Elmore

In August 1910, the former manager of the Palace, Simon Mackintosh, recalled an appearance at the theatre a little over three years previously by an artist named Belle Elmore. Her "turn" was apparently "a most interesting one" and she was said to have been a "great hit with the Dundee audiences" who recognised her as an "artiste of ability" and were not slow to demonstrate their appreciation. She became a "prime favourite" and her week-long visit was said to be an extremely successful one.

It was an estimation of Miss Elmore's abilities, the like of which has rarely been heard subsequently. Her reputation is that of a poor performer whose talent did not match her ambition. This is often illustrated by way of an incident that is supposed to have occurred at the beginning of 1907 when the Variety Artistes' Federation organised a strike over wages and conditions. While top stars such as Marie Lloyd were themselves well paid and able to dictate their own terms, they took their places on the picket lines in support of their less well-off colleagues. On one occasion when her fellow strikers attempted to stop Belle Elmore crossing the lines, Marie Lloyd is reputed to have said: "Don't be daft. Let her in and she'll empty the theatre."

Certainly, Elmore was not in the top league of music hall artistes and had fallen well short of her original ambition to be an opera singer, but she did earn several favourable, if rather underwhelming, mentions in the press. The theatrical paper *The Era* noted that she "dances and sings merrily"; the *Portsmouth Evening News* said she was "a dainty comedienne…very well received", while the *Western Daily Press* described her as "pleasing". She was never destined to progress up the bill, though, and in later years devoted much of her energy to the Music Hall Ladies Guild.

Why, then, was this, at best middle-ranking music hall star and her visit some three years earlier being talked about in Dundee in 1910? The answer was that she had been murdered and her remains found buried in the cellar of her home at 39 Hilldrop Crescent, Camden Town, London. The chief suspect was her husband – a 47-year-old American homeopathic doctor and salesman by the name of Hawley Harvey Crippen.

Dr. Crippen might have got away with the murder had he not panicked following a visit by Chief Inspector Walter Dew of Scotland Yard, on 8 July 1910. Crippen had previously told friends that Belle – or Cora as he knew her[9] – had died while on a trip to California, but suspicions were aroused when he went to France with his secretary (and lover) Ethel Le Neve soon after his wife's supposed death. Crippen told Chief Inspector Dew that he had invented the story of Belle's death and that she had, in fact, left him for another man, and he was merely trying to avoid the humiliation and scandal. Dew believed the story and left. It was only when he discovered that Crippen and Ethel Le Neve had disappeared in the wake of his visit that his suspicions were reignited.

On the day that the news of Belle Elmore's murder broke in July 1910, the *Evening Telegraph* reported that Crippen's description had been circulated among the Dundee police force and that they were keeping a look out for him, watching the railway stations and steamers and making periodic visits to local hotels and lodging houses. Although the city was a major port, it might have been thought that this was just a routine precaution, repeated in cities up and down the country. It appears, though, that the possibility that Crippen was in Dundee was being taken seriously by the police, and two detectives from Scotland Yard travelled to the city on Saturday, 16 July aboard the steamer *London*.

If he had been hiding in the city, however, Crippen would surely soon have fled after reading the lead story in the *Telegraph* on Monday, 18 July which asked, "Is H. H. Crippen in Dundee?" before going on to report the visit of the two detectives. Together with Ethel Le Neve (who was dressed as a boy), Crippen was in fact arrested aboard the *Montrose* having almost reached Canada. He was found guilty of murder and was hanged at Pentonville Prison on 23 November 1910. Le Neve was acquitted of being an accessory after the fact.

If Crippen had not been in Dundee following the murder of his wife, is there a possibility that he was with her in the city when she made her appearance at the Palace? He was certainly thought to have been touring the provinces with her at this time, and theatre manager Simon Mackintosh said that he believed Crippen had been in Dundee. A performer who appeared on the same bill as Belle Elmore at the Palace Theatre in Glasgow told the press

---

9   Belle was born into a Polish family in New York and her original name was Kunigunde Mackamotzki. She adopted the Anglicised name Cora Turner before taking on the stage name Belle Elmore.

that the doctor had definitely accompanied Belle when she appeared there in 1907: "Of course we saw a good deal of Crippen. He seemed very devoted and they were apparently a very happy couple. He did not speak much, but Belle was vivacious and full of fun."

It is likely that the trip to Glasgow was part of the same tour that came to Dundee and there is every possibility that there were those in the city who encountered a small, nondescript man with a moustache and gold-rimmed glasses, unaware that they had, in fact, met someone who would become a permanent fixture of Madame Tussaud's Chamber of Horrors and one of the country's most infamous murderers.

James Berry

Whether or not Hawley Harvey Crippen ever attended the Palace Theatre, it is certain that in December 1895 one killer did enter the theatre and indeed stood on its stage before a cheering audience who had paid between 3d. and 2s. for the privilege of seeing him. Many others outside had failed to gain admission, so great was the demand for tickets. Heading up a bill that included Dr. Denno the magician, Vox the "marvellous ventriloquist" and Parvo "the negro impersonator", was a man who had, in fact, killed 131 people in the space of seven years. The reason that the stage was not stormed by the local police to arrest this serial killer was that every one of his victims had been killed legally. Between 1884 and 1891, James Berry had been the public hangman.

Berry's act consisted of him talking about his experiences as an executioner and also showing a series of lantern slides portraying various criminals and scenes from the interior of Newgate Prison. The audience sat enthralled, perhaps as much by being in the presence of the former executioner himself as by his anecdotes.

This was James Berry's first appearance in Dundee as a public performer but it was not his first trip to the city. His previous visit had been in April 1889 in what was then his professional capacity. He had not been able, he told the press, to see any of the locality at that time as he had not been allowed to leave his hotel. He had travelled to the city to hang a wife murderer by the name of William Henry Bury. Bury, who came to Dundee from the East End of London, was the last man to be hanged in Dundee and is thought by some to have been the notorious serial killer Jack the Ripper. This was an opinion with which his near namesake Berry agreed, later writing: "I became firmly convinced in my own mind that Bury was the man who had introduced such a reign of terror into the East End of London, and years of calm reflection in retirement have made me more convinced than ever that I was right." In his memoirs published in the *Weekly News* in 1927, he recalled two mysterious visitors from London who came to witness the hanging:

> "There were two strangers in the prison and who they were nobody knew except the men who examined the order for their attendance. Two quiet-looking men in suits of a London cut, they watched the man die from behind the little crowd at the edge of the scaffold, and then, with their faces strangely marked by excitement, they walked up to me.
> 'Well, Berry, what do you think?'
> 'Oh, I think it's the man right enough.'
> 'And so do we. There can be no doubt about it. You'll find there will be no Whitechapel crimes after this. You've put an end to 'Jack the Ripper's' games.'
> The men assured me that they were officers from Scotland Yard sent down to take observation in the prison of Dundee when Bury the Princes Street murderer, died by my hand, to find out from me if he had made any remarks which could be taken to refer to the sensational London crimes, and to report thereafter to the Crown."

Berry also described what happened when he went into the condemned cell:

> "When I walked into the cell he looked at me almost defiantly, and then he twisted his face up into a sneer. He was the first to begin the conversation.
> 'I suppose you think you are clever to hang me?'
> Now, there isn't much in that question when you see it in cold print, but had you heard it spoken you would have thought as I did at the time. The man about to die laid particular emphasis on the last word he spoke. He talked as if he thought himself to be one who stood head and shoulders above every other criminal who had passed through my hands. Meanwhile the detectives had drawn near and were straining their ears to catch any word which might fall from his lips. I looked at him and waited.
> 'I suppose you think you are clever because you are going to hang me,' he repeated. 'But because you are to hang me you are not to get anything out of me.'"

Although there was much speculation in the press on both sides of the Atlantic at the time he was hanged that William Bury might be Jack the Ripper, James Berry's conviction that this was the case does not seem to have emerged into the public domain until years later. There is no mention of either Bury or the Ripper case, for example in Berry's 1892 book, *My Experiences as an Executioner*. As with everything Ripper-related there are arguments and counter arguments regarding this. The information might have been regarded as too sensitive in the immediate aftermath of the hanging, some would argue, and furthermore it may have taken a few years for Berry to have finally become convinced that he had hanged the Ripper. In the years following the killer's reign of terror, rumours as to his identity still abounded and further murders in all sorts of locations were attributed to him. It might only have been at a few years distance that Berry realised that the Ripper killings had, in fact, stopped after he hanged Bury and that the full meaning of the events of April 1889 had come home to him. A cynic might argue that for an entertainer and public speaker being "the man who hanged the Ripper" was a more valuable asset than simply having hanged a man who viciously murdered his own wife as the result of a domestic dispute.

"Many crimes," Berry had told his Dundee audience in 1895, "were committed during a fit of drinking." He had never, he said, hanged a teetotaller. There is a certain degree of irony, then, that Berry himself sought succour in alcohol for many years. It seems that the responsibility of his occupation weighed heavily on him. He became an opponent of hanging, not least for its effect on the executioner himself. He wrote: "I now hold that the law of capital punishment falls with terrible weight upon the hangman and that to allow a man to follow such an occupation is doing him a deadly wrong."

Haunted by his past and exasperated at the way he treated his family as a result of his drinking led Berry to consider suicide in 1904. He boarded a train with the intention of throwing himself out of the window in the tunnel between Leeds and Bradford. Instead, his final desperate prayers were apparerntly answered when he encountered an evangelist on the train and underwent a religious conversion.

The James Berry who appeared at the Kinnaird Hall in Dundee in April 1906, then, was a changed man. His appearance in the city this time was announced in the Public Meetings column of the *Courier* and not the Entertainments section as before. His first words on stage, before a hushed audience, were: "My prayer is that the Lord may give me two hundred souls for every soul I have launched into eternity." Berry was appearing under the auspices of the Dundee Tent Mission and his principal objective was to tell of his religious conversion and convert others. It is difficult to disagree, however, with the *Courier* journalist who wrote of the vast numbers who had turned out to see him that "one could not help arriving at the conclusion that they had been drawn not so much by religious enthusiasm as by a strong desire to gaze upon the man who played so grim a part in many of life's tragedies".

The audience's curiosity would be rewarded with stories of Berry's life as an executioner, but they often had a religious slant – such as the story of two brothers who had been convicted of murder and were hanged together. They had knelt together on the scaffold and prayed for the prison officials and the hangman. "These young brothers are in Heaven," declared Berry.

James Berry died in 1913 aged 61 at his home in West Yorkshire. As we have seen, he had made only three known visits to Dundee during the course of his life, each time in a different guise. On the last occasion he was a preacher, before that a music hall entertainer, and before that a public executioner and maybe, just maybe, the man who hanged Jack the Ripper.

3
Relics

Perhaps the best way to approach Dundee is by train over the Tay Bridge. That particular journey affords a fine view of the city, one that is dominated by two hills, the Law and Balgay. It was this journey and this view that inspired the late Dundee entertainer Stuartie Foy to write a song with the title "Coming ower the Tay Brig tae Bonnie Dundee".

It is surprisingly rare, nonetheless, on a train journey over the bridge, to hear anyone even mention the magnificent view, let alone break into song about it. The sight that is more commonly commented upon seems to indicate that the eyes of many passengers, whether tear-filled as the song's lyrics suggest that Stuartie Foy's were or not, are directed downwards into the murky waters of the River Tay. What seems to capture people's imaginations are the surviving piers of the old Tay Bridge which collapsed in 1879 but which still trace out its span across the river.

Some might question the wisdom of pointing out to one's fellow passengers, particularly any of a nervous disposition, on a train crossing the Tay Bridge that a previous train crossing a previous Tay Bridge landed in the river and that all the passengers drowned when that bridge collapsed. There is little doubt, though, that the empty plinths standing forlornly in the water provide a more effective reminder of the tragedy than any statue or memorial ever could.

When the second Tay Bridge was being planned, it was decided not to use the piers or any parts of the old bridge in the construction of the new one and it was thought that they would be removed. Indeed, the matter was taken to court as an attempt was made to force North British Railway Company to remove the piers, leading to the matter being debated in Parliament. William Henry Barlow, the designer of the new bridge, though, said that removing the piers would cause too much disruption to the river bed and it was eventually decided to leave them in place.

Just as the piers still rise through the waters of the Tay, so there are other places in Dundee where the past breaks through into the present in the shape of physical remnants of past events. Sometimes, though, the passage of time has divorced these artefacts from their original meaning or the story that surrounds them. This chapter attempts to put some of these relics back into context.

The Last Flag

At 12 noon on Wednesday, 4 June 1746, an unusual procession left Edinburgh Castle led by a detachment of soldiers from Colonel Lee's Regiment. The procession involved much pageantry and included many of the capital's civic dignitaries but was particularly notable for the presence of John Dalgleish, the chief hangman of the city, and several chimney sweeps, each of whom was carrying a flag or banner.

The flags that Dalgleish and the chimney sweeps carried were taken to the Mercat Cross in the capital's High Street, where a bonfire had been prepared for them. A herald announced that "these scraps of silk and braid" would be burned by order of the Duke of Cumberland. These were the flags or colours that had been captured at the Battle of Culloden earlier that same year when Cumberland's army had defeated the Jacobite rebels under Prince Charles Edward Stuart (perhaps more commonly remembered as Bonnie Prince Charlie).

Each flag, beginning with the prince's own banner, the one carried by the hangman, was named as it was held over the flames and burned. In all, fourteen were burned that day and others later suffered the same fate. Very few of the Jacobite colours that flew at the fateful Battle of Culloden are known to survive. One – carried by the Appin Stewart Regiment – is in the National Museum of Scotland in Edinburgh, while another is in the McManus Galleries in Dundee.

The Jacobite flag which survives in Dundee consists of a St Andrews Cross with a thistle above it together with a ribbon bearing the Latin motto of the Stuart dynasty: *Nemo me impune lacesset*, which translates as "No-one provokes me with impunity". It was carried by Lord Oglivy's Regiment at Culloden.

Indeed, some have speculated that it dates from the previous Jacobite Rebellion in 1715.

The Lord Ogilvy in question in 1745 was David, son of the Earl of Airlie, and his regiment was recruited from the Angus area. Lord Ogilvy and the 1st Battalion of the regiment were with Prince Charles at Edinburgh following the Battle of Prestonpans and accompanied him on the march into England, when the Jacobite army reached as far south as Derby. Ogilvy was among those who advised the prince to turn back rather than press on to London.

Lieutenant Colonel Sir James Kinloch of Kinloch raised a second battalion of Ogilvy's regiment comprising around 600 men. In late 1745, the members of the 2nd Battalion held Dundee for the Jacobite cause and gained more recruits there. They were also involved in the victory at Inverurie before reuniting with the 1st Battalion and fighting at the Battle of Falkirk in January 1746. The Jacobites were victorious once more but failed to take advantage of their success and their campaign ended in disaster on the moor of Culloden on 16 April that year.

Following the defeat at Culloden, Ogilvy's regiment showed much more composure than some of their contemporaries and retreated intact from the field. They made their way to the pre-arranged rendezvous at Ruthven Barracks in Badenoch where they were told by the prince that the situation was hopeless. They then marched home again to Glen Clova as a unit and dispersed. The well-drilled and disciplined nature of Ogilvy's troops helps to explain the survival of their banner. Other regiments simply dispersed on the battlefield and fled the scene – no doubt caring little for the emblems of a defeated cause.

In the wake of the Battle of Culloden, Sir James Kinloch was captured and held at Perth. Records were kept of the 113 Jacobite prisoners examined there between April and July 1746. The entry for Kinloch says that he admitted that "he was a Lt. Col. of a Regiment of Foot in the Pretender's eldest son's army, and fought at Falkirk and Culloden". His brothers Charles and Alexander were also captured and made similar admissions. Two of Charles Kinloch's servants, John Duncan and John Ogilvie, perhaps truthfully or perhaps in fear of their lives, declared that they "only looked after the horses for Mr. Kinloch while he was with the rebel army and never bore arms".

Sir James Kinloch was imprisoned at Inverness and then sent on board the *HMS Winchelsea* to London. There, he was sentenced to death as were his two brothers but, like them, Kinloch was eventually reprieved, though he was not released until August 1748. His lands were forfeited – though eventually regained by another branch of the family – and it was a condition of his release that he lived in England. He died in 1776.

The Culloden banner was kept in the Kinloch family and handed down as an heirloom. Indeed, so precious was the flag said to be to the family that it was hidden under the mattress of the bed upon which the head of the family slept. It remained in the ownership of the family until the early twentieth century.

On Tuesday, 27 April 1920, the contents of Logie House, the Kinloch family residence at Kirriemuir, were put up for auction. Of all the items sold, the Culloden Flag aroused the most interest, eventually selling for £750 to a fine art dealer from Glasgow named Robert Lauder, who outbid several potential purchasers from the United States. Lauder was keen that there should be an opportunity that the flag might stay in Scotland and found a purchaser in John Henderson Stewart of Fingask Castle. Stewart later presented it to the Dundee Museum at the Albert Institute. It has been in the possession of the museum ever since – a tangible link to that fateful day in April 1746 when the Jacobite Rebellion was crushed in the last battle to be fought on British soil.

The Lochee Crucifix

At the back of the Immaculate Conception Church in Lochee (more popularly known as St Mary's Lochee), there is a life-size crucifix. It might be thought – quite correctly – that there is nothing particularly unusual in the sight of a crucifix in a Catholic church, but a second look reveals this particular one to be perhaps a little too large for the foyer area that it occupies. The crucifix is situated in an area that is often busy and there is nowhere for worshippers to sit or kneel and contemplate the cross. It seems unlikely that the sculpture was commissioned for that particular space or originally planned to be in that location, and that, indeed, is the case. This is the story of how it came to be there.

The Immaculate Conception Church was officially opened in 1866, having been designed by the architect Joseph Hansom, the man who had invented the Hansom cab. Prior to the opening of St Mary's, Catholics in Lochee had worshipped at a property situated off Liff Road known as The Walton (later known as Wellburn).

That a new Roman Catholic church was needed in Lochee is testament to the large number of Catholic immigrants who had made their way to the suburb from Ireland in the wake of the Great Famine of the late 1840s. These immigrants were attracted to Dundee by the prospect of work in the jute mills and to Lochee in particular by the chance of employment at Cox Brothers' Camperdown Works, which at its height employed 5,000 people. Such was the extent of the Irish population in Lochee at around the time that the church opened, that the area around Albert Street (later known as Atholl Street) gained the nickname of "Tipperary".

Lochee's Irish population may have escaped destitution in coming to Scotland but many still lived in poverty. The level of poverty among the Catholic congregation in Lochee is vividly brought to life in the text of an announcement that was read out at the church in 1886: "In future the 8.30 Mass on Sundays will have no collection and all are invited to attend in their everyday working clothes. Anyone wishing to air their good clothes are requested to do so at the later Masses and not cause unnecessary embarrassment to those less fortunate."[10]

Against this background, the church played a major part in the lives of the immigrants, not only attending to their spiritual needs but providing a ready-made social structure and leadership in the form of the clergy.

For the most part, large-scale Irish immigration to Dundee does not appear to have been accompanied by the problem of religious sectarianism to the extent that occurred elsewhere in Scotland. It has been suggested this might be because the immigrants to Dundee were largely from one side of the religious divide and so the problems of their native land were not imported. The large number of female immigrants is also cited as a reason for the relative lack of sectarian strife. Nonetheless, religious and cultural differences between the Irish and the native population meant that there was always the potential for conflict, and one man, perhaps more than any other, seemed determined to tap in to this potential.

"Ex-Monk Widdows" or "Frater Aloysius" first lectured in Dundee at the Steeple Church in December 1878. At that meeting, it was reported, he detailed experiences as a Franciscan monk and his reasons for renouncing Roman Catholicism and becoming a Protestant. So captivated were his audience, that another lecture was arranged the following night at the same venue. Despite the enthusiasm of the audience, these events seem to have passed off peacefully. Lectures on religious matters would not have been uncommon in Dundee at this time and while the personal religious history of the speaker was unusual,

---

10   St Mary's Lochee, 125th Anniversary commemorative booklet

Widdows would hardly be the first Roman Catholic priest to vehemently denounce his previous allegiance to the Church, given that both Martin Luther and John Knox had been ordained as Catholic priests. What seemed to mark him out from other Protestant preachers of the time was the strength of his denunciations of Catholicism and the lengths to which he went to demonstrate them, always appearing in his monk's habit and staging mock representations of Catholic ceremonies. While Widdows would claim that he was merely educating people as to the errors of Rome, many Catholics saw it differently and viewed his actions as deliberately offensive and provocative.

A few months later, in April 1879, Widdows was back in Dundee to deliver some lectures in the Kinnaird Hall in Bank Street. His reputation seems to have grown in the intervening period and on the first night the hall was packed both with those who wanted to hear him and those who sought to oppose him. A large number of Catholics had paid to get into the meeting, while hundreds more gathered outside.

Widdows came onto the stage, dressed in his customary habit, to the sound of much booing, hissing and shouting from his opponents in the audience. Police officers guarded the steps leading up to the stage while senior officers sat on the platform. After the initial introductions, Widdows got up to speak but there were constant interruptions from the audience. There were also persistent demands that he remove his habit as he had no entitlement to wear it and his doing so was offensive. He refused and instead fell onto his knees to pray but his words were drowned out. Getting up he went to the side of the stage, saying "I will show your God" and produced a large Communion wafer and proceeded to eat it. This led to uproar in the audience which went on for some time. Widdows sat calmly throughout. In a bizarre interlude that was later described as an attempt to pacify his opponents, Widdows played some tunes on the harmonium including "God Save Ireland" while his opponents joined in. When he had finished, hostilities resumed once more.

At around 9.15pm, Dundee's Provost, William Brownlee, arrived in the Kinnaird Hall after having been sent for. Brownlee took to the stage, though he too found it difficult to get a hearing. "Ladies and Gentlemen," he said, "I hope you will now quietly disperse to your homes without any further annoyance. It is quite clear that there can be no lecture." Even after this, there were demands that the "ex-monk" remove his robes. At the Provost's suggestion, Widdows left the hall, accompanied by some detectives for his own protection and to cheering and jeers from the crowd.

Some of the protesters rather optimistically asked for their money back on the basis that there had been no lecture. One man told Provost Brownlee about the depth of feeling that Widdows's visit had engendered: "I have now been twenty years in Dundee and in all that time we have lived in harmony with the Protestants and it is not right that this man should come here and disturb the harmony and insult us." The meeting at last broke up peacefully with three cheers for the Provost, Mr Dewar, the superintendent of police, and Mr Dunbar the Fiscal.

On 8 April, a meeting of several hundred Catholics in Tay Street was addressed by local priest Father Clapperton, who said that he had co-operated with the authorities to ensure that there was no rioting. He said that they had made their point against Widdows and they should "let him lecture his friends as long as he pleases". Clapperton's conciliatory tone was not to everyone's liking and one man, Lawrence Phin, said to great applause that they should go "armed" to Widdows's next lecture on Wednesday night.

The ticket price for this lecture, which was entitled "the Mass as taught in the Church of Rome", was doubled to two shillings in an effort to price the protesters out. Nevertheless, tension was high in Dundee on the day that it was due to be delivered. Widdows himself had to be rescued from a mob by police when he was recognised near the West Port. In the early evening, crowds of protesters thronged Bank Street and Reform Street and there was a heavy police presence. It was only when Father Clapperton appeared and made an announcement that the evening's lecture had been cancelled that the people dispersed.

What one party saw as a victory against those who would mock their religion, another saw as an attack on their right to free speech. The letters pages of the press were filled with letters making this case and meetings were held on the subject. So high were tensions that a detachment of troops was sent to the city at Provost Brownlee's request and around 200 special constables were drafted in to protect a meeting that Widdows was to give on 24 April. This meeting appears to have passed off relatively peacefully, though, and after this life in the city appears to have gradually begun to return to normality.

"Ex-Monk Widdows" made several more visits to Dundee over the next few years, and while these were invariably controversial, there was never another disturbance on the scale of that of April 1879. Tensions remained, however, and Widdows's very presence in the city always had the potential to cause these to spill over.

In March 1883, the Franciscan fathers came to Dundee to preach a mission at St Mary's Lochee. Their preaching evidently inspired the parish priest, an Edinburgh man of Italian descent, Father Peter Butti. He decided to set up a "Calvary" – a life-size depiction of the crucifixion of Christ – on top of a rockery in the church grounds so that the congregation could visit it on their way to and from the church itself. On 15 April, a large number of people attended the solemn blessing of the site, which was situated in the relative seclusion of St Mary's Lane, off the main High Street of Lochee.

For Father Butti and the Catholic population in Lochee, the timing was to prove unfortunate. "Ex-Monk Widdows" was due to address another meeting at the Kinnaird Hall just three days later. The subject of his lecture on this occasion was "Monks before the World and Monks in the Monastery" – comparing monks as they appeared to the world unfavourably to how they appeared "behind the scenes". He had, he said, lectured before on this subject in Dundee but he proclaimed it to be "inexhaustible". Widdows also welcomed the formation of a new Protestant Association in the city and that it should teach children about "the terrors of Popery".

He told those attending the meeting that if they wanted to see what monks could do, they only had to go to Lochee, where they would see a crucifix set

This old postcard view appears to show the crucifix in place outside the church on the left hand edge of the image

up by the side of the road as in foreign countries. He had passed the church a couple of days before and had seen the crucifix for himself "with the figure of Jesus hanging on it and children kneeling before it". That image, he asserted, had been "put up by two Franciscan monks". While he did not object to Roman Catholics worshipping as they pleased, he considered it the duty of Protestants to see that in granting freedom to Catholics, they did not encroach on their own. Widdows cited the Book of Exodus ("thou shalt not make unto thee any graven images") as the reason for his objection.

In an age where many people do not profess any religious belief and where there is generally greater tolerance among those who do, it is difficult to fully appreciate the depth of feeling that Widdows was able to exploit. The Reformation in the sixteenth century had seen the removal of religious icons from churches and the almost total destruction of medieval stained glass, religious sculpture and painting in Scotland in the name of Protestantism. To some, even the presence of a religious sculpture in a public place was a threat to the Reformation settlement itself and an attempt to re-establish the Old Religion.

In the few days that the crucifix was in place before Widdows's visit, there does not appear to have been any protest against its presence in the church grounds. In the immediate wake of his lecture, however, the letters pages of the local press became filled with hostile letters. "One Disgusted" wrote: "If the authors of this outrage on decency intended this as a means of attracting those outside their own Church, I venture to say their object has miserably failed. The only feelings one can have on gazing at the repulsive sight are disgust and contempt for the religion that stoops to such artifices. If, on the other hand, it is merely intended as an aid to the devotions of those who belong to their own sect, the proper place to have the erection is in their own place of worship." "A. Citizen"'s letter was more succinct but no less forthright: "We are Protestants and what we have protested against and still protest against, is the mummery of Roman Catholicism, and as a Protestant country, we claim our right."

"Do the Lochee Papists wish to provoke a riot? If they do not they will instantly remove their wooden god from the streets into their church for it is a thing which the Protestants of this country will not stand," wrote a correspondent named Iconoclast, adding that had the crucifix been put up in the open at the foot of Tay Street, it would have been down the next day. Iconoclast went on to say, "I am not intolerant. I would not prevent Papists from worshipping or kissing toes of wood, stone or brass…but I say that these degrading practices must take place in their own chapels and shall not be made causes of offence to Christian eyes."

A.B.C. had made a special trip to see the "blasphemous and contemptible statue" and concluded that the "Romish Church" was "becoming more degraded and sinking down into the miry slough of Popery". "Plain Protestant", meanwhile, concluded that if the Presbyterians of Lochee were to stand "this disgusting sight" much longer, then "the Reformation was a work in vain".

An editorial in the *Courier* said that there had been nothing of the kind seen in Scotland "these three centuries" and said that many people would view the presence of the crucifix as "the thin end of the wedge". It was acceptable for Catholics to have such symbols in their churches but it was a "somewhat different proceeding to erect crucifixes in our streets similar to those at which wayfarers on The Continent are expected to cross themselves as they pass or kneel down and perform their devotion". This was, the newspaper said, "imprudent" and almost certainly illegal.

The *Aberdeen Weekly News* said that the crucifix was something that no Scottish Protestant could tolerate and that there was a danger of a riot in Dundee unless Bishop Rigg instructed his priests to take the "offensive image" inside the church. Catholics could not expect that they would be allowed to erect crucifixes in public as if the Reformation had never been. "Let them keep their symbols inside their churches," the paper said.

Protests against the crucifix were not restricted to those who made their arguments in the pages of newspapers. Hostile crowds began to gather outside the church on a daily basis. One middle-aged woman had to be forcibly ejected after entering the grounds and throwing stones at the crucifix, perhaps seeing herself as a latter-day version of Jenny Geddes, the woman who is reputed to have thrown her stool at James Hannay, Dean of Edinburgh in St Giles Cathedral, when he began to read from a new prayer book that was too Catholic-sounding for her tastes.

On 27 April, under the cover of darkness, someone entered the church grounds and painted over the figure of Christ with tar. When this was discovered, it was obviously distressing for the congregation. For Father Butti, it was the final straw and he had the crucifix removed. After being cleaned, it was placed at a side altar to the right of the main altar in the church. In 1900, a new altar dedicated to Our Lady of Sorrows was placed in that position and the cross was moved to the back of the church where it has stood ever since.

The story of the Lochee crucifix is, of course, in particular a story of attitudes to Roman Catholicism and Irish immigrants in late nineteenth-century Dundee. There are surely parallels, though, to be drawn with the treatment of modern-day immigrants and minorities, religious or otherwise, and lessons to be learned about how they are treated and how the fears and concerns of the indigenous or majority population are handled. There are surely lessons to be learned, too, about the extent to which such fears and concerns can be whipped up into a frenzy by a single individual.

"Ex-Monk Widdows", the man who had fanned the flames of the Lochee crucifix controversy and indeed, some would say, had caused the whole incident, was in fact born George Nobbs, in a Norwich workhouse in 1850. He was baptised, not as a Roman Catholic, but as an Anglican. He appears to have joined the Catholic Capuchin Franciscans at Peckham when he was 17 and his time with the order seems to have lasted around eight years – some of it spent in Canada where his anti-Catholic career appears to have begun.

In 1888, some five years after the Lochee incident, Widdows was sentenced to ten years hard labour for indecent assault against a teenage boy. It was not his first conviction for such an offence – he had been jailed in Canada as far back as 1875 – and nor would it be his last. Each time he was released, he simply began his lecture tours again. He died in 1936 at the age of 86, by which time the Lochee crucifix had been inside the church for more than half a century and the controversy that had once surrounded it would have been remembered only by the older members of the congregation.

The booklet produced for the centenary of St Mary's Lochee in 1966 described the presence of the crucifix at the back of the church as standing as "a silent witness to days which are happily now over and which have given place to ones of more tolerance and understanding"[11]. It is difficult to disagree with that assessment. If it is possible to take pride in a speculation, then we can perhaps be proud that the likelihood is that if the crucifix were to be returned to its previous position outside the church today, it would not be attacked by Christians of other denominations, followers of other religions or those of no religious belief at all on the grounds that it does not represent their own way of seeing the world. (We would, though, also have to be ashamed of the high likelihood that it would be vandalised for no ideological reason whatsoever.) It seems unlikely, though, that the crucifix will ever be placed outside the church

---

11   *St Mary's Lochee, Dundee 1866-1966*: souvenir brochure (1966). Glasgow: J.S. Burns

again and it remains in place at the back of the church. If it is noticed at all by those who pass by, it is as the object of religious devotion that Father Butti intended it to be.

Relics of the City Churches

The objection to certain types of religious imagery that fuelled the trouble over the crucifix in Lochee has its roots in the Protestant Reformation of the sixteenth century. Because such things were seen by the reformers as encouraging idolatry, many thousands of statues, paintings and other works of art were destroyed in the upheaval of those times. Consequently, relatively few such pre-Reformation artefacts survive today and for obvious reasons, among those that do, few are to be found at their original locations.

Although it does not depict any religious imagery, there must be a certain degree of irony in the fact that the only surviving pre-Reformation stained glass in Scotland that remains *in situ* is to be found in the Magdalen Chapel in Edinburgh's Cowgate, which is home to the Scottish Reformation Society[12]. Closer to home for Dundonians, a pre-Reformation baptismal font is to be found outside Liff Parish Church. In his 1940 history of that parish, the former minister Arthur Dalgetty describes how the font was found among some rubbish when the old hearse-house was cleared out in 1933, adding that it shows the ill treatment that such things got at the time of the Reformation.[13]

There are more pre-Reformation survivors in the centre of Dundee. Look up at St Mary's Tower, more commonly referred to as the Old Steeple, and you will see two small, weather-worn statues nestling in their alcoves on the outside of the building. One, of St David of Scotland, can be seen on the south side while the other – a Madonna and child – is visible on the west.

Of course, the Old Steeple itself, Dundee's oldest building, survived the Reformation and much else besides, but the church of which it forms part has an even longer history. It was founded around 1190 by David, Earl of Huntingdon, brother of King William the Lion and dedicated to the Virgin Mary. Originally outwith the boundary of the town, it was known as St Mary's

---

12 The chapel was built in 1541 for the trade guild the Incorporation of Hammermen and would have originally been Roman Catholic.
13 Dalgetty, Arthur B., *The Church and Parish of Liff* (1940), Dundee: Harley & Cox, pages 71-72.

in the Fields or simply "the kirk in the fields". The original church building was burned down by the English army under Edward I who invaded Dundee in 1296 and 1303. There were further invasions in 1336 under Edward III and 1385 under Richard II. In the early fifteenth century, work began on rebuilding the church, and around 1480 the tower was completed.

Much of the rebuilt church was lost in the aftermath of another English invasion in 1548 when a fire destroyed the nave and the north and south transepts, leaving only the choir and the tower standing. The following century saw the church devastated again when the Marquis of Montrose attacked Dundee in 1645. Six years later came the invasion of Dundee by General Monck, and at this time, part of the church buildings suffered the indignity of being used as a stable – something that was to be repeated in the next century at the time of the Jacobite Rebellion.

Throughout all the upheaval to the church building, the Old Steeple stood aloof as the scene around it changed. The rebuilding of the church was a painfully slow process which had been ongoing since the sixteenth century and suffered the many setbacks previously mentioned. Gradually, though, the church – or rather churches – took shape. As each section was completed, it became home to a separate congregation. St. Mary's Kirk at the east end of the building was the first to be completed, and another church known as the South Kirk was later established in the south transept. In the mid-eighteenth century, the north transept was rebuilt and North or Cross Church was founded there. Finally, the nave was rebuilt to accommodate a fourth congregation, St. Clement's (or Steeple) Kirk. The four churches, though each belonging to the national Church of Scotland, were completely separate entities but shared one bell tower in the shape of the Old Steeple. The poet and humorist Thomas Hood, who lived in Dundee in the early nineteenth century, summed up the situation in this way:

> "And four churches together with only one steeple,
> Is an emblem, quite apt of the thrift of the people"

Thomas Hood died in 1845 at the age of 45, but by the time of his death the four churches that he had written about had been destroyed again. Early in the morning of Sunday, 3 January 1841, a fire broke out in the passage between the South Church and the Steeple Church. The fire spread quickly and soon engulfed the building, burning until the following evening. The wave of destruction had not only affected the structure itself but had destroyed the priceless Burgh Library. In the final analysis, however, was not the "great conflagration of 1841" as it became known, which ultimately destroyed remnants of the four churches. Part of the fabric of the old buildings survived the fire but the decision was made to remove these and construct a new home for the City Churches to a design by the architect William Burn.

At least one relic of the old churches does survive, however, in the shape of the stonework of a rose window which was once a prominent feature of the building. In James Thomson's *History of Dundee*, published only a few years after the fire, there is an account of the collapse of the window:

> "After a moment of suspense the flames burst with irresistible fury through the beautiful Gothic window facing the street in an immense mass of inconceivable brilliancy carrying with it every portion of mason work, the glass having been previously destroyed. At this moment the scene was truly sublime. The assembled populace were driven back from the fire by the intensity of the heat and looked on with mixed feelings of astonishment and apprehension. At that fearful crisis every hope of saving any portion of the edifice seemed by common consent to be abandoned for an instant every exertion of the firemen was paralysed and the groups who huddled together on the street looked on in almost total silence subdued by the grandeur of the scene."

On 7 August 1873, a meeting of the council was held, which among other things, decided to re-issue Thomson's history of the town. The same meeting also resolved that the ancient sculptured stones lying in the ground around the churches "should be removed into the first Chamber of the Steeple for preservation and that the other old stones, should be given to the Recreation Ground Committee to be placed in Balgay Park".

Balgay Park had only been acquired for Dundee a few years previously and was officially opened by the Earl of Dalhousie in September 1871. The rose window was embedded in the earth in the park where it still sits today, providing the setting for a floral display. A plaque placed beside the window by the organisation the Friends of Balgay, provides an explanation of its origin.

There is one more link to the past to be found, back at the City Churches in St Mary's at the east end of the building. Just below a memorial to those who died in the First World War stands a small reading desk. At some point during the desk's long history a notice was added which explains its story: "This

The remains of the rose window in Balgay Park

reading desk is composed mainly of carved wood, which before the year 1688 formed part of the pulpit of the High Church of Dundee [as St Mary's would have been known]. In that memorable year, it was taken down, and thrown aside among some lumber, till Bishop Rait, having heard of its existence, searched it out and purchased it for £1 5s."

James Rait was the Bishop of the Diocese of Brechin in the Scottish Episcopal Church between 1742 and 1777. Bishop Rait had the historic pulpit erected in the Episcopal Chapel of St Roque in the Seagate. In 1812, the congregation of that church – the predecessor of the one that worships today at St Paul's Cathedral – moved to premises in Castle Street. There, the pulpit was re-assembled and used for its original purpose for another twenty-seven years. In January 1839, however, it was removed to allow for alterations and expansion of the chapel brought about by a growing congregation. The ancient pulpit was broken up at this time and the pieces distributed among the members of the congregation.

Some of the wood came into the ownership of a cabinetmaker called William Smellie. Forty years later, in 1879, Smellie's son fashioned the wood into a reading desk and it was presented to St Stephen's Church in Broughty

Ferry at a bazaar held there in October that year. Although a familiar landmark today, St Stephen's was built in 1871 and had only become an independent parish in 1875, four years prior to the presentation.

The sign attached to the desk appears to have been added during its time at St Stephens as it refers to the presentation. It ends with what was undoubtedly Smellie's intention "that the relic has again found a place of rest, honour and usefulness in the National Church of Scotland", and finally the words "Adsit Omen". These last two words effectively mean "may what is said come true". However, it was not to be – at least not at St Stephen's.

It is not clear when the reading desk was removed from St Stephen's but the most likely time for such a thing to occur would be when there was a major structural or organisational change in the church, and in 1929 St Stephen's underwent both. Not only did that year see the reunification of the Established Church of Scotland and the United Free Church of Scotland but it also saw a major refurbishment of the church building. The chancel was remodelled and a new organ installed together with a new pulpit, choir stalls, lectern and Communion chair. It seems likely that there was no place for the old relic in this reordering.

Exactly what happened to the reading desk after its removal from St Stephens remains a mystery. It was in 1987 that it was finally located in a furniture restorer's workshop in Dunfermline. The desk was returned to St Mary's under the supervision of the then minister and later Moderator of the General Assembly of the Church of Scotland, William B. R. Macmillan. It remains there to this day, a silent witness to the long history of the church and the people who have worshipped there over the last 800 years. It seems that the relic has finally found its "place of rest, honour and usefulness". Though perhaps, given its long and varied history, we should add, "Adsit Omen".

The Ungracious City – the story of the Caird Fountain

Jute Mill owner Sir James Key Caird was one of Dundee's greatest benefactors – as the continued presence of the Caird Hall and Caird Park in the city testify to this day. These were not the only examples of his philanthropy, though. In total, between 1895 and 1914, he donated £240,940 to various good causes and organisations in Dundee and elsewhere. His donations within the city and its environs ranged from paying off the debts of both the Dundee Royal

Infirmary and Sidlaw Sanatorium to paying for a purpose-built cancer hospital at the infirmary and funding research into the disease. He also donated many Egyptian artefacts to the city's museum. Outwith Dundee, he helped to fund Sir Ernest Shackleton's *Endurance* expedition to the Antarctic and paid for a new insect house at London Zoo. Sir James was not, however, the first member of his family to seek to provide something of benefit to the citizens of Dundee. In 1861, his father, Edward, who started the family business, put a modest proposal to the Provost. He wrote:

Dundee 24 April, 1861

Dear Sir,

I am desirous to have a drinking fountain erected for the public, and would do so at my own expense, in the form of a pillar of polished Peterhead granite, 5 or 6 feet high, provided the Magistrates and Town Council will kindly grant permission, and give a site on the High Street, and supply the same with water from the Lady Well.

Hoping this will receive a favourable consideration,

I remain, dear Sir, yours truly,

Edward Caird

A drinking fountain was no mere decorative accessory in the mid-nineteenth century. Rapid growth in the population of cities in the wake of the Industrial Revolution had led to problems with sanitation. Dundee, for example, had suffered several outbreaks of cholera in the early years of the century. In the epidemic of 1832, more than 500 people died of the disease in the city. In London in August 1858, there was a phenomenon known as "The Great Stink" when the summer heat exacerbated the smell of untreated human waste and industrial effluent on the banks of the Thames. This led to renewed efforts there to improve the sewage system and provide clean drinking water. The following year the Metropolitan Free Drinking Fountain Association was set up by Samuel Gurney MP and barrister Edward Wakefield. Their intention was to supply free, clean water to the masses. They insisted that no fountain would be "erected or promoted by the Association which shall not be so constructed as to ensure by filters, or other suitable means, the perfect purity and coldness of the water". Their first fountain, paid for by Gurney, was opened on 21 April 1859 at the Church of St Sepulchre-without-Newgate on Snow Hill.

Free public drinking fountains soon became enormously popular throughout the country and so, in 1861, when Edward Caird offered to pay for one in the centre of Dundee, it would have been thought that his offer would be immediately accepted. Instead he received no reply. Undeterred, on 3 August, Caird wrote again, this time addressing his letter to both the Provost and magistrates of the town, presumably thinking that he had more chance of a reply if he wrote to more than one person. He also included mention of a donation that he had received, again, it seems, in the hope that this would mean that an answer would be soon forthcoming. He wrote:

Gentlemen,
Some time ago I wrote you, requesting permission to erect a drinking fountain of polished granite on the High Street, and I have not yet received an answer.

A gentleman has sent me £10 towards this object, and I hope, since you have taken so long to consider of it, the answer will be favourable, otherwise this gentleman's subscription must be returned to him and my purpose to provide a drink of fresh cold water to the thirsty be frustrated

The favour of your reply will oblige, Gentlemen, yours respectfully,
Edward Caird

Again, Caird received no reply. In November, Provost David Jobson retired and was replaced by Charles Parker. Perhaps Caird thought he might have more success with the new man because seven months after his original offer was made, he wrote again:

Dundee, 26th November 1861

Gentlemen,
I have on two occasions addressed you – namely on 4th April and 3rd August, as per copies of my letters enclosed, to neither of which have I received any answer or acknowledgement.

Allow me again to beg your attention to my request for liberty to erect a drinking fountain for the public on the High Street,

I am, Gentlemen, yours respectfully
Edward Caird

Having not heard anything by 9 December, the persistent Caird wrote to the new Provost directly:

Dear Sir,

I have three times – 24th April, 3rd August and 26th November – addressed letters to the Provost and Magistrates of Dundee and to none of which have I received any answer. The subject is the erection of a drinking fountain on the High Street.

Your attention will very much oblige dear Sir,

Yours faithfully

Edward Caird

This time, Parker replied, saying that he would bring the matter before the Property Committee. The committee met on 17 December, and Caird's latest letter was read out. The official minutes record what happened next:

"The meeting having considered said letter, as also the minutes of the meeting of 1st May last, at which it was resolved that such permission ought not to be granted, for this reason that such an erection would obstruct the traffic on the street."

It seems that Edward Caird's original letter had, in fact, been discussed by the council shortly after it was received but they had not bothered to inform him of the decision reached. The latest rejection of his offer was confirmed by the council on Christmas Eve. Caird wrote another letter, this time to the *Advertiser*, dismissing the council's argument that the fountain would obstruct traffic: "few towns possess such a spacious High Street as Dundee. If I had not thought some place could be easily found for such an unobtrusive but useful ornament, I would not have stirred in the matter. The authorities in several large cities such as Glasgow and Liverpool, have found room for several of these fountains in great thoroughfares. Hundreds and thousands make use of them daily, a sufficient proof that they are a great boon to the public."

In January 1862, the matter came before the council again when Councillor Cooper moved that it should be referred back to the Property Committee who should seek Mr Caird's views on the matter and see if he would be happy to see the fountain placed elsewhere. This was too much for Bailie Scott, who accused Mr. Cooper of creating work for the Council and Property Committee, who had quite enough on their hands. Scott went on: "if Mr Caird cannot by the exercise of his own judgement find any other site than the High Street, let him consult with his friends, and I have no doubt they will find plenty of sites.

Then, let him produce a plan and a written description of his fountain, and I am sure the Town Council will take the proposal into their most favourable consideration but to throw out a bone of contention like that, and to disturb the council with vain offers like that, is not the way to proceed, and so long as that is done, we should have nothing to do with it."

Despite Bailie Scott's vehemently expressed disapproval, the motion was passed and the council agreed to look again at the proposal.

In June 1862, Councillor Cooper proposed that the fountain should be placed in front of the Town House in the High Street, where it would not be an obstruction to traffic. Other councillors, however, still saw Caird's gift as a problem. Mr Butchart queried the expense of taking water to the fountain and of supplying the water. Bailie Scott protested at the idea of the High Street being dug up to lay pipes to the fountain, perhaps at the expense of the Police Commissioners.

Nevertheless, in January 1863, it was agreed to place the fountain at the west end of the Town House. Some councillors remained unhappy. One asked who would pay for its upkeep and if Mr Caird expected the council to pay for any damage it might sustain. By this time Edward Caird must surely have begun to regret his decision to donate a fountain to Dundee. It is little wonder that an *Advertiser* editorial expressed regret at "the carping spirit in which Mr Caird's generous gift has been received".

In February, an attempt was made at the council to rescind the permission for the site, but this motion was rejected and the fountain looked set to be built. On 31 July, however, as the councillors filed into a meeting they were served with notice of suspension and interdict. The action had been brought at the instance of five local businessmen, whose premises were near the proposed site. They were: George Lloyd Alison, wine merchant; James Feathers, clothier; Joseph Rickard, innkeeper; John Austin Gloag, solicitor; and wine merchant and former Provost of Dundee David Jobson – the very man that Caird had first written to regarding the fountain. Together, this group were soon to be known by the local press as "the ungracious five".

The five were soon the focus of public anger. Letters were written to the press and a petition was presented to the Provost asking him to "call on an early day, a public meeting of the inhabitants, in order to ascertain their mind as to the proposed erection of a fountain by Mr Caird, and to consider whether such would be an obstruction or ornament to the town". He was also asked to "consider the propriety of an expression of sympathy towards Mr Caird on his being dragged into a court of law, in his laudable endeavours to beautify the town".

Neither Caird nor the council, however, were willing to take the matter back to court. Caird wrote to Provost Parker:

"When I offered to place a fountain in the High Street of Dundee, similar to those which have been erected in the crowded streets of the Metropolis and other large cities in England and Scotland, and when the Town Council granted a site, I had no idea that my intention and their resolution would be 'interdicted'. The fountain is now ready. I have no wish to force it upon the town by entering into law proceedings and as the Town Council by refusing to vindicate their own rights, have admitted that they cannot give the site, I am prevented from having the pleasure of presenting it to the Town."

Caird feared that any other site that the council offered him would be susceptible to a similar legal action and began to consider presenting the fountain to some other town. An Arbroath correspondent to the *Advertiser* bemoaned the way that Caird had been treated by Dundee and said should the fountain be handed over to his town it would stand as "a memorial of Mr Caird's benevolence and a standing monument of shame and grace to Dundee". Caird had been associated with Arbroath in his younger days, but turned down a formal offer to place the fountain there.

On 1 September 1863, the meeting that Provost Parker had been petitioned to hold took place in the Corn Exchange Hall (later the Kinnaird Hall) in Bank Street. The hall had an official capacity of around two thousand but many more were present that night as the *Advertiser* reported:

"The working men with a discernment that does them credit treated the question as peculiarly *their* question and packed the room from end to end. Seen from the platform the large hall was one sea of heads, the people having built themselves into all the avenues between the seats until they were as compacted together as the stones in a wall. We never saw the great hall so full; we never saw a meeting so enthusiastic."

The overwhelming sentiment from those present and, no doubt, from the hundreds who were turned away was in favour of Mr. Caird and his fountain. "Such a meeting cannot be ignored" proclaimed the *Advertiser*. A committee was appointed to see what could be done to make the fountain a reality.

Edward Caird must have watched in bemusement, as later that same month his fellow philanthropist Sir David Baxter managed to successfully gift a 38-

acre site to the town for a public park, given Caird's own difficulty in handing over a drinking fountain. At the park's opening ceremony George Alison, one of the "ungracious five", who was there in his capacity as a major in the Dundee Volunteers, was hissed by the crowd.

Public discontent about the fountain may have remained, but the situation had reached a total impasse. The months, and indeed, years began to slip away with no resolution in sight. In April 1865, the Committee of the Dundee Working Men's Association wrote to Edward Caird to ask the current state of affairs. He thanked the committee members for their interest but there was, unsurprisingly, more than a hint of exasperation in his reply:

"You know the cause of delay and there is no hope now of the interdict being removed which hinders the fountain being erected on the High Street or any other public street in Dundee, so that this gift to the inhabitants of Dundee, which I thought to be both ornamental and useful is lying at Ashton Works a useless thing, till I find opportunity to have it erected elsewhere."

The fountain was not erected elsewhere, however, and remained a "useless thing" at Ashton Works for another fourteen years. It was not until 1878, following the demolition of the Union Hall at the west end of the High Street and the consequent widening of the street at that point, that the authorities once again turned their attention to Caird's gift and, luckily for them, found that he was still amenable to the idea. On 24 September that year, a site for the fountain was finally approved.

On 27 May 1879, work began on the foundations for the fountain and on 25 July that year, some eighteen years after Edward Caird's first letter to the council, the water was finally turned on. In the evening, people gathered around the fountain and drank a toast to Mr Caird, coupled with what was presumably a somewhat less sincere one to the local authority.

In the years after it was put in place, the fountain became a familiar landmark and popular meeting place as well as adding ornamentation to the High Street and fulfilling a practical purpose. Popular with the public, surely Mr Caird's gift would at last be treasured by those in authority? The evidence would appear to indicate that this was not the case.

In 1901, someone signing himself "Citizen" wrote to the *Evening Post* speculating as to what the figure on top of the fountain might say if it could speak and came up with following:

"What am I and the edifice upon which I stand? Once, no doubt, we were things of beauty but alas! Neglect has robbed us of our charms. Oh that the

The Caird Fountain in the High Street

powers that be would order us to be washed and re-clothed with paint and gilt, so that our nakedness might be hidden from strangers within our gates; that no more I may hear them say 'If this is the way you treat your gifts, oh, citizens of Dundee, no wonder they are so few'."

Despite "Citizen's" warnings, the fountain continued to be neglected. In September 1926, the figure that the correspondent had brought to life a quarter of a century earlier, finally took matters into its own hands and, together with its base, tumbled off the top of the fountain, in the process injuring a young boy who was getting a drink. At a subsequent meeting, even the City Engineer was unsure as to whether the fountain was the responsibility of the Works Department or Public Health Department.

It was not just neglect that meant that the fountain's days were numbered. The reason that had been given for the initial rejection of Edward Caird's offer, that of traffic congestion, might have been a contentious one in 1861, but by the 1920s, Dundee's streets were undoubtedly becoming busier. The area around the fountain was now a major stopping place for trams, and motor traffic was also increasing. In January 1927, the tramway manager intimated that the fountain should be removed to ease congestion, perhaps to a site at the Mains Loan entrance to Caird Park. As if to prove his fears, in early February four people were injured when a tram and a bus collided near the fountain.

On 15 February, the fountain was dismantled and put on the back of a lorry for transportation to its new home at Caird Park. The *Evening Telegraph* commented that "unlike the old Town House, the passing of the fountain has been unwept, unhonoured and unsung. Not a voice has been raised in protest. But then it had no claims to be either antique or architecturally aesthetic."

Of course, there could have been a new life for a drinking fountain in the setting of a public park, but this was not to be. Robbed of its original function, the fountain fell further into disrepair until all that remains today is the granite plinth which sits upon its original stone base, still bearing the legend "Caird Fountain erected 1879" around the side.

Edward Caird died in 1889, and his son James in 1916. While Sir James Caird's principal gifts to Dundee, the Caird Hall and Caird Park, have been much appreciated over the years and regarded as being among the city's greatest assets, his father's modest gift of a drinking fountain must rank among the least appreciated donations Dundee has ever received. As we have seen, Caird senior's gift was in turn ignored, rejected, complained about, criticised, regarded as a nuisance, subjected to legal action, neglected, removed, dumped and forgotten.

Perhaps there is still a way for the city to make amends. The site in Dundee's High Street where the Caird Fountain was erected in 1879 is still a busy traffic area but the main part of the street near the former site of the old Town House is completely given over to pedestrians. This was Edward Caird's own preferred site for the fountain. Would it not be possible for the fountain to be recreated on its original plinth and placed there? Alternatively, a new design could sit on the plinth. So much of the centre of Dundee that Caird himself would have recognised – including the Town House itself – has gone for good but a restored or reimagined Caird Fountain would be a decorative feature with a genuine history. If it were not possible to place it there, then surely some of the public space that the waterfront development has opened up would provide a home? Modern concerns over the proliferation of single use plastic bottles have seen drinking fountains return to popularity and, indeed, in 2019, a modern "top-up tap" was installed in the City Square. Perhaps, more than 150 years after he first proposed it, Edward Caird's gift can, at last, be graciously accepted and take up a prominent place in the city.

4
The Passing Show

One of the more unusual "firsts" claimed for Dundee is that the first scientific dissection of an elephant took place in the town in 1706. The procedure was carried out by a local doctor, Patrick Blair, after the creature collapsed on the road between Broughty Ferry and Dundee. Blair's findings were published in *Philosophical Transactions of the Royal Society of London* in 1710, and as a pamphlet entitled *Osteographia Elephantina* three years later. This work provided a useful basis for subsequent study in this area. Indeed, one of Blair's discoveries – the appearance of a supposed "sixth toe" on the elephant's front foot – was only successfully explained by a study conducted by the Royal Veterinary College, London as recently as 2011.

The citing of this undoubtedly impressive fact, though, often ignores the elephant in the room (or rather on the road) and the fact that such a creature should be in the vicinity of Dundee in the first place. The female Indian elephant had been exhibited throughout Europe since the late 1680s. Patrick Blair himself described what happened next: "she came at last to Scotland, where after some stay at Edinburgh[14], they conducted her to the north and by long and continuous marches hastened to Dundee in their return. The beast

---

14 The elephant's trainer, Dutchman Abraham Sever, petitioned the Edinburgh Town Council for permission to show the creature to the local population on 31 October 1705. In 2019 a document was discovered in Edinburgh City Archives in which a baker named Adam Kerr protested to the Edinburgh Dean of Guild Court about the tenant above him. The space, at Fishmarket Close, was rented by Sever who was keeping the elephant there. Kerr complained that his shop and oven were being ruined and exposed to dung and water coming down.

much fatigued fell down within a mile of Dundee. After many endeavours (which proved ineffectual) to get her on her feet again they digg'd a deep ditch to the side of which she might lean to rest herself but soon afterwards there fell great rains, so that after lying a whole day in the water, she died the next morning, being Saturday the 27th April 1706."

The unfortunate elephant's death demonstrates that even in the early eighteenth century, Dundee was an established venue for travelling shows. In the course of the three centuries since, many circus troupes and travelling performers have followed in her footsteps. The nineteenth and early twentieth centuries in particular saw a succession of truly remarkable shows, exhibits and artists arrive, some of whom could justifiably advertise themselves as being "world famous". For most of those participating in these shows, Dundee would have been just another blurred memory – yet another town in a seemingly endless list of venues and performances. For those watching, on the other hand, such a show might be a once-in-a-lifetime experience and provide a lasting and indelible memory. At the very least, they provided a chance for many to escape from the grim realities of life in Dundee and, however temporarily, enter another world.

The Greatest Show on Earth

At the beginning of September 1899, an advertisement appeared in the Dundee press announcing the impending arrival of one of the most spectacular travelling shows ever seen in the city. Indeed, the organisers, Messrs Barnum and Bailey, had for many years famously billed theirs as being "the Greatest Show on Earth". Certainly, the advertisement seemed to offer much to justify this description. Barnum and Bailey would be "presenting every kind of marvellous attraction – an imperial programme of nearly 100 acts in three rings,[15] on two stages and racetrack". There would be two menageries and the whole undivided show would be exhibiting under twelve new pavilions with a daily expense of £1500 for each of its three days in Dundee. Two performances would be given daily, but the doors would open an hour beforehand to allow patrons time for "a saunter through the menageries, a view of the remarkable living human curiosities and the collection of prodigies".

---

15 Events took place simultaneously in these three rings. This aspect of Barnum and Bailey's circus is the probable origin of the phrase "three ring circus" for a noisy and confused situation. The expression came into popular use about this time.

Ordinary seat prices ranged from one to four shillings while, for those who could afford it, private box seats were available for seven shillings and sixpence. Children under 10 years old would be admitted at half price on all but the one shilling tickets. As the next cheapest seats were two shillings, though, this meant that the lowest priced tickets for adults and children alike were one shilling each. Many large working-class families, particularly those millworkers who found themselves involved in a strike when the circus rolled into town, must have been glad to read the words "watch for the street parade" at the end of the advertisement.

The circus was to be situated at Fairmuir. An application had been made regarding the use of the more central location of Magdalen Green but this was home to the Dundee Horticultural Society's annual flower show on 9 September, only two days before Barnum and Bailey were due to arrive, and it was feared that the site might not be ready in time for the opening of the circus. Fairmuir had long been the setting for livestock fairs, and since 1845 had housed one of Dundee's oldest annual fairs – Stobb's Fair (which had relocated from its previous situation at Stobsmuir). By the last decade of the nineteenth century, however, it was reported that Stobb's Fair had "lost much of the boisterous mirth which pervaded it some years ago" and the remnants of Dundee's medieval fairs had entered a period of terminal decline. Barnum and Bailey's Circus, on the other hand, seemed to represent the future of popular entertainment.

Despite an early morning downpour, the weather on the first day of the circus's stay in Dundee soon turned to glorious sunshine, which ensured that there would be a high turnout for the street parade. At a few minutes before nine o'clock the procession left Fairmuir and made its way along Strathmartine Road and meandered into the centre of town via Main Street, Dens Road and Victoria Road. (Even Barnum and Bailey, it seems, balked at the prospect of guiding elephants down the Hilltown.) Vast crowds lined the route and every tenement window and other vantage point seemed to be taken. Many workplaces had allowed their workers to go out and watch the parade.

The procession moved along Bell Street, Euclid Crescent, Meadowside and Ward Road before heading down North and South Tay Street and into the Nethergate and High Street. Many circuses and menageries had visited Dundee before, but nothing on the scale of this parade had taken place in the city. It was led by a platoon of mounted police and a military band followed by the spectacular sight of a team of forty horses driven by a single man. Then came

Barnum and Bailey's circus makes its way down Dens Road

the wild animals: tigers, lions, panthers, hyenas, bears and wolves with their trainers in what were described as "open dens" before numerous horses, chariots and riders including "eight golden chariots containing wild beasts". Twenty-two elephants, a caravan of camels and a team of zebras pulling a carriage were among the highlights of the next section before a series of carriages based on fairy tales such as Cinderella's coach. A large part of the final section of the parade was given over to a re-enactment of Christopher Columbus's reception at Barcelona by the King and Queen of Spain after his first trip to the New World.

There can be little doubt that the parade would have made an indelible impression on those who saw it, not least because of the incongruity of seeing such extraordinary things in such familiar surroundings. As the procession wound its way up Commercial Street and back the way it had come, it was followed by what was to become a steady stream of people heading for Fairmuir throughout the day.

Their appetites whetted by the street parade and days of building excitement in the city, expectations among those making their way to Fairmuir must have been high – which was just as well according to a preview article in the

Courier: "The visitor to Barnum and Bailey's must go prepared for something stupendous," the paper had said. "If he saunters up to the entrance and walks in as though patronising an ordinary travelling exhibition, the probability is that he will be so overcome with the magnitude and splendour of the spectacles as to be unable to follow, much less appreciate them."

It is easy to imagine how the visitor could be overwhelmed. The menagerie alone contained hundreds of animals. Among the highlights were the elephants (sadly, though, not including the legendary Jumbo, who had died in a railway accident some fourteen years earlier). The current major attraction was Johanna, billed by Barnum and Bailey as a "giantess gorilla" but regarded by zoologists who had examined her as a large chimpanzee. Johanna impressed visitors with her ability to understand certain commands given by her keeper and to eat her dinner from a plate while seated at a table (albeit without the aid of a knife and fork). The *Courier* went so far as to say that a close observation of her general conduct would "go far towards persuading some folks that after all Darwin may not have been so wrong in his much-buffeted theory". Not all of Johanna's human-like characteristics came naturally, however, as the *Courier* article went on to observe: "She dresses – or is dressed – in garments of brilliant hue disdaining not boots or stockings." More shocking to modern sensibilities, though considered harmless and amusing at the time, was Johanna's penchant for smoking cigars.

It is not clear from the reports of the circus in the local press if the menagerie included a walrus. If it did it is likely that few of the visitors realised the creature's connection to Dundee. In 1885, it was reported that a young live walrus had been brought to the town by Captain Adams aboard the whaler *Maud*. The walrus was sold to animal dealer William Leaburn for £120 but was later reported to have been sold to Barnum and put on a train bound for London before being shipped to New York.

In the same tent as the menagerie, the visitor would see what were known as "the prodigies". Vastly changed attitudes since Barnum and Bailey's visit to Dundee over a century ago mean that the idea of exhibiting what was described as a "stupendous collection of living freaks" or "curious human beings from everywhere" seems strange, if not downright abhorrent. It is still possible, though, to imagine the excitement for the schoolboy of 1899 in seeing Hassan Ali, the Egyptian giant or Khusania, the Hindoo dwarf, not to mention Miss Delphi, the orange-headed girl who, it was reported, was regarded as one of the mysteries of life that philosophers could not solve. Visitors could also hope to encounter a double-bodied Hindoo boy, an armless wonder, an elastic skinned man, a human pin cushion or a tattooed brother and sister from Providence City, Rhode Island. There was also Sol Stone, who could give the correct answer to mathematical problems instantly, and Wade Cochran, who could perform a similar feat with dates. Putting his head to work in a more physical sense was Billy Wells, the hard-headed man, who allowed granite blocks to be broken on his head with a sledgehammer. Wells, who was almost 60 at this time, placed only a thin cushion of cloth between his head and the stone to prevent cuts to his scalp.

After the prodigies, the visitor would pass into the main tent and to a bewildering array of performances taking place simultaneously in the circus's three rings and the hippodrome track which surrounded them. Among the attractions flashing past the spectators' eyes were everything from trapeze artists the Silbons, billed as the "Masterly Monarchs of the Air", to a group of trained Alaskan seals. At one point, seventy horses were introduced into the arena, while at another a frenzied chariot race took place around the track. The *Courier* reporter attempted to describe the scene: "while one's attention is concentrated perhaps on a daring aerial show, it is almost immediately diverted to an equally clever act in another ring and the next moment to a performance even more meritorious in another part of the huge tent. A prize is offered to the individual who can see the whole show. Needless to say, it is still begging for an owner…".

The brilliant sunshine continued into the second day of the circus's stay in Dundee and this helped to boost attendances. It was estimated that around 30,000 people made their way to Fairmuir each day. Special trains brought people to Dundee from the surrounding countryside and nearby towns.

Barnum and Bailey's first two days in Dundee may have been greeted by glorious sunshine but they were not so lucky on Wednesday, 13 September, the last day of their stay in the city, when heavy rain fell all day.[16] Nevertheless, thousands of people braved a muddy Fairmuir in order to see the final performances. Soon after eight o'clock at night, the well-rehearsed process of dismantling the circus began. Spectators emerging from the main tent were said to be astonished that the menagerie and the prodigies had gone while they had been watching the show. By a little after midnight, the whole site

---

16 In the two weeks after the circus left Dundee, performances were cancelled at Montrose, Paisley and Dumbarton due to bad weather, and another performance at Glasgow had to be abandoned.

had been cleared and Barnum and Bailey's entire outfit had been packed onto trains. At half past one in the morning the last of these left Fairmuir goods yard for its next destination: Aberdeen. As the "the Greatest Show on Earth" left Dundee, many in the city must have been reflecting that it had truly lived up to its billing.

General Tom Thumb

When "the Greatest Show on Earth" visited Dundee in 1899 it was accompanied by only one half of the Barnum and Bailey partnership – James A. Bailey, though the circus still bore both names. The other partner, Phineas T. Barnum, had died eight years previously. Barnum had been in Dundee, however, more than half a century before the arrival of the circus. On that occasion, in 1846, the show he was presenting was on a much smaller scale in every sense. Barnum had been accompanied by one of his most famous discoveries – General Tom Thumb.

General Tom Thumb was born Charles Sherwood Stratton in 1838 in Bridgeport, Connecticut to parents of average height and was a larger than average baby at birth. He grew at a normal rate for the first six months of his life but remained at just over two feet tall until he was nine. His height increased slowly later in life but never went over 3 feet 4 inches. Stratton came to the attention of Barnum when he was around 4 years old. The showman entered into a partnership with his father, Sherwood Stratton, and the boy learned to sing and dance and do impressions as well as to smoke and drink for amusement of the public. A tour of America in 1843, during which the 5-year-old Stratton was billed as being 11, was an immediate success.

Stratton and Barnum left the United States in 1844 for a tour of Europe that was to last for more than three years. The General made an appearance before Queen Victoria, who was apparently very much amused. This royal meeting proved to be the catalyst for an extremely successful tour and more audiences with European royalty. The tour included, as Barnum later recalled, with only a little of his customary exaggeration, "nearly every town in England and Scotland". It reached Dundee at the end of January 1846, where General Tom Thumb was to appear at the Bell Street Hall.

Advertisements in the press and on posters prior to his arrival made much of the General's performing for the crowned heads of Europe and his having played to more than 2,000,000 people in the preceding two years. "The little General is in fine health and spirits," readers were told, "[he] has not increased one inch in height nor an ounce in weight since he was *seven months old*. He is 14 years of age, 25 inches high and weighs only 15 pounds." The performances or "levees"[17] would include his "various extraordinary performances and costumes including songs, dances, ancient statues, imitations of Napoleon and Frederick the Great, Highland costume, citizen's dress and the unique and elegant new French court dress".

The show took place four times daily and lasted an hour and a half on each occasion. Admission was one shilling or sixpence for children under 10 years old. The final show each evening was at quarter to nine "in order to accommodate the working classes" and all tickets to this performance were sixpence. The General's "miniature equipage" paraded the streets daily and there was also an exhibition of the gifts he had received from royalty.

General Tom Thumb was well received in Dundee, attracting large audiences to his levees and occupying the attention of the public to such an extent that poor attendance at a lecture in the Watt Institution at this time was blamed in part on the presence in the town of "Tom Thumb". Much of this attention, it must be supposed, was based on a curiosity as to the General's actual physical appearance rather than the quality or otherwise of his songs or impressions, but his adoption of Highland dress, a few lines of Scottish dialect and dancing the Highland fling endeared him to local audiences.

Nevertheless, the press reports of the time concentrate on his appearance. An article in the *Courier* stated: "Few who have not seen the General can have the slightest conception of his pigmy size – the actual height and weight representations of his advertisement giving but a most inadequate idea of his appearance." The sinews and muscles of his arms were said to be particularly strong and at one point the General was carried round the hall while hanging by his hands from a small rod. Another article noted: "His personal appearance is most prepossessing – there is no symptom of disease or weakness about him. On the contrary, he is well formed of comely proportions, lively and active. He goes through his exercises in a sprightly and playful manner, and appears to very much enjoy the wonder and delight of his spectators." The "little rogue" the paper noted, particularly enjoyed the attention of the ladies, for whom he had a great penchant, and frequently kissed, "with much grace and vivacity."

---

17 A word for a formal reception.

The success of the tour made Barnum and Stratton extremely rich. As well as the scheduled appearances, the General would appear in wealthy households for an astonishing $50 a time. It is not known if he made any such appearance in the Dundee area, but it was reported in the *Courier* that he made a charity appearance at the local lunatic asylum and performed before "a numerous orderly and delighted audience composed principally of patients".

A year after his first visit to Dundee, General Tom Thumb was back in Bell Street – but only in the form of a waxwork in an exhibition mounted by Mr. John Springthorpe. He did return to the same venue in the flesh but not until 1858 by which time he was reported to have grown "stouter but no taller". Nobody seemed to notice that the General was also aging at a different rate to other people. Twelve years earlier he was billed as being 14, which would make him 26 in 1858, but now his age was given as a more accurate 20 years old. One thing did remain the same over the period, however - the ticket prices. It is difficult to imagine an artist visiting Dundee today and charging the same prices as twelve years previously.

Public interest in the "small specimen of a gentleman", as he was billed, remained as high as ever and the intervening years had seen him honing his skills as an entertainer: "his intellect is riper and he is more lively and amusing", said the *Courier*. "His entertainment is really a treat and visitors are allowed no time to weary between his songs, dances and lively conversation," added the *Advertiser*.

Nine years passed before General Tom Thumb's third and final visit to Dundee and much had happened in his life in the intervening period. On 10 February 1862, he had married another Barnum artiste by the name of Mercy Lavinia Warren Bump (known as Lavina Warren). She was 21 years old and 32 inches tall and was billed by Barnum as "the smallest woman alive" and "the little Queen of Beauty". The wedding itself was a typical piece of Barnum theatre. Another of his diminutive stars, "Commodore" Nutt, was the best man and the bridesmaid was Lavinia's sister Minnie. Crowds lined the streets of New York as the bride arrived at the Grace Episcopal Church in a miniature wedding carriage. The reception took place at the Metropolitan Hotel and among those who donated gifts to the happy couple were President and Mrs Lincoln. The wedding was a publicity coup for Barnum and pictures of the wedding party were widely sold. In future, the General would be joined on his tours by his wife, Commodore Nutt and Minnie Warren.

There had been changes in Dundee too since the last visit of General Tom Thumb. The Bell Street Hall was no longer used for entertainment following a tragic accident there in 1865 when twenty people were crushed to death. The General and his entourage were to appear this time at the Kinnaird Hall in Bank Street, which had opened in 1858. They took up residence in the nearby Lamb's Temperance Hotel in Reform Street – a somewhat ironic choice for the diminutive performer who had his first taste of alcohol at around the age of five.

Crowds gathered in Reform Street in the afternoon of 21 March 1867, the day of the first performance and watched the General's miniature coach – complete with a miniature coachman and drawn by two Shetland ponies – leave the hotel and drive up and down. There was disappointment for those who had hoped to catch a glimpse of the performers though – they had left by a back door and made their way to the hall in an ordinary cab.

The little party took to the stage of the Kinnaird Hall at exactly three o'clock. Each took a turn to entertain the audience. Highlights included the General himself making his customary appearance as Napoleon, and Commodore Nutt singing "Billy O'Rourke" and "Johnny comes Marching Home" complete with drummer boy costume and drum solo. "Mrs Thumb" sang "The Female Auctioneer" and Commodore Nutt and Miss Warren sang a duet as did the General and his wife. At one point the whole company danced a polka. At the interval, the General and the Commodore went among the audience selling photographs of themselves, and the ladies did the same from a small raised platform.

The appearances at the Kinnaird Hall were to be General Tom Thumb's last in Dundee. He died in 1883 at the age of 45 as the result of a stroke. Many will consider that he was exploited by P.T. Barnum. If this was the case, it was not in a financial sense. There is no doubt that Barnum's intervention made him rich. Indeed, at one point when the showman got into financial difficulty it was the General who bailed him out, and the two eventually became business partners. If he was exploited at all, it was in the sense of being taken around the world as a sort of exhibit for the amusement of others. To concentrate on this aspect, though, is perhaps to ignore the benefits and opportunities that came his way as opposed to the kind of life that might have faced Charles Stratton had he stayed in Bridgeport, Connecticut.

Chang and Eng – the Siamese Twins

In 1830 a pair of conjoined twins were exhibited in Dundee. The idea of displaying "Siamese twins" for public entertainment seems to modern sensibilities to encapsulate the worst of the nineteenth-century's freak show mentality. The term "Siamese twins" was long used to describe any pair of conjoined twins but it has its origin in the particular set of twin boys who appeared in Dundee on that occasion. The twins had been born in Siam (now Thailand) in 1811 and were named Chang and Eng. They were joined at the chest by a band of flesh which had originally left them permanently facing each other. Somehow, their bewildered peasant mother had managed to work out a programme of exercise for them to gently stretch the band so that they could stand side by side. One twin, Chang, was one inch shorter than his brother, though, giving the pair a somewhat lopsided appearance.

Chang and Eng came to the attention of the Western world after they were discovered in 1827 by a Scottish merchant called Robert Hunter. Hunter was, at that time, one of the few Westerners in Siam, and indeed, he was for a long period the only British trader there. After a protracted period of negotiation, Hunter managed to get the agreement of the twins' mother and the Siamese government to take them out of the country. The twins left Siam on 1 April 1829 on board the American ship *Sachem*, which was captained by Hunter's business partner, Abel Coffin.

They first went to America, but in November 1829 they arrived in London for the tour that would bring them to Dundee. The tour was a great success and the "wonderful and extraordinary Siamese Boys" or the "United Brothers" as they were billed, soon became famous throughout the country. By the time they reached Dundee, Chang and Eng were not merely being presented as something to be stared at by audiences. They had spent their time in America working up an "act" which included demonstrating their strength by carrying the heaviest member of the audience about the hall and challenging others to a game of draughts or chess, playing battledore and shuttlecock (the precursor of modern badminton), building up to a finale which included rapid somersaults and back flips.

The twins were obviously intelligent and quick learners. They learned to speak English and to read and write. They were perhaps a little too shrewd for their next manager – one P.T. Barnum – with whom they enjoyed an uneasy relationship but who nonetheless made them very rich. Robert Hunter, meanwhile, kept in touch with them over the years, passing on news of their mother and family to them. One letter the twins wrote to Hunter shows that they had fond memories of his native country. They told him: "If you should go to Scotland give our very warmest remembrances to our friends of your acquaintance in that country."

It was to be thirty-eight years, though, before the Siamese Twins returned to Scotland, and to Dundee in particular, by which time they were 57 years old – "old grizzled men who have spent a life beyond the average duration" according to one newspaper report. Advertisements made much of the likelihood that this would be their last visit with slogans such as: "Last opportunity of witnessing Nature's Greatest Living Wonder" and "Their like was never seen before and probably never will again – Don't fail to see them." Chang and Eng had not, however, been appearing continually since their previous appearance in Dundee. Indeed, they had ceased touring in 1839 and had settled near Wilkesboro, North Carolina where they bought a plantation and lived the lifestyle of typical Southern gentlemen of the time – even to the extent of owning slaves. They had also become naturalised US citizens and adopted a Western surname – Bunker. In 1843, they had married two sisters, Sarah and Adelaide Yates, and between them went on to have twenty-one children.

Like many Southern landowners, the twins' finances suffered badly as a result of the American Civil War which ended in 1865. Unlike many others, though, they had an obvious way to recoup some of their losses – by returning to the road. Desperation drove them to ask Barnum to manage them again. Their subsequent appearances in New York were not too successful but Barnum had another idea, as he later recalled: "I sent them to Great Britain where, in all the principal places, and for about a year, their levees were always crowded."

So it was that Chang and Eng found themselves appearing at the Kinnaird Hall in Dundee in January 1869. There was a certain degree of irony in the fact that age had reduced them to being, to a great extent, the passive exhibits that they had avoided being on their previous visit. A *Courier* reporter gave this poignant impression of their demeanour at this time: "They are affable and like to talk to visitors of their varied experiences. It was impossible to look at them yesterday as they stood in the area of the Kinnaird Hall without feelings of melancholy interest… there is a subdued tone of sadness – resigned it may be, but still sadness – pervading the countenances of those strangely-linked brothers."

The underlying reason for this air of melancholy was given as the fact that the twins were in Europe not only to make public appearances but to seek an operation which would separate them. They were said to be doing this at this late stage in their lives out of the fear that one of them would die and that the other would, in turn, die as a consequence. To Phineas T. Barnum, even this sad state of affairs could be a selling point. He wrote in his autobiography[18]: "In all probability the great success attending this enterprise was much enhanced, if not actually caused by extensive announcements in advance that the main purpose of Chang-Eng's visit to Europe was to consult the most eminent and medical and surgical talent with regard to the safety of separating the twins."

The "most eminent and medical and surgical talent", however, including Sir James Young Simpson of Edinburgh, advised against an operation and the Siamese Twins remained joined together for the rest of their lives. They both died on the same day – January 17, 1874. Chang died first and following his death a doctor was called to perform an emergency separation so that Eng might live on. Unfortunately, he arrived too late. Chang and Eng died as they had lived – together.

Buffalo Bill's Wild West

Buffalo Bill Cody rode into Dundee in the early hours of the morning of 17 August 1904. The legendary soldier, scout and one-time buffalo hunter was not on a horse, though, but aboard a special train accompanied by the 700 members of his Wild West show in some forty-nine carriages. Buffalo Bill's Wild West and Congress of Rough Riders of the World was on its most extensive tour of Great Britain to date. While Dundee slept, this finely tuned organisation was busy bringing its version of the Wild West to the Esplanade extension, ready for a three-day stay in the city.

The show had come to Dundee directly from Kirkcaldy where it had spent the previous night. The *Evening Telegraph* had sent a reporter to that show to give Dundonians an idea of what they could expect. The reporter was also to meet his boyhood hero Buffalo Bill himself – a prospect which he seems to have particularly relished. His article begins: "Buffalo Bill! The very name sent a thrill through every vein in my body. Mental pictures flashed before me. I was transported to the prairie. I saw death-struggles with fearsome Indians, blood-curdling battle-cries rang in my ears, scalps dangled before my eyes, rifle and revolver

---

18   Barnum, P.T., *Struggles and Triumphs or Forty Years Recollections*, (1872) Buffalo, New York: Warren Johnson & Co, page 854.

The Wild West in Dundee

cracked, tomahawk and arrow whizzed through the air, and then – victory! There stood my hero in the midst of prostrate redskins, calm, cool and collected." The reporter's real-life meeting with the great man took place in the somewhat more prosaic setting of a tent in Kirkcaldy but left him no less impressed: "His is a truly striking personality. Decidedly handsome in appearance, tall, broad chested and with shoulders well thrown back, he is alert and graceful, without affectation, in every movement, and his 58 years which seen to rest so lightly upon him, are only betrayed by the silvery locks that fall in artistic coils from below his wide brimmed sombrero." Our intrepid correspondent's delight when he received a cordial invitation to accompany Colonel Cody to Dundee in his personal railway carriage can be readily imagined.

Who, then, was this impressive figure making his way to Dundee that summer's evening? William Frederick Cody was born on February 26, 1846 in Iowa. His life of adventure really began at the age of 14 when he became a rider for the pony express. After America's Civil War, in which he served in the Union Army, Cody came to the occupation that gave him his nickname: buffalo hunting. He was contracted to do this in order to feed construction workers working for the Kansas Pacific Railroad. His own estimate of the number of buffalo he killed in an eighteen-month period is more than 4,000.

It was his involvement in General Philip Sheridan's 1869 campaign against the indigenous American population, during which the Cheyenne were driven from their lands in Kansas, Nebraska and Colorado that paved the way for Cody's transition to being a figure who seems to straddle the divide between fact and fiction. Shortly afterwards, he appeared in a novel, *Buffalo Bill, the King of Border Men*, and a few years later was appearing in person in a play called *The Scouts of the Prairie*.

In 1883, Cody founded his own show, "Buffalo Bill's Wild West", which eventually became the phenomenon that came to Dundee in 1904. Over the years the show included such iconic figures as sharpshooter Annie Oakley, and Sitting Bull, the Lakota chief who defeated General Custer at the Battle of Little Bighorn. As the reality of the Wild West receded into history it was Buffalo Bill's version which captured the public imagination, particularly in Europe, and which would go on to dominate Hollywood's representation of the West. By the time the show reached Dundee, Cody had entered into a partnership with James A. Bailey and it had taken on some of the characteristics of a circus and now included a sideshow. Particularly observant Dundonians would recognise that the show also included Jake Posey, the man who had been in charge of the team of forty horses that featured in the visit of the "Greatest Show on Earth" some five years earlier.

Ticket sales for the Wild West's Dundee performances were greater than had been anticipated and around ten thousand people attended the first show on the afternoon of 18th August 1904. The show began with the music of a cowboy band before the performers entered the area beginning with the Indians resplendent in their war paint and shouting loudly. They were followed by a seemingly endless procession of the other groups involved in the show including Lancers, Cossacks, cowboys and US and Japanese Cavalrymen. Finally, when the whole company was assembled came the entrance of Buffalo Bill Cody himself.

The show itself consisted of a series of events such as the horse race involving participants described as an Indian, a cowboy, a Cossack, a Mexican and an Arab, and demonstrations such as that carried out by the veterans of the 5th US artillery who showed considerable skill and dexterity in dismounting, charging and firing their field guns with great speed. Buffalo Bill himself gave a shooting demonstration. Mounted on a galloping horse, Cody shot at glass balls that were thrown in the air as he passed by – successfully breaking every one, of course. A particular highlight of the show was the re-enactment billed as "The Battle of The Little Big Horn or Custer's Last Stand". It was a thrilling spectacle, if somewhat lacking in historical accuracy, portraying the "Indians" as the villains of the piece.

Though the show went well, that first afternoon of the Wild West's stay in Dundee was marred by tragedy. As expected, the show proved to be a magnet for the local children. Among those who made their way to the site was a group of young boys from the Benvic Road area. The boys were playing on the esplanade extension wall when one of their number, a 10-year-old named John Fraser from Cleghorn Street, fell into the Tay. The alarm was raised and one of the cowboys from the Wild West show ran along the wall and threw a lifebuoy into the water, but Fraser was too far out and soon disappeared from view. His shoes and stockings were later found on the esplanade wall.

The evening show was afflicted by torrential rain causing the large crowds to run for cover. The performers, though, did not curtail the show in any way. This caused particular problems for Carter the Cowboy Cyclist whose act, billed as a "Leap through Space", was dangerous enough in normal conditions, as the *Evening Post* explained: "He starts from a height of 92 feet above the ground, sweeps down the declivity and with a huge leap crosses a broad chasm some 35 feet above the ground." Despite the rain on this occasion, he managed to cross the "chasm" but when the bicycle hit the wet track on the other side it skidded causing him to lose control. The bike turned over some half a dozen times and it was feared that he was badly injured. He was helped onto a horse and out of the arena having suffered only minor injuries.

Such was the wave of excitement that the Wild West appeared to have unleashed in Dundee that a newspaper report appeared to imply that it had caused the death of a Lochee man. John Glass had talked of nothing else but the show on the day he saw it and was still talking about it at breakfast the next morning when he collapsed and died. A doctor, though, attributed his death to an underlying heart condition.

Attendance at the afternoon show the next day was boosted by around two hundred young news vendors for the *Evening Post* who had been given tickets to the show by their employers. The boys and girls gathered at the *Evening Post* offices where they were given refreshments before making their way to the show. Their enthusiasm was palpable as the *Courier* reported: "every item on the programme was closely watched and forcible expression given to the high pitched feelings of the youngsters. Not until the last horse had left the ring did their interest for a minute flag and it was with visions of bucking broncos and daring cowboys that they returned to their homes and beds there to dream of the Red Indian in his far-off Western Home." The Wild West evidently had a big impact on children throughout the city.

Performances on the final day of the Wild West's stay in Dundee were again affected by heavy rain but the Cowboy Cyclist completed his performances unscathed this time. There can be no doubt that the Wild West's stay in Dundee had been extremely successful, with 72, 400 people attending – an average of around twelve thousand per show – a higher proportion than anywhere else the tour had visited recently other than Glasgow.

After the final performance, the company began the well-rehearsed business of dismantling the show and loading it onto railway carriages. This time though, the operation was not to proceed without a hitch. A special wagon that contained the fuel which was used to light some of the smaller tents caught light. Although the wagon was immediately detached, the fire was by this stage threatening to ignite adjoining buildings. Fred B. Hutchison, the manager of the exhibition, and Mike Coyle, its superintendent, swiftly took charge of events, and mud and sand were thrown onto the wagon. The fire was eventually brought under control but only with the assistance of the Dundee Fire Brigade under Captain Weir.

From the vantage point of more than a century later, it is still possible to imagine people's excitement when a show like the Wild West came to Dundee and the spectacle that it must have created in the city, but the passage of time has given us other perspectives as well. It is hard not to feel a tinge of sadness for the Native American members of the show who, despite reports that they were treated very well by Cody, had essentially been reduced to playing a role in creating a mythology which belittled and demonised them.

Blondin

On 30 June 1859, a man walked in a straight line for a little over one thousand feet and caused an international sensation. This was because the straight line in question comprised a rope three inches in diameter and was suspended 160 feet above the Niagara Gorge on the US-Canadian border. The fearless tightrope walker had been born Jean-François Gravelet in St Omer, Pas-de-Calais, France some twenty-five years earlier but became known to the world by the name he had borrowed from a former employer – Blondin.

Blondin completed the Niagara crossing on several further occasions, each time with a more daring twist than the last – such as walking the rope blindfold, on stilts or while pushing a wheelbarrow. On one occasion, he carried his manager, Harry Colcord, on his back, and on another he took a stove, stopped halfway across and cooked himself an omelette.

These exploits brought Blondin international fame and he was in particular demand in the United Kingdom. The Prince of Wales himself had already witnessed one of the Niagara Crossings and had reputedly refused an invitation to make the return journey on the tightrope walker's back. Blondin's first appearance in Britain was at the Crystal Palace in London in 1861, and the following year saw him embark on a tour which brought him to the altogether less glamorous setting of Dundee's docks.

For weeks before his visit, there were posters in the town announcing that the "hero of Niagara" would be arriving soon to undertake "daring feats" and give "wonderful performances". The Dundee public did not seem to have been impressed by this, however, as a contemporary report suggests that under a thousand people turned out to Messrs Calman and Martin's shipbuilding shed at the Victoria Dock to see him perform.

Some put the low turnout down to a mix up whereby a telegram had been received in the city to say that Blondin's visit had been cancelled. Any casual observer would have noticed, though, that Dundee's citizens were well aware that the visit was going ahead. As soon as news of his arrival in the town began to spread, crowds flocked to the vicinity of the British Hotel where he was staying, hoping to catch a glimpse of their hero.

There were other theories put forward as to the relatively poor attendance. One that was suggested by some at the time but just as quickly dismissed by others was that the ongoing religious revival in Dundee had left the town's inhabitants in such a high-minded moral state that they were above such vulgar entertainments. It would only take a glance at the attendances at other forms of popular entertainment available at this time to convince that there was at least a potential audience for Blondin's exploits in Dundee. Indeed, it is possible that the Dundee public had had, if anything, too much of this particular type of spectacle. Blondin's fame had spawned many impersonators, and Dundee had only recently played host to one of these. Appearing over two nights at the Corn Exchange at the beginning of September, she was billed as "The Female Blondin". Her advertisement promised that she would "wheel a loaded barrow extending from the stage to the ceiling and perform other feats of daring not equalled by Blondin himself". It was a risky business impersonating Blondin, however, for another "female Blondin" had been seriously injured a few weeks before while yet another (or perhaps even the one who appeared at Dundee) was killed while performing at Aston Park in Birmingham the following year.

The most likely explanation for the lack of attendance at Blondin's appearance in Dundee is the question of cost. The cheapest ticket prices, although advertised as being one shilling, were, in fact, one shilling and sixpence. This may have been considered by some to be a fair price for admission to one of the nation's top venues such as the Crystal Palace in London, but relatively few, it seems, were able or inclined to pay such a price for admission to one of Dundee's dockyards or to sit in a hastily erected rickety "grandstand" – particularly when it soon became apparent that at least part of the show could be seen for free. The *Courier* reported that there were to have been arrangements made to prevent outsiders from seeing anything but that these arrangements had not been made. Consequently, people crammed into every available space to see Blondin. The paper noted that a portion of the "non-paying public" were on Marine Parade at the front of the shed while others were in the adjoining sheds and "thousands" more were gathered around the gate of Victoria Dock.

For those gathered, whether paying or non-paying, there was to be a delay before Blondin made his appearance. They watched as the rope was suspended some thirty-five feet in the air and attached to either end of the shed – a distance of over a hundred and fifty feet. The band of the Dundee Volunteer Rifles kept the crowd entertained, until finally at six thirty – an hour and a half after the gates had opened for the paying audience – a cab arrived containing Blondin.

Blondin ascended to the platform to the cheers of the spectators. He stood to take in the view (and no doubt to increase the tension) for a moment or two before taking up his balancing pole and then beginning, as the *Courier* observed, to walk along the rope "so lightly and gracefully and with such an entire appearance of confidence… that seemed at once to be imparted to the spectators". More applause greeted his arrival at the other end of the rope, but Blondin does not appear to have taken the opportunity for a rest. He was soon back on the rope – this time pausing in the middle to perform a series of acrobatic feats such as standing on his head and hanging from the rope by his hands and then his legs and then one leg only. He lay face down on the rope and pretended to be a swimmer. He then stood on one leg before walking and somersaulting backwards and finally running along the rope.

If this was not enough for the enthralled crowds, Blondin returned to the rope with his eyes blindfolded and a sack over his head that came down to his knees. He began this journey across the rope in an ultra-cautious manner, making the odd stumble and drawing screams and gasps from the spectators, who then proceeded to laugh at themselves when they realised that it was all part of the act as he completed his walk at his normal pace.

The show's finale involved Blondin carrying the "same gentleman across the rope as he did at the Falls of Niagara". Whether or not this passenger was actually Harry Colcord is not clear from the reports. A newspaper report describes him as "being much heavier and about six inches taller than the muscular Blondin". Whoever he was carrying, Blondin walked the rope seemingly unaffected by the extra weight and potential problems with balance. It was reported that not a muscle of the "same gentleman" moved on the journey across. Once the pair were safely across to the other side, Blondin slid down the rope.

As the band struck up the national anthem, Blondin's appearance in Dundee was at an end. He returned to the British Hotel to spend the night before heading to Edinburgh in the morning. The Dundee appearance would long be remembered, not so much for its spectacle as for its poor attendance, but as the *Courier* report put it at the time: "there was no actual want of interest in the affair, although it was not the interest profitable to [the show's promoter] Mr Kyle. Indeed, Blondin's visit to the town was…decidedly sensational."

Three Bears

Not every circus-style show that exhibited in Dundee had the genius for showmanship of a Phineas T. Barnum or a William Cody behind it. Some were altogether more makeshift affairs. One such event was planned for the morning of Thursday, 7 November 1878, by John Woods, a general dealer from the Greenmarket on what was then some vacant ground in Commercial Street near the top of the Seagate. A tent had been erected and the two prize exhibits were to be brought to the site from a cellar in the Nethergate on the back of a barrow in a wooden cage with a metal grill. This ramshackle transport was the cause of much excitement and soon gathered a following crowd as it clattered its way along the cobbled streets. The procession had almost reached

ESCAPE OF A POLAR BEAR AT DUNDEE

A nineteenth century illustration of the scene in John Jamieson & Co's shop

its destination when one of the occupants managed to escape from captivity. Fortunately, the cage was divided into two compartments, meaning that the other remained a prisoner. Nonetheless, the escape was still a cause of great alarm and understandably so – a polar bear was loose in Dundee High Street.

John Woods and his assistants gave chase as the crowd that had been following the barrow scattered in all directions. One woman took shelter in the shop of Messrs John Jamieson & Co, a clothier and outfitter. The shopkeeper went to the door to find out what was happening only to find a polar bear rushing at him. Fleeing back into the shop in terror, he, together with the woman, climbed up onto the counter.

The shop was soon filled as Mr. Woods and his men arrived followed by a crowd of curious onlookers and self-appointed experts in bear capture. The bear, meanwhile, had ignored the terrified man and woman on the counter and instead knocked over a display figure. It then caught sight of itself in a mirror – something which appeared to cause it great distress as it growled and pawed at the glass, trying to get at what it must have believed to be another bear.

The animal made several attempts to escape by the door, but finding it closed, tried to exit via a window after climbing onto another counter that was situated in front of it. After this too had failed, it made its way behind the main counter by means of a gap between it and the wall. The gap was just large enough for the bear to get through.

The bear was now trapped in the back shop and several men climbed onto the counter, hoping to capture the creature when it re-emerged. A former sailor named James Coullie made a noose and dangled it into the gap. When the polar bear at last attempted to re-enter the shop, Coullie expertly caught the creature in the noose and returned it to Mr. Woods. Luckily, no one had been harmed during the incident and the polar bear's adventures no doubt provided a boost to Woods's ticket sales.

This was not the first time that a bear had caused panic on the streets of Dundee. Four years prior to the incident with the polar bear, a Russian brown bear had terrified people in the Wellgate area when it too escaped from a show. The bear escaped in George's Place, a street that ran off of the old Wellgate. People ran into the Wellgate itself and some took refuge in a coal dealer's shed. This was an unfortunate choice, however, as the bear followed them. The *Dundee Advertiser* described the scene inside the shed:

> "The coals were stacked against the walls, and men and women, boys and girls scrambled up the heaps, presenting to the eye of the bear when they reached the rafters an amphitheatre of frightened faces gazing on him "down among the coals". Apparently concluding that it would be useless further to "bear" the coal market, the animal turned away, no doubt with feelings of contemptuous disgust, and once more reaching the street retraced his steps as if with the intention of returning leisurely to his den."

The bear did not return to his den, however, but proceeded up Idvies Street to Victoria Road. There the creature made its way into a crockery shop, breaking dishes and terrifying the owner in the process. On the way out of the shop, it met a small boy. The *Advertiser* report says that it "made a snap at his head and bit rather severely some of the fingers". Not surprisingly, the child ran off screaming.

The bear then entered a baker's shop. The baker tried to scare it off by throwing the nearest object – a four-pound loaf – at it. He successfully managed to hit the creature between the eyes, but rather than driving it out or angering it, he only succeeded in persuading it to lie down on the floor and eat the loaf. This ultimately proved to be sufficient distraction to allow the animal to be recaptured by its owners.

The most famous bear to be displayed in Dundee lived almost a century after the two previously mentioned, and unlike them, lived out its entire time in the city in captivity. Jeremy the Bear achieved national fame as the face of the breakfast cereal Sugar Puffs from the launch of the product in 1957, featuring on the packaging and in advertising campaigns and television commercials. The European brown bear, who was actually a female, was eventually replaced by a cartoon version and entered retirement.

The bear was kept for a short time at Cromer Zoo in Norfolk where the future rector of Dundee University, Stephen Fry, was among the children who visited. In his autobiography *The Fry Chronicles*[19], he describes how the bear was the first celebrity he ever saw in the flesh – or rather in the fur. He was clearly overwhelmed by the experience, writing: "believe me, what the A-listingest Hollywood babe or pop idol is to a child now, Jeremy the bear was to me then".

Jeremy was transferred to Camperdown Park, eventually becoming the centrepiece of the new Wildlife Centre. The bear hit the headlines again in 1986 after biting the arm off of a 10-year-old boy who had entered the zoo after hours with some friends. The animal was not blamed for the incident and escaped the threat of being destroyed. Instead, Jeremy lived on until 1990 and remained the park's star attraction as have the other European brown bears who have replaced him.

---

19 Fry, Stephen, *The Fry Chronicles* (2010), London: Penguin, page 7

5
Modern Myths

In a field at Balkello Farm to the north of Dundee, there is a Pictish sculptured stone which has long been associated with a local myth. There are, of course, many versions of this myth but the basic story involves a farmer at Pitempton who had nine daughters, one of whom was sent to fetch water from a local well. When she did not return, another daughter was sent. She, too, failed to return and another was sent and so on until all were missing. The father himself then went to the well where he found a dragon or serpent resting after devouring his daughters. He ran off and gathered his neighbours to kill the creature. Chief among them was Martin the blacksmith, who had been betrothed to one of the daughters.

The dragon was driven to Strathmartine where the people urged Martin to strike it dead. ("Strike, Martin!", they cried – supposedly giving the area its name.) He did – but the creature staggered on and died at the spot where the stone now stands. The legend is remembered in an old rhyme:

It was tempted at Pitempton,
Draiglet at Baldragon,
Stricken at Strike-Martin,
and killed at Martin's Stane.

The story lives on today in local place names. There still exists, among others, a farm at Pitempton, a Baldragon Academy and a Nine Maidens pub. A statue of the dragon itself adorns the city centre.

Like all such myths, it is impossible to pin down its origins. Was it simply an attempt to explain the markings on the Pictish stone? Do the place names come from the story, or was the story created to explain the origins of the place names? Might the legend have been an echo of an older story from Glen Ogilvy on the other side of the Sidlaws about Saint Donevald, who was reputed to have lived there in the eighth century and who also had nine daughters?

The passage of time and the lack of documentation means that we cannot have definitive answers to any of these questions, but there are some more modern myths, however, from the nineteenth and twentieth centuries that it is possible to, at least, investigate and perhaps reach a conclusion as to their origin. This chapter attempts to rediscover the truth behind four such stories.

"God will in time supply their place"

At St George's Chapel, Windsor there is a monument to Princess Charlotte Augusta of Wales, who died in November 1817, the day after giving birth to a stillborn son. Princess Charlotte was 21 years old and the heir presumptive to the British throne. Her grandfather was King George III, and her father, the Prince Regent at the time of her death, would later become King George IV. The entire country seemed to enter a period of mourning following the tragic death of this young woman and her child. Shops closed their doors and people donned black armbands. The princess's husband, Prince Leopold, wrote of two generations being gone in a moment, while the future Lord Chancellor, Henry Brougham, wrote: "It really was as though every household throughout Great Britain had lost a favourite child."

The monument at Windsor, which was paid for by public subscription, depicts Princess Charlotte ascending to Heaven while an angel raises up her child and weeping figures back on Earth mourn her loss. It is still a very moving and poignant sight even two centuries after the death of the woman it commemorates.

There is another monument to Princess Charlotte, though, besides the one at Windsor. It is situated just off of the main Broughty Ferry to Dundee road at West Ferry and consists of a memorial stone set into a wall. Time has faded the words on the stone, but a modern metal version displays the original inscription. It reads:

The plaque to Princess Charlotte at West Ferry

"Sacred to the memory of Her Royal Highness the late Princess Charlotte Augusta, daughter of His Royal Highness the Prince Regent, Consort of His Serene Highness Prince Leopold of Saxe Gotha, and Heiress of the British Crown, being just delivered of a still-born son, died on the 6th November 1817, aged 22 [sic] years, much lamented by all the nation, who hoped to be blest in her succession.

> But death's strong hand struck such a blow,
> As like has laid their bodies low;
> Which stroke cost many mournful sighs,
> But trusts their souls are happy 'bove the skies;
> So therefore now our grief must cease,
> God will in time supply their place."

It is a strange place, to say the least, to find such a monument, but a local legend offers an explanation for its presence and one which includes a very different account of the circumstances surrounding Princess Charlotte's death to the official version. This legend claims that she and her husband Prince Leopold were visiting his homeland towards the end of her pregnancy. It was said to be Leopold's intention that the baby should be born there due to the better medical facilities, but Charlotte's father, the Prince Regent, insisted that they return to England for the birth, and the couple agreed. Their ship, however, was caught in a fierce storm and took shelter in the Tay Estuary. There, Charlotte went into labour. She was taken ashore to a nearby cottage where her baby was born and where, tragically, they both died. The occupants of the cottage were sworn to secrecy and the bodies of the princess and her son were smuggled back to London by coach. When the official announcement was made it was claimed that they had both died at Claremont House in Essex.

In 1901, when a cottage in the grounds of a property known as Viewpark in West Ferry was being demolished, workmen found the stone tablet inscribed to the memory of Princess Charlotte. The owner of the property at that time had it mounted into the boundary wall. The metal plaque was placed there in 1986 after redevelopment of the site, as by then the wording on the stone had become largely illegible. Is it possible, then, that there is some truth in the local legend and that the stone was placed originally at the cottage in secret acknowledgment of the truth of the story? Is there a message also in the final rhyme of the inscription? Surely it should read: "So therefore now our grief must cease, God will in time supply their *peace*" – rather than "place". Might this error be a hidden clue as to the significance of the "place" where the tragic events occurred?

If the legend were true, though, why would the princess and her child be said in official records to have died at Claremont? This is perhaps the easiest aspect of the mystery to explain. If Princess Charlotte and her child had died in inappropriate circumstances, then questions would surely be asked. As things stood, so shocking was her death that people sought a scapegoat. Some sections of the public blamed the Prince Regent and his estranged wife for not attending the birth, while others blamed Dr Croft, the physician who attended the princess. Indeed, such was the pressure on him that three months after Charlotte's death Croft shot and killed himself while attending another patient. If it emerged that the princess, who was second in line to the throne, had really died in the lowly cottage home of a total stranger without proper medical care or attention, and if it was realised that that situation had come about only because there had been an attempt to have the heir to the British throne born in a foreign country, then the anger directed against the monarchy would only have been increased. While the princess was popular in the country, her father and grandfather were not.

If it is relatively easy to explain a "cover up" in the wake of the death of the princess and her son, then more difficult to explain are the reports of Charlotte's presence at Claremont immediately prior to the birth. A report in the *Morning Post* on 3 November 1817, three days before the birth, for example, stated:

> "Yesterday the weather proving remarkably fine, the Princess Charlotte took her usual airing in her chaise and continued out for about two hours. The princess and Prince Leopold assembled their principal attendants and all their domestics for divine service in the morning, which was performed by the Rev. Dr. Short. Soon after the service Her Royal Highness rode out in her small chaise in the park, and occasionally walked in the pleasure grounds. Prince Leopold accompanied his Royal Consort in her airing."

There were other similar reports in the press of Princess Charlotte taking the air in the park in the days before giving birth. If the authorities had good reason to lie about the location of her death and that of her child in the event that they happened at Broughty Ferry, they would have had little reason to lie about events before the birth when they did not know what was to happen. Even if it were to cover up the fact that the couple were away and that the child might be born abroad, they would surely have said that she was confined to her room and not appearing in relatively public places before numerous witnesses.

Something else that points towards there being no truth in the legend is to be found – or rather not found – in the newspaper report of the discovery of the stone in 1901. The short article in the *Courier* of 6 December does not mention the story of Princess Charlotte's death happening in the locality. In fact, it says, "As to the reason for the stone's location where found there is only conjecture to fall back upon." If the legend were well known then it would surely have been referred to in the piece and the discovery of the stone taken as pointing towards its veracity. Of course, it might be that it was just that the journalist who wrote about the discovery was not familiar with the story. Even if this were so, it would surely have been well known to others in Broughty Ferry and Dundee. That being the case, it might have been expected that the paper's correspondence pages would have been filled in subsequent days with local people amazed at the possibility that the old story they had heard as children might be true. There appears to be no such correspondence – and while not conclusive, this points to the legend growing up in the wake of the discovery of the memorial and not predating it.

The *Courier* article concludes with a bit of conjecture, saying of the stone, "it is surmised to be the handiwork of a former occupant". This conjecture, as it happens, turns out to be accurate. To find out the true story of the Princess Charlotte memorial, we must travel back to 1822, when another article appeared in the same paper. This was a guide to the attractions of the Broughty Ferry area and contains the following passage:

> "… and if the feet of the invalid will carry him far as the unique abode of the primitive schoolmaster, he may walk into a garden whose paths are twined into more mazes than the Cretan labyrinth or the approach to the celebrated bower of the frail Rosamond. There, too, he will find a series of monuments as novel the walks are intricate. Enter the left hand – the owner will not be offended – and first, you have a cenotaph to the Princess Charlotte, next a monument, somewhat in the fashion of a kirk, set up in honour of the Reformation; after this comes a cone to the battle of Waterloo, then tribute to Mr. Pitt, after that cone to the battle of Leipsic, [Leipzig] then a monument to John Knox and lastly, one to his late Majesty George III."

Princess Charlotte's monument, it seems, was at one time only one of several that adorned the intricate pathways of the garden of a schoolteacher – but who was this man? Almost thirty years after the first article appeared, it was reprinted in the *Advertiser* under the heading "Antiquarian Gleanings". This reprinted article named the schoolmaster in question as one Alexander Small. This article also included descriptions of the other monuments, besides that to the princess. One was said to have "a rude resemblance of Gothic Cathedral, with tower and spire rising from the centre of the roof" and bore the inscription:

> Sacred to the memory of the Establishing of the Protestant Reformed Religion in Scotland.
>
> Reader, now credit ye the news it brings,
> And put no trust in earthly things;
> Since ye share in this donation,
> Trust God in Christ for your Salvation.

The article continues:

> "In the middle of the north wall of the garden, betwixt two pyramids or cones, one in the north-west and the other in the north-east corner, there was a tablet bearing the following inscription:

Built by Alexander Small, teacher here, in memory of the late Mr. Pitt, sometime prime minister in the reign of His Majesty King George III. Also, two Pyramids, the lesser in memory of the famous Battle of Leipsic, the greater in memory of the decisive victory of Waterloo by the Duke of Wellington, June 18th, 1815."

The inscription on the monument to John Knox read:

"Built to the memory of John Knox, who
By Grace Divine with zeal did shine
In the Protestant profession,
And in his day did fast and pray
To procure the Reformation.

By A. S., as were the other monuments here."

The last monument bore the inscription:

"To the memory of his late Majesty King George Third
a Gracious Sovereign - in a word,
of Godliness set an example,
fear'd the Lord, and revered his Temple,
and from his accession it appears
he'd reign fifty and nine years.
Died 1820"

Reading the inscriptions for the other monuments appears to put an end to speculation that the final two lines in the memorial to Princess Charlotte hid some sort of code, rather than simply being a poor attempt at rhyming. Small had managed to rhyme "profession" and "Reformation" and "temple" and "example". The newspaper reports that Small had also written "several epitaphs in the old Ferry churchyard, and also that of the South Ferry" before going on to offer an implicit criticism of his poetical abilities when it says of the garden monuments: "whatever may be thought of those" as a preamble to expressing disgust at the conduct of those who demolished them.

According to the newspaper, the inscriptions were transcribed from the monuments on 28 January 1829, and the report states that it was soon after this that Alexander Small died at the age of 84. His wife was around the same age and her death followed so soon after that of her husband that they were buried together on the same day.

It is a strange twist of fate that caused the monument to Princess Charlotte to surface. It was surely the only one of Alexander Small's memorials that was capable of spawning a legend: the memorial to the Reformation or the ones to the Battles of Leipzig or Waterloo would undoubtedly have been taken at face value had they turned up and it is unlikely that anyone would have seriously considered the possibility that John Knox, William Pitt or King George III had secretly died at Broughty Ferry if their stones had been uncovered. The sad circumstances around the princess's death, however, as well as her young age and her relative historical obscurity a century after her death, make her an ideal candidate for a romantic conspiracy theory, however far-fetched.

The other individuals commemorated in Small's garden each have memorials somewhere in Scotland today. For example, there is a statue of William Pitt the younger in Edinburgh's George Street. There are several statues, too, of John Knox – notably at Edinburgh's New College and Glasgow's Necropolis as well as in his birthplace of Haddington, and George Square in Glasgow is named after King George III. By accident rather than design, Dundee has gained the only memorial in Scotland to the relatively neglected Princess Charlotte Augusta, and by a quirk of fate has placed that memorial at the end of Victoria Road – a street that is named after a queen who would never have come to the throne had the princess and her child not died in 1817.

The White Lady of the Coffin Mill

On 2 September 1945, at a ceremony on board the *USS Missouri* in Tokyo Bay, the Japanese formally surrendered, thus bringing an official end to the Second World War. When a large crowd gathered in a Dundee street two days later, a passer-by might well have suspected that people were gathering in belated celebration of the official end of hostilities. Those who had assembled, however, had not come to mark the end of the war or anything quite so earthly – instead, they had turned up to look for a ghost.

The crowd was gathered outside the large and forbidding building which still stands today between Lower Pleasance and Brook Street. The building's official name at that time was Logie Works but it had long been known locally by the suitably sinister name of the Coffin Mill. While that name conjures up a

The bridge at the Coffin Mill where the White Lady is said to walk

horror film like an image of a factory containing a production line of coffins, it is said to be derived from the unusual shape of the central courtyard of the works. Coffins are unlikely ever to have been manufactured on the premises, though in 1945 part of the building was occupied by a firm of wholesale cabinetmakers, who might conceivably have had a sideline in coffins.

The reason that so many people had congregated was because it had been reported that the Coffin Mill's resident ghost, the "White Lady", had been seen. This legendary figure is said to haunt the factory and, in particular, the narrow iron bridge that spans its central courtyard linking the two parts of the building. She is said to be the ghost of a young female worker who had died in the mill as the result of a horrific accident when her long hair became entangled in her loom.

By 10 o'clock at night the crowd had grown so large that it came to the attention of the police, and several officers attended the scene. After they had assured the crowd that there was no ghost on the premises, a large number of people went away. Later, however, more people turned up to look for the ghostly visitor and some damage was done to the building when some of the younger members of the crowd, no doubt bored by the White Lady's non-appearance, started throwing stones at the building. The gathering only finally dispersed after a policeman and night watchman made a full tour of the building, shining a torch from every window.

The following evening a crowd gathered at the Coffin Mill again, but the White Lady, it seems, was overcome by shyness once more and did not put in an appearance. Her disappointed public soon began to abandon the scene. The legend of the White Lady has persisted over the years, but she never again got such an audience as she did in 1945. A contributor to the *Evening Telegraph* calling himself "Frank-in Stane" turned to poetry to sum up the White Lady mania that had so briefly gripped the area at that time:

> Have you seen the White Lady?
> The cry's gaen roon,
> It's the dread o' the Bairns
> And the talk o' the toon
>
> Have you seen the White Lady?
> She's young and she's fair
> She walks through the mill
> When there's naebody there
>
> Have you seen the White Lady?
> They're seeking her still
> On the auld iron brig
> At the auld coffin mill
>
> Some say that she died
> Wi' her hair in a loom
> Some swear that she fell
> Through the brig to her doom
>
> It might be a tale
> That the auld people tell
> So I made up my mind
> That I'd see for masel'
> But while I stood waitin'
> The White Lady's play
> The Right Lady came
> And she hauled me away!

The Coffin Mill has since been converted to housing and given the more wholesome sounding name of Pleasance Court – but it retains much of its original outward appearance including the "auld iron brig" that the White Lady is reputed to haunt. The Lady herself, however, though still occasionally talked about, is conspicuous by her absence. Could it be, nonetheless, that there is a grain of truth in the story that gave birth to the legend. Was there really ever a tragic accident at the mill involving a woman with long hair?

Several attempts have been made to identify such an event at Logie Works but no trace of the long-haired woman has so far been found. Accidents involving women having their hair caught up in machinery were certainly not unknown in Victorian factories. Such accidents caused horrific injuries and were often fatal. In January 1900, for example, a 15-year-old girl named Jane Murray was killed at South Dudhope Works, not far from Logie Works. Her hair had been caught up in the rollers of a carding machine and when she used her hand to try to release it, it was drawn in too. By the time the machine was stopped, the unfortunate girl was dead.

There were fatal accidents at Logie Works too, but none matching the story of the White Lady. In 1873, for example, a man named Alexander Menzies was killed when a lift he was travelling in with two colleagues plunged to the bottom of its shaft. The men had been employed to replace the worn-out rope on the very lift in which Menzies was killed. There is one horrific accident, however, that may have provided the origin of the White Lady story. It is a tragic event that dates back to the mid-nineteenth century and which seems to have been forgotten over the years.

Logie Works was opened in 1828 by Messrs A and D Edward to spin flax, though it later, like the majority of Dundee's mills, dealt with jute. Like many of the earliest mills it was situated in the area around Scouringburn (later Brook Street). The Scouring Burn itself, which still exists today, though long since piped underground, provided a ready-made source of water for the factory's 30 horse power steam engine. In 1833, the building was expanded and there were subsequent additions over the years. By 1846, there were two steam engines totalling 160 horsepower and driving 14,068 spindles in a factory with forty power looms. Eighteen years later, there were five engines with a combined 260 horsepower, 17,000 spindles and 600 power looms. The workforce at this time comprised 2,500. The middle years of the nineteenth century, then, were a time of great expansion for Logie Works, but this time and location also provided the setting for one of Dundee's worst ever industrial accidents.

At the east end of the premises near the iron bridge was a three-storey building which was separated from the main body of the mill by a strong partition wall and bounded on the east by a narrow lane. On the ground floor of this building and built partly below the level of the street was a boiler room containing four boilers. On the floor above this was an area for drying spun yarn. There were few people on this floor but the two further levels above were used for preparing flax and these were occupied by around thirty – mainly female – workers and much heavy machinery. Adjacent to the boiler room on the ground floor at the entrance to the courtyard was a porter's lodge.

At around one o'clock on 15 April 1859, an enormous explosion was heard all over Dundee. One of the boilers at Logie Works had exploded. An eyewitness later told the press how he had seen a sudden cloud of steam emerge before the whole building above the boiler house perceptibly rose into the air and crashed down into a "mass of ruins". When the cloud of dust and steam cleared away it was clear that the entire building was reduced to rubble, burying its occupants.

The workers from the adjacent mill in Logie Works were, of course, the first on the scene and soon began to clear the rubble, aided by people from the immediate area, which, at that time, was mainly home to Irish immigrants. The sights which met their eyes as they tried to clear the debris and extricate the dead and injured must have been truly appalling. A report in the *Saturday Post* published the next day gives an impression of the extent of the horror:

"The poor victims were in many instances scalded and mangled so horribly that their relatives could not recognise them. One young woman was found gasping for life, her mouth fixed open, dreadfully scalded and her arms literally boiled. She died soon after reaching the infirmary. Another woman was found lying across a sharp iron beam with a quantity of heavy machinery above her. She was of course quite dead and nearly cut through… Some of the women were found in the preparing machines at which they had been working. One of them was carried into the counting-room in a state of excruciating torture, so scalded that the features could scarcely be recognised."

That last unfortunate woman who had been discovered, like so many of the Irish workers in Logie Works, to be a Roman Catholic, had at least the comfort of the Last Rites, performed by one of several priests who attended the scene. Various Protestant ministers were also there to offer consolation to the injured and dying. It is doubtful, though, that even any of these clergymen, who would have been familiar with the worst of Dundee's slums and the sickness and death that went with them, would have been prepared for the hell that confronted them that day in the Scouringburn.

Bodies continued to be pulled from the rubble, including that of a dyer named Adam Doig. His corpse was said to be "quite charred", while that of another man was found missing the whole of one hand and the fingers of another, the feet and shoes having been shrivelled by the fire. Elsewhere, a boot was found with a woman's foot still inside it. Some of the bodies, according to a report in the *Advertiser*, were "so mangled that they had lost the appearance of humanity".

Some people did escape the explosion, though. The porter's lodge adjacent to the boiler room was entirely demolished by the blast but its occupants – a man and two boys – were said to have survived. The works manager, Alexander Taws, also had a narrow escape. He had just crossed the iron bridge that linked the two sections of the mill when the explosion occurred. With one of its supports obliterated, the bridge was left dangling from the north wing of the works. Meanwhile, one of the firemen who stoked the boiler had just left for his dinner and so escaped death. His colleague, Joseph Clark, was not so lucky and was found dead in the ruins, with his hand still on his shovel.

News of the explosion spread quickly through the town. Among the first to arrive at the scene were members of the Edward family, who owned the works, as well as Provost Jobson. Within a short time, a vast crowd had gathered. As well as the merely curious, this consisted of many who feared for friends and relatives. Large numbers of police stopped them from getting too close to the scene. The *Courier* reported that: "The scene was painful in the extreme when a wounded sufferer or mangled body was recognised by a disconsolate parent or other friend. But the most of the dead bodies were so much injured that recognition was a matter of great difficulty and the identification of the whole was not completed until the next day."

Relatives also flocked to the infirmary in search of their missing loved ones in the hope that they might be among the survivors. One woman, searching for her niece, failed to find her among the injured. A doctor, though, heard a faint cry of "Auntie" from one of the patients. It turned out to be the missing woman. Such were the poor girl's injuries that her aunt had failed to recognise her.

As night fell, it was becoming apparent that there would be no more survivors, but the search for bodies continued throughout the night and into the next morning, with the last of these being recovered around 3 am. In all, sixteen bodies were removed from the destroyed section of the factory. Work continued on Saturday to clear the rubble and resumed again on Monday. By the end of that day three more of the injured had died in the infirmary, bringing the total number who died as a result of the disaster to nineteen. Of these three were men, two were boys and the other fourteen were women.

The works owners Messrs A and D Edward seem to have made generous provision for the families of the deceased and they also carried on paying the wages of the injured. It is unlikely, though, that they would have made any such provision for the 300 or so people who would have found themselves out of work until the necessary repairs were made at the factory. The Edwards did, however, arrange for the burial of some of those killed.

Nine of the dead were buried directly from Logie Works by the firm. A succession of coffins left the works that weekend – which raises the possibility that this might be the true origin of the name the Coffin Mill. Ann Taylor was buried on Saturday, 16 April in the Howff. The following day, six hearses arrived at the works to take the bodies of Mary Young, Margaret Craig, Catherine Collins, Ellen Gowans, Charlotte Crammond and a 9-year-old boy called Thomas Wake to the New Burying Ground at Constitution Road. They departed in two journeys, each followed by a large crowd which included many of the workmates of the deceased. The fireman Thomas Clark was buried at Erroll and his body was also accompanied part of the way by a large crowd of mourners.

The body of Margaret Mitchell was kept at Logie Works until Monday 18 April so that her mother could travel to Dundee from Aberdeen for the funeral. Margaret Mitchell herself had only just arrived in Dundee the day before the disaster and had gone to Logie Works with her friend Ellen Mackay on Friday, 15 April to look for work. Shortly after their arrival, the manager had been called away and asked them to wait in the lodge house, but instead they waited outside and were caught up in the explosion. Ellen escaped with burns and a scalp wound but Margaret was tragically killed.

The remaining bodies were released to their families for burial. Among these were the bodies of 17-year-old Agnes Jamieson and her 15-year-old sister Jemima, as well as that of 15-year-old Thomas Newall.

As to the cause of the explosion, two main theories emerged in the days that followed the incident. One was that the boiler was being overworked and another was that there was not enough water in the system. An investigation by Henry Forsyth, the procurator fiscal at Forfar, however, taking into account the opinions of professional engineers who examined the site, seems to have concluded that the wall of the boiler had been extremely thin at the place where it first gave way. This had not been detectable because the defective part of the boiler was situated in an inaccessible position.

Perhaps because it was an industrial accident at a time when such things were regarded as being an occupational hazard, the memory of the terrible explosion at Logie Works seems to have faded remarkably quickly. There would certainly have been no question of any memorial being erected to those who died. A local worthy named McIntosh saw fit to commemorate the tragedy in verse, but the result was hardly fitting. Only a fragment of this poem is known to survive and so it is not clear whether it was an unintentionally inappropriate attempt at sincerity, such as those later produced by William McGonagall, or a tasteless attempt at humour:

> Factory operatives, all take warning,
> For death and judgement to prepare,
> For you know not when a boiler,
> May burst and blow you in the air!

The collapsed section of the building was rebuilt and the iron bridge once again connected the two sections of the works. This is the bridge that the White Lady is reputed to haunt, and perhaps the tragedy provides the origin for that legend. Had any of the doomed female workforce crossed the bridge that day in 1859, as the works manager Mr Taws had done, then they would have been saved. With this knowledge, it would not be surprising if many felt a sense of unease looking at the factory and the bridge in particular in the years that followed the disaster. As time passed, this unease seems to have been passed down like a folk memory, though its origins were forgotten until there only remained a vague knowledge of some horrific accident having taken place there. The White Lady, in that sense, is a ghost – the ghost of past events. The only people who would ever have been truly haunted by the spectre of the Coffin Mill, though, are surely those who witnessed the horrific scenes in the Scouringburn that fateful day in 1859 and the friends and families of the killed and injured in so horrific a fashion.

Mary Buik and the Death of Admiral Nelson

The Dundee Women's Trail is a collection of twenty-five plaques positioned around the city, which together with an accompanying book and website, tells the stories of many of the remarkable women born in or associated with Dundee. Included in the trail are some truly exceptional individuals such as the pioneering astronomer Williamina Fleming, the Christian missionary Mary Slessor, the suffragette, teacher and city councillor Lila Clunas, and Florence Horsburgh, Dundee's first woman MP and the first female Conservative cabinet minister. Perhaps one of the most remarkable stories of all, however, is that of Mary Buick (or Buik), who was born in Dundee in 1777.

The story, or one version of it at least, goes something like this. When she was 20, Mary married a fisherman from Cellardyke in Fife named Thomas Watson. When Watson was compulsorily recruited into the service of the Royal Navy by a press gang shortly afterwards, Mary did not want to be parted from him and ran after the press gang asking them to take her as well. She secured a place aboard her husband's ship working as a nurse. Husband and wife both served aboard HMS Ardent in the early part of 1801 during the Battle of Copenhagen. Incredibly, in the middle of that battle, Mary give birth to a daughter.

The story then takes an even more remarkable twist when the Watsons were transferred to *HMS Victory* under Admiral Lord Nelson and both were present on the flagship during the Battle of Trafalgar in 1805. Thomas, it is said, headed a gun crew while Mary tended the wounded. After Nelson was killed, it was Mary Buik who helped to prepare his body for embalming. Another Cellardyke man on board, Malcolm McRuvie, is said to have looked after their daughter, Mary, while her mother undertook this historic duty.

The Watsons survived the Battle of Trafalgar and eventually found their way back to Cellardyke, where they ran a public house. Their daughter, Mary, who had been born during the Battle of Copenhagen lived to be 90 years old. The story of Thomas Watson and Mary Buik and, in particular, Mary's part in dealing with the death of Nelson, was passed down through the generations. Given the importance of the battle and the heroic status afforded to Nelson, it is easy to see how this story could have captured the imagination of so many down the years. Nevertheless, the question remains – is it true?

There is no doubt whatsoever that Thomas Watson and Mary Buik existed. Records show that Thomas was born in the Parish of Kilrenny in 1765 and Mary was born in Dundee twelve years later. The couple were married in Dundee on 18 December 1797. This was not Thomas Watson's first marriage. He had married a Margaret Thomson in Kilrenny in 1786, but she died of consumption seven years after they had wed. At the time of Thomas Watson's marriage to Mary Buik, the records show that both parties were resident in Dundee and Thomas's occupation is given as "sailor" rather than "fisherman". The term "sailor", of course, could be used to refer to anybody who made a living from going to sea and so does not preclude him still being a fisherman but it might imply that Watson was already in the navy or working on a commercial vessel at the time of the marriage.

It seems highly likely that Thomas Watson was coerced into the navy as press gangs were highly active in this period. Contrary to popular myth, though, the gangs generally did not kidnap unsuspecting civilians who had no experience of life at sea. There was no shortage of such volunteers. It was, rather, those with a nautical background such as fishermen or merchant seamen who were most keenly sought. It is not surprising, then, that such gangs would turn their attention to the Fife coast and other areas heavily dependent on fishing. Sometimes informers would pass information about an intended victim or chalk the door of their house.

In his 1887 book *Our Old Neighbours or Foklore of the East of Fife*[20], local historian George Gourlay gives a vivid account of the attempts of young Thomas Watson to avoid the press gang:

> "Take, for instance, poor Tammas Watson, watched and hunted till the whin bushes of Kingsmuir were as familiar to him as the rocks on which he had waded from childhood, though even there he was not out of danger, chased as he was by the fiery young Comptroller on horseback, till he took like the fox to the coal wastes at Lochty; or when he was tracked as a thief by the Anstruther beagles, who tried, though vainly, to bribe or threaten every herd boy on the hillside. Three times he approached so near the old home as to see his mother sitting at the window, but there was likewise the red napkin, that sign of danger, as when the beacon is blazing on the bar, so that he had as often to fly to the muirs; till on the ninth day his feet began to swell with fatigue and cold."

It is clear that this is the same Thomas Watson, as Gourlay goes on to tell how "Tammas" married "the plucky Dundee lass, Mary Buik, who, like a true wife, had shared his perils in the battle and the breeze".

---

20 Gourlay, George, *Our Old Neighbours or Foklore of the East of Fife* (1887), Anstruther: George Gourlay, page 108.

Whether he was eventually caught by the press gang or joined of his own volition, Thomas Watson certainly found himself in the navy. Records show that he served on *HMS Ardent* from 1799. What, though, of Mary Buik and her life "in the battle and the breeze"? Surely women did not go to sea at this time? Certainly, the official position was that they did not. The *Regulations and Instructions Relating to His Majesty's Service at Sea* issued by the Admiralty stated that women were not allowed to be taken to sea and the only ones who should ever be permitted on board a ship at any time were "such as are really the wives of the men they come to, and the ship not too much pestered even with them". It is clear, nonetheless, that women – whether officers' wives, nurses or passengers – did travel aboard Nelson's ships. As they were not paid, however, their names were not entered in to the official records. It is possible to be sure, however, that Mary Buik accompanied her husband as far as Yarmouth – as there she gave birth to the couple's first child in 1799, a boy named John. The entry for his christening at St Nicholas's Church gives Mary's maiden surname as "Bewick" – one of many variations of its spelling. The spelling of names was much more fluid in this period as many people – including Mary Buik – could not write.

HMS Ardent's records show that half of Thomas Watson's wages were instructed to be paid to Mary Buik from the time he joined the ship but that these payments stop at the end of February 1801. Could this be when she joined him on board? Certainly, the fleet that took part in the Battle of Copenhagen, including the *Ardent*, assembled in Yarmouth harbour at the beginning of March, finally setting sail on the twelfth of that month, under Admiral Sir Hyde Parker, with Vice Admiral Lord Nelson as second in command. The British were intent on reasserting their naval supremacy and breaking up the league that had been set up by Denmark, Sweden, Prussia and Russia, to enforce free trade with France. Knowing that the ships were likely to be going into conflict, might this not have been an opportune moment for a nurse to come on board?

What, though, of the couple's young son, John? Surely Mary could not have taken him to sea? Sadly, these were times of high infant mortality and it seems likely that John did not survive. Children were often given the names of an older sibling who had died, and in 1806, the Watsons named another son John.

If the story of Mary Buik giving birth on board the *Ardent* is true, then it seems likely that she would have been heavily pregnant at the time she boarded. The pregnancy might not, however, have lasted its full term. This would not have been the first time that the stress of a battle situation had brought about a premature labour. This had happened to Mrs. Daniel McKenzie on board *HMS Tremendous* in 1794, during the action against the French that became known as "the Glorious First of June". Her child was named Daniel Tremendous McKenzie. Years later, in a highly unusual move, he was awarded the Naval General Service medal, with his rating listed in the official records as "Baby".

There is no such record for Mary Buik's daughter, Mary Watson, but her birth aboard the *Ardent* did make it on to an official document – albeit some fifty years later. In the 1851 census, by which time she was married and living in John Street, Cellardyke, her place of birth was given as "aboard *HMS Ardent*, 64-gun ship, at sea". It is clear that she, at least, believed that that was where she had been born, and given that Mary Buik was still alive and living in Cellardyke at the time that the information was given to the census enumerator, there seems little reason to doubt it. Certainly, all the evidence that exists seems to support this and none has so far emerged to contradict it.

Immediately after the birth of Mary Watson and the Battle of Copenhagen, however, is the point where the legend of Mary Buik appears to diverge from the evidence. The legend has the Watsons and their child transferred to *HMS Victory* under Nelson's command. The records show, however, that Thomas Watson was discharged from the *Ardent* on 11 April 1801, the day after the Battle of Copenhagen, to *HMS Bellona*. It seems unlikely that Mary would have gone with him, while nursing so young a child. In any case, the following year, the *Bellona* was "laid up in Ordinary" – effectively mothballed – at Portsmouth and its crew paid off. This appears to raise the possibility that the Watsons might have transferred to the *Victory* at this point thus allowing for them to be present at the Battle of Trafalgar in October 1805. This would not be possible, however, as at the time that the *Bellona* was laid up, the *Victory* was undergoing an extensive refit that would not be completed until April 1803.

It is possible to be certain that the Watsons did not join the *Victory* following her refit, as from July 1803, Nelson began a blockade of the French at Toulon which lasted until 1805. In June 1804, the Kilrenny parish records show that "Thomas Watson, fisher in Cellardyke and Mary Buick or Boyack his spouse" had a daughter named Anne. It appears that the couple had returned to Cellardyke following Thomas Watson's discharge from the *Bellona* and that he had resumed his former occupation. The next time the Watsons appear in the parish records is in July 1806 when their son John was born. Again, Thomas Watson is referred to as "fisher in Cellardyke".

For Thomas Watson and Mary Buik to be present aboard the *Victory* at the Battle of Trafalgar, they would have had to have left Cellardyke again in between the births of these two children. Thomas would have had to re-join the navy and persuade the authorities to take his wife on board once again as a nurse. The couple would have had to board the *Victory* at Portsmouth before she set off on 14 September 1805 for her date with destiny. While this would be possible, it appears, on the face of it, to be highly unlikely. They would either had to have taken both their 4-year-old daughter Mary and 15-month-old daughter Anne aboard the *Victory* or have left one or both with someone else on dry land. While it was not uncommon for older children, usually boys, to be employed at sea as "powder monkeys", helping to load the artillery, it is difficult to imagine that such young children, who could not be pressed into any kind of service, would be allowed on a ship just about to head into battle.

Furthermore, there does not appear to be any record of the Watsons being on board the *Victory*. This is not surprising with regard to Mary Buik, but surely some record of Thomas Watson's service would survive. A variety of sources, such as the navy pay-books, record the names of those who served on the ship but none refers to either Thomas Watson or Malcolm McRuvie, the other man from Cellardyke, who supposedly looked after Mary Buik's child while she attended to Nelson's corpse.

Again, it is possible that Thomas Watson's presence on the *Victory* at Trafalgar was unrecorded, or that his name is noted in some record that has not yet surfaced, but it is unlikely, given the importance of both the ship and the battle, that the records were not well maintained and preserved. Indeed, it is the very importance of the setting that helps to sow seeds of doubt as to the veracity of the legend of Mary Buik. Not only is she said to be at sea at a time when it was unusual for a woman, but she is present at what is arguably the most important naval battle in history. Not only is she said to be present at this battle, but she is on board the flagship. Not only is she said to be present on board the *Victory*, but she is there at, or shortly after, the most important event that takes place on board – the death of Admiral Nelson.

As we have seen, the evidence appears to point to there being at least a kernel of truth in the story – that Mary Buik did go to sea with her husband. Her time on board ship appears to have been brief, however, and both she and Thomas Watson were back in Cellardyke by 1804. Much as we may wish to believe it, there does not appear to be any documentary evidence that she was present at the Battle of Trafalgar in 1805, and again she was known to be in Cellardyke the following year.

Were it not to be true, then, where might this story have come from? Everything points to this being the type of legend that was passed down through the Watson family and the local community at Kilrenny and Cellardyke. Indeed, every recorded version of the story seems to owe its origins to this part of the Fife coast. There seems to be little doubt that Mary Watson junior, who lived to be 90 years old, believed that her mother had attended to Nelson's body after his death. It is any corroborating evidence from elsewhere that is missing. Perhaps the whole thing can be traced back to a winter's evening by the fireside in a house on the Shore at Cellardyke, where an already exciting tale was spun and expanded to incorporate one of the defining moments of the age, producing a story that stayed in a young girl's consciousness until her old age, when there was nobody left that could contradict it.

Thomas Watson died in 1831 after a long illness and Mary Buik died in 1854 at the age of 77. They are buried together in Kilrenny Kirkyard. For the time being, the truth of the story is buried along with them. All that remains is the legend and such facts as are available. From these, we know that Mary Buik followed her press-ganged husband to Yarmouth and was most likely to have been at sea with him during the Battle of Copenhagen, where she gave birth to a daughter. We also know that she had at least a further six children, some of whom predeceased her. She also endured the anxieties of being married to a fisherman and ran a public house. Surely a woman like this does not need Horatio Nelson to justify her place on the Dundee Women's Trail?

The Lonely Italian of the Blue Mountains

The prime minister's wife, Mrs Cissie Baldwin, was wearing a smart cape over her black gown of black Zingara satin. The cape, of fine *velours de laine*, was encrusted in crystal motifs forming a paisley design. Her large picture hat was adorned with a diamond ornament on one side and a large floral decoration of black and white plumage on the other. The Duchess of Atholl had donned a black ensemble under her long coat of musquash fur. Her outfit was topped with an ostrich feather in her hat. It was June 1925 and the ladies were being driven towards one of the most notorious slum areas in Dundee's history – the Blue Mountains.

The women were, in fact, dressed for the presentation of the Freedom of the City of Dundee to Mrs Baldwin's husband, Stanley, which they had just attended in the Caird Hall. Together with their husbands, as well as Sir John Gilmour, the Secretary of State for Scotland, Lady Gilmour and Lord Provost William High and his wife, they were on their way to see some of the worst housing in Dundee. The entourage sped towards the West Port, past the flag-waving children of Tay Street School.

Go to the West Port today and you will find a small street named Johnston's Lane which stretches between the old and new Hawkhills at the back of the Globe Bar. In 1925 these streets were known as Hawkhill and Scouringburn and the area entering by a pend off Johnston's Lane called Barron's Court was known as the Blue Mountains. The entire area behind Johnston's Lane, essentially that which is occupied by a car park today, was home in the 1920s to hundreds of people.

On the day of Stanley Baldwin's visit a large crowd had gathered in front of the pend and the prime minister had to pass through lines of cheering children, many of them barefoot, to enter it. Mrs. Baldwin handed the children flowers from the bouquet that had been presented to her at the Caird Hall. Going through a narrow, whitewashed passage, Baldwin emerged into a cobbled courtyard with rickety staircases leading off it and up to the houses. It was thought that he would be content just to see the poverty of the area from the courtyard, but the prime minister wanted to see the houses themselves and headed off up one of the staircases. The Duke of Atholl, Mrs. Baldwin and Sir William and Lady High followed him. When they all entered the first house they came to – a single room housing five people – there was no room for anybody else. The prime minister remarked upon the number of religious symbols on the walls. There was little else of note in the house apart from some rudimentary furniture. The Duke of Atholl engaged the householder in a conversation about what was perhaps the only thing that they had in common – their army service.

As they emerged, the duke is said to have remarked to Baldwin: "What a terrible conscience the landlord of this property must have."
The prime minister replied: "That is just what I have been thinking myself."
The party moved along a passageway so dark that they had to grope the walls with their hands to find the point where it turned left. There, they visited more houses whose conditions were no better than that those that they had just encountered.

When Baldwin returned to the courtyard it was obvious that his trip to the Blue Mountains had affected him. He was heard to tell the Secretary of State for Scotland: "That is the worst of the cursed system", before resolving to come up with ways to get rid of such conditions. Meanwhile, an official told a reporter from the *Glasgow Herald*: "these are not our worst houses even. I wish I could get the Prime Minister to see some in the Overgate."

If the Blue Mountains represented among the worst of Dundee's housing conditions, the prime minister's next destination was representative of the very best. The housing scheme at Logie had first been proposed by the City Architect James Thomson in 1918. Logie was seen as a suitable space for high quality housing, close enough to the city centre but still with "space in profusion for gardens and allotments".

The development, which eventually was built as Scotland's first local authority housing scheme, was heavily influenced by the Garden City movement which had been founded by Ebeneezer Howard at the turn of the century and had seen the construction of both Letchworth Garden City and Welwyn Garden City in Hertfordshire in England. Logie's streets curved off a tree-lined central boulevard and the houses had space for gardens and allotments. The scheme also included a municipal heating scheme which supplied central heating and hot water to the houses. So proud were the authorities of the scheme that a special platform was built at one end of the development to allow passers-by the opportunity to take in the view. The contrast with the Blue Mountains could not be clearer.

The Dundee writer David Phillips, in his book *The Hungry Thirties* speculates that the reason Stanley Baldwin was taken to the Blue Mountains in the first place was to show the contrast with the Logie scheme and the extent to which the council was making improvements in the city[21]. Baldwin, himself, however, in the speech he made accepting the Freedom of the city, said that it had been proposed that he visit Dundee's great public buildings and factories but he had asked instead to see "what the city of Dundee is doing to face the housing question in its poorest quarters".

Whatever the truth of how he came to be there and whatever the political differences that many in Dundee would have had with him (and these would have been numerous, particularly during the General Strike, less than a year after his visit), Stanley Baldwin is surely to be commended for actually visiting

---

21 Phillips, David, *The Hungry Thirties* (1981), Dundee: David Winter and Son Limited, page 43.

A view over the "Blue Mountains"

the area. It is difficult to imagine any modern prime minister of whatever political persuasion, actually stepping into the latter-day equivalent of the Blue Mountains and visiting houses at random.

In the days after Baldwin's visit, a vigorous debate took place in the correspondence pages of the local press. The controversy being discussed did not involve the rights and wrongs of the prime minister's itinerary or of how best to deal with slum dwellings or indeed the intricacies of housing policy in general. Instead, it was the type of debate that Dundonians appear always to have enjoyed and to be happy to discuss until the exasperated editorial staff feel the need to insert a notice saying "Thanks to all who wrote" – namely how did the area known as the Blue Mountains get its name?

The story that the Baldwins had been told when they asked of the name's origin was that the area was once home to an Italian tenant who was homesick for his native land and had painted a mural featuring mountains and mostly using the colour blue. When the *Glasgow Herald*'s reporter had asked a policeman at the time of Baldwin's visit for an explanation, he had been told a similar story. A wall outside the Italian's window, it was said, had blocked out nearly all his light and so he had painted the blue mountains and sunny sky to remind him of his home country. The *Herald* report goes on to say: "And today these wretched backlands which the Corporation of Dundee have condemned for a clearance scheme still bear a title which commemorates the artistic revolt of this stray visitor from the colourful Mediterranean"

This romantic story was very appealing but was not universally accepted. A correspondent calling himself "Dundee Man" wrote to the *Evening Telegraph* disputing the tale of the homesick Italian, saying that the explanation that he had always heard was that the buildings in the area were the first in the city to be slated with blue slates. Looking up from the level of the Overgate district these blue roofs were a landmark. Their appearance had earned them the nickname "Blue Mountains".

The supporters of the Italian launched a counter attack. "West Port" wanted to know by what authority "Dundee Man" had pronounced the explanation of the blue slates. He or she had always heard the story of the Italian, who it was said, had lived there seventy years earlier. "Sky Blue" was even more outraged by "Dundee Man"'s letter and warned him to keep his "hands off" – "Leave us the Legend of the Blue Mountains and the homesick Italian. Blue slates – indeed."

"A Doubting Thomas", like his biblical namesake, was not prepared to believe without proof. He asked for anyone who had actually seen the legendary painting or heard of the testimony of anyone who had seen it to come forward. It seems that no one did, but if "West Port"'s dating of the incident was accurate, this was always going to be unlikely.

Another theory that was presented by some who wrote to the press was that the area got its name because of the habit of the local housewives in years gone by of applying "blue cam" to their window sills. "The sight of many window sills aglow with 'blue cam' brought the name 'Blue Mountains'," wrote "Searcher".

"Rover" had brought up yet another possibility – the romantic sounding name for the area was obviously an ironic comment. Its origins lay in the one-time popularity of a song called "The Blue Alsatian Mountains", which included the line:

This song will pass away
But the blue Alsatian mountains
They do watch and wait alway[s].

"Rover" noted that though Dundee's Blue Mountains had watched and waited for years, they too would soon pass away.

Meanwhile, someone with the initials GW had a more elaborate explanation and said that they had always heard the name in conjunction with "the Nile" in the expression "Up the Nile to the Blue Mountains". The phrase, the writer understood, was coined after one of the Egyptian campaigns by returning British soldiers, who likened the Overgate to the Nile and West Port to the junction of the White and Blue Niles, with the Blue Mountains (of Abyssinia) in the background. This explanation, however, does not appear to have attracted many supporters.

The Blue Mountains correspondence went on for several days causing someone using the name "Get a move on" to write that "it would be more fitting to find out the cause of buildings such as the Blue Mountains rather than waste time as to the origin of the name". Eventually, though, it was brought to a close in the customary manner.

Like most nicknames, the name "the Blue Mountains" was probably in common usage long before it appeared in print or in any official documentation. Nevertheless, there are certainly references to the name in the local newspapers which pre-date Baldwin's visit by many decades. When the question of the location of the Blue Mountains was asked during a case at Dundee police court in 1879, it was reported to have caused much laughter. A 1901 article, meanwhile, used the nickname and described the area even then as being "long synonymous with sluminess".

What, though, was the true origin of the name? If we dismiss the overly complicated "Up the Nile to the Blue Mountains" theory presented by "GW" and the "blue cam" theory (on the grounds that at the time that it was fashionable to apply this, it was done in various parts of the city and would not have been exclusive to the area), then we are left with two main suggestions – the homesick Italian and the blue slate roofs.

The homesick Italian tenant is the most romantic, but seems the least likely, of these two. For one thing, the buildings in the area and the nickname given to them long predated large-scale Italian immigration to Dundee or indeed to Scotland in general, which did not begin until the later nineteenth and early twentieth century. That is not to say, though, that there were not Italians in Dundee before that time. Their number, though, at any given point in the early to mid-nineteenth century is likely to have been in single figures and composed of people staying for a limited time.

Among the first to settle on a more permanent basis in the city was Giuseppe (or Joseph) Gonnella from Barga in Tuscany, who came to Dundee sometime in the 1850s. Gonnella's pioneer status is demonstrated by the fact that even in later decades, it fell to members of his family to act as Dundee's Italian Consul. Joseph Gonnella was a maker of plaster figures and so was clearly of artistic bent. Could he be the homesick Italian? After a century and a half there remains proof that he was in Dundee and was Italian and artistic but surely no evidence could survive to suggest that he was homesick? Amazingly, it seems that there does in the form of a classified advertisement that appeared in the local press on 26 October 1860:

SIGNOR J. GONNELLA, Manufacturer of Plaster of Paris FIGURES &c., being about to return home to Italy, wishes to inform the Inhabitants of Dundee, that he will SELL OFF his WHOLE STOCK, in that shop No. 23 REFORM STREET, commencing the Sale by Private Bargain, ON TUESDAY first, 30th October when Great bargains will be given. The Remaining Portion of the Stock will be Sold by Auction on FRIDAY Evening, 2nd November commencing at Seven o'clock.

For whatever reason, it seems that Gonnella did not return to Italy but instead remained in Dundee and married a local girl named Agnes Robertson in 1861. No evidence has so far emerged, though, to tie him to the Blue Mountains area. His address at the time of his marriage was listed as Bell Street. His wife, however, hailed from Hawkhill. Perhaps the best we can say is that if the homesick Italian of the Blue Mountains ever really existed then Joseph Gonnella is the most likely candidate.

This leaves the theory of the blue slates. One of those who wrote to the press in the wake of Baldwin's visit was a man named James Downie, who said that he had been born in the Blue Mountains in 1867 when the area was the property of his grandmother, Elizabeth Whitton. He went on to recount the story of the origin of the name as he had heard it from his mother – that there had indeed been some tall buildings in front of the Blue Mountains area where the building with the clock stands today. These buildings were among the first in the city to have slated roofs and people in the neighbourhood called them the Blue Mountains.

The Dundee historian AH Millar refers to these buildings in a 1924 article as the "Barns of Blackness" and states that they were erected by Alexander Hunter, who purchased the Estate of Blackness, which included the West Port area, in 1740. Indeed, William Crawford's Plan of the Town and Harbour of

Dundee in the 1770s shows "barns" in this position. The West Port would have been a chiefly rural area at this time and the barns would have been prominent structures. Millar suggests that the barns gave their name to Barn's Court (or Barron's Court).

A 1901 article on the history of the area in the *Evening Telegraph*, written to mark the opening of the Blackness tram route, explains that the barns "in time fell upon degenerate days and by and by became part and parcel of the delectable neighbourhood known as the 'Blue Mountains'". This article also attributes the origin of the name to the blue slate roofs.

It seems most likely then, that the "Blue Mountains" area owed its name to the presence there of some early examples for the area of slate roofs, either on the "Barns of Blackness" themselves or nearby buildings. Just as the origin of the name had faded into history by the 1920s, so too has the memory of the area itself faded from the general consciousness. A few short years after Stanley Baldwin's visit, most of the slums in the area had been demolished but the "Blue Mountains" name persisted for many years until the entire area was eventually cleared. Standing in the car park that occupies most of the site today, it is difficult to imagine that the area was once home to so many people and was so infamous, let alone that it was somewhere that would ever have been visited by a prime minister.

6

Our American Cousins

Nineteenth Century

Dundee's relationship with the United States of America in the nineteenth century is usually portrayed as a one-way affair consisting of the export of both people and materials from the city to the other side of the Atlantic. There were occasions, however, when what was happening in the New World found an echo in Dundee when some of those most closely associated with the major events of the period, such as the fight against slavery, the Civil War and the assassination of Abraham Lincoln, came to town.

Few visitors from the United States, however, have caused as much of a stir as a couple of students claiming to be American who paid a visit in the early years of the century.

American spies

According to legend, during the Napoleonic Wars, the good citizens of Hartlepool in England hanged a monkey that had been washed up on the beach. There was a real fear of invasion from France at this time and when a French ship was wrecked off the coast near the town, the local fishermen kept a watchful eye out for survivors. There was to be only one – the monkey, which had been the ship's pet and was dressed in a military uniform. Unable to understand the creature's strange gibbering, the fishermen mistook it for a French spy and after being put on trial, the poor creature paid the ultimate price from the mast of a fishing boat. Some deny that the event ever happened, while others point to the more sinister possibility that it was a young boy who died at the hands of the fishermen. The name powder-monkey was given to the children employed on warships to prime the cannons with gunpowder. It might be that over time people had forgotten that the term was applied to children and had assumed that a real monkey had been killed.

Whether the story of the Hartlepool monkey is true or not it gives an idea of the atmosphere that prevailed in the country at this period and the tangible fear of a French invasion that existed. Any foreign stranger had to be looked at with suspicion as there was a real possibility that they might be a French spy. It was against this background, in August 1801, that two students from Edinburgh University set out to tour Scotland on foot. Nevertheless, by keeping a low profile, it might have been thought that they could avoid any potential trouble, but Englishman John Bristed and his American companion Andrew Cowan fully intended to travel in disguise and spy on people, albeit not for the French authorities. Bristed wrote in his account of their trip:

> "The sole purpose for which we set off on our expedition, was to see and to investigate the manners of the great body of the people, and to obtain a knowledge of their situation. In order to effect this purpose, we deemed it necessary to travel in such a condition as would, in all probability, induce the people whom we met to treat us without any disguise of fictitious and artificial civility, and show their native character, whatever it may be, in all its outlines and features. We, therefore, assumed the garb of poverty…"

Bristed and Cowan's attempts to blend into the background, dressed as sailors, seems to have been singularly unsuccessful. Their attempt at the "garb of poverty" does not appear to have been overly convincing and their outfits, particularly Bristed's cat-skin cap and green spectacles, caused much hilarity among the bystanders on the pier at Leith. Bristed also decided that he would be an American:

> "… we knew that their nation was a favourite with the Scottish and that the Caledonians, as yet, so despise and dislike the English and the Irish, that, had it been known that we were natives either of Ireland or of England, we should

never have gained the least information, but should have returned no wiser than when we set out."

After passing through Fife, where they aroused some suspicion among the natives, the pair crossed the Tay on the ferry from Newport, where they met Jonas Watson, a Dundee tobacconist. Watson recommended that while in Dundee they should stay at the inn kept by Peter Cooper at Fish Street near the docks. On arrival at Dundee, Bristed and Cowan duly made their way to the inn. Cooper was, at first, reluctant to let them stay, saying that there was no room. Bristed later wrote how the landlord had "cast an impudent, insulting and disdainful look at our unhappy garments". The pair, however, were intent on staying because they were tired and feared that they might not find anywhere, and also because, as Bristed put it, "a great mob began to gather round the door to stare and to gape at us and our exhibition".

Rather than quietly plead their case with the landlord they harangued him with their "full artillery of words, shot off in a continued volley", telling him of the number of Scottish people who were successful in America. Whether Cooper was beguiled by this or simply worn down, he decided to let the travellers stay and they were shown to what Bristed referred to as a dark and dismal room upstairs, at one end of which stood two beds in a dreary recess.

In the room, Bristed began to write in his journal, and after some tea and eggs, he and Cowan began an intellectual discussion on the relative merits of the Roman playwrights Plautus and Terence. Their debate was interrupted when the landlord burst into the room, telling them that there were two gentlemen downstairs who wished to talk to them. Cowan asked that the men come up to the room.

The two strangers explained that they were magistrates of the town and that they had had no less than four reports that strangers of a "very dangerous and suspicious appearance were gone into Cooper's public house". One of the men, Patrick Sterling, explained that given the fear of a French invasion they had to investigate. Cowan and Bristed told him that they were Edinburgh students of American birth on a tour of Scotland. They had no written evidence to prove this, though, and while Sterling may have been satisfied with their verbal explanation, his companion was not and he asked them once again for identification, much to the indignation of Cowan, who launched into a verbal assault on the magistrate for his impertinence at repeating the question. Mr. Sterling then concluded that he could not let the pair go unless they could produce at least a reference from "some gentleman or other" proving that they were what they said they were.

The justice's clerk was sent for and he too interviewed the pair with suspicion, asking them about their professors and other eminent men in Edinburgh. Bristed reeled off several names of those with whom he said he was acquainted including one Walter Scott (though the name was perhaps not quite as impressive as it sounds today – Scott was, at this stage, yet to publish any of his novels and most of his poetry). He finally settled on a bookseller named Laing. "Every man in this country, that has any pretensions to intellect or acquirement, knows Laing," he said, "pray, sir, do you know that celebrated bibliopolist?" The clerk admitted that he did not and rather than leave the inference hanging in the air, the arrogant Bristed could not help but hammer home his point in the face of a man who had the power to lock him up. "I leave you to draw the conclusion with regard to yourself; I assert that every man in this country who has any pretensions to intellect or acquirement, knows Laing; but you do not know Laing."

Nevertheless, it was agreed that a letter would be sent to Laing, which Bristed composed in his own pretentious style:

Dundee, August 6th, 1801.

Dear Laing,

I am at this moment at Dundee on my road to the Highlands, but having no credentials, or letter, or testimonials, setting forth who and what I am, the prudent and cautious inhabitants of this town have, with all laudable sagacity and wisdom concluded that I am a French spy, and have detained me accordingly. In vain I have attempted to show the absurdity of such a supposition, and am forthwith to be put into the gaol of Dundee till farther ken can he taken of me. One of the magistrates, Mr. Sterling, has behaved as handsomely and liberally as man can do, I cannot say much for the politeness and civility of our two other examiners. I request that you would have the goodness merely to certify that you know A. Cowan and J. Bristed to be medical students at the university of Edinburgh, and you will greatly oblige

Your humble servant,

John Bristed.

While the other magistrate went to fetch the constables to take the students into custody, pending a reply to their letter, Sterling told them of the rumours that were circulating about them, as Bristed later recalled:

"Some declared that we were French spies, come with a determination to murder all the people in the land: others said that we were English deserters, who wished to hide ourselves in Dundee; some insisted upon it that we were Irish rebels, and ought to be hanged on the spot, as a specimen of British justice and an example of Dundee loyalty to the sovereign of this empire; others again contented themselves with mercifully insinuating that we were wandering Jews, and should be put into the round-house for a few days, and then publicly whipt through the town, after which we might be sent about our business."

Bristed and Cowan chatted to Sterling, apparently making light of the fact that they were to be sent to prison but perhaps attempting to change his mind. When the other magistrate returned with the constables, Sterling told them to wait outside. Might there be anybody in Dundee, he asked, who might know them. Bristed unhelpfully replied that they knew no more of Dundee more than they did of Grand Cairo. Sterling, however, seemed determined to bring an end to the matter and went out, returning some time later with Patrick Nimmo, a doctor in the city who had been a medical student at Edinburgh. He immediately recognised the pair as did another former student, John Watson, who was an apothecary in Dundee.

Bristed and Cowan were at last free to go, although a local militia captain suggested to Sterling that they should be enrolled in his company as a punishment for the "terror and alarm" that they had spread among the inhabitants of Dundee. Luckily for the students, Sterling did not take up the offer and instead they spent the night at Cooper's inn. The landlord's attitude towards them had softened by this stage and he even went to the post office to retrieve the letter to Laing.

That evening, they had dinner with John Watson (Patrick Nimmo had a previous engagement). Watson told them of the events of the day and how the whole town had been in uproar: "men women and children were seen issuing out of doors, hanging halfway out of the windows, and choking up the main streets with a press of mortal carcasses thronged together, and demanding the immediate execution of the two bloody-minded terrible spies". Watson's own brother had told him of the capture of the two spies and how gallows were to be erected in the High Street to hang them. Watson, however, had already seen the pair walking up from the quay. Though he and Bristed were not acquainted, he had recognised him by his green spectacles, which he said were of "some notoriety" when they both attended classes at Edinburgh.

For someone who helped save him from prison or perhaps even execution, Bristed seems particularly ungrateful towards Watson when the latter did not enter into the intellectual discussion that he and Cowan had embarked upon. He wrote: "his dull, anxious frightened and confused looks evidently shewed that he was unable to comprehend a hundredth part of what we said." When Watson began pulling nervously at the frill of his shirt, Bristed saw it as a slight against the checked shirts that he and Cowan were wearing. Cowan told the hapless apothecary: "Sir, fashion is the badge of slavery; it argues a mind dull, hebetated, timid and frivolous, which has not the power to ascend the elevated height of individuality of character."

Watson wanted the pair to stay in town the next morning so that they might "parade the streets of Dundee" – not, according to Bristed, because the town contained anything particularly worth seeing, but so that "the sapient and humane inhabitants being all agog with expectation might have their laudable curiosity gratified by staring at two men arrayed in sailors' jackets". In what was perhaps their wisest decision since arriving in Dundee, Bristed and Cowan decided to make a low-key exit the following morning at 5 am, when they took the road for Perth. In the front of Bristed's journal was a testimonial designed to stop them getting into such a predicament later in their journey:

> Mr Bristed and Mr Cowan, two young gentlemen of America, now students of medicine at the university of Edinburgh, having been brought before me this evening as suspicious persons or vagrants who could give no good account of themselves did satisfy me of being what they said they were by producing two gentlemen of this town, well known to me who attended the classes along with them and bear testimony as to their characters.
>
> Patrick Sterling
>
> Dundee 7th August 1801
>
> Patrick Nimmo
> John Watson
>
> By our joint testimony we have delivered from durance vile our two fellow students.

The letter appears to have worked to the extent that the rest of their journey seems to have passed without major incident and the two survived the trip unscathed. Andrew Cowan became a doctor, and in 1803 published a book entitled *Anthropaideia: Or a tractate on general education*. Bristed too wrote several books, including the story of his travels with Cowan. He became a lawyer, practising in London and New York. He later was ordained as a clergyman and became rector of St. Michael's, Bristol, Rhode Island. He married a daughter of merchant and real estate mogul John Jacob Astor.

The story of Bristed and Cowan's visit to Dundee can be portrayed as if it was a case of a wholly ignorant population panicking at their first encounter with visitors from elsewhere, but this was certainly not the case. Dundee was a busy seaport in this period and people, particularly at the area around the docks, where Cooper's inn was, must surely have been accustomed to foreign visitors.

The fear of French spies was certainly a factor in the turn of events and reflected a real feeling in the country at this time. In August 1803, a French teacher in Dundee, M. Dugour (or Du Goure) was arrested on suspicion of being a spy. He was taken into custody in Edinburgh and held at the castle until October. It had been reported that a French colonel's commission signed by Napoleon himself had been found among his papers. After a thorough investigation, though, Dugour was released without charge and given permission to stay in the country.

The real cause of the panic surrounding the visit of the students appears to be that they drew attention to themselves from the beginning due to their outlandish appearance and their arrogant inclination to attempt to assert their intellectual superiority over everyone they met by talking in terms that few would understand, including Latin quotations, while at the same time seeking to "investigate the manners of the great body of the people". It is hard to escape the conclusion that another pair of students could have successfully made a quiet visit to the city, even in the period of the Napoleonic Wars.

Harriet Beecher Stowe

"So," President Abraham Lincoln is reputed to have said on being introduced to Harriet Beecher Stowe at the start of the American Civil War, "you are the little woman who wrote the book that started this great war." This story may or may not be true (the two certainly met in 1862 but what was said is not certain), but the very fact that people are prepared to consider that it might be serves to illustrate the place that Stowe's anti-slavery novel *Uncle Tom's Cabin* has in history. It certainly acted as a powerful condemnation of slavery. It was written in the wake of the 1850 Fugitive Slave Law which stated that anyone who refused to assist in the capture of fugitive slaves or who helped them could be fined up to $1,000 and jailed for six months. Stowe disobeyed the law herself by hiding runaways but was encouraged to do more by her sister-in-law Isabella Porter Beecher who wrote to her saying: "… if I could use a pen as you can, Hatty, I would write something that would make this whole nation feel what an accursed thing slavery is".

Like many nineteenth-century novels, *Uncle Tom's Cabin* first appeared in weekly instalments, featuring in the anti-slavery newspaper the *National Era* from 5 June 1851 to 1 April 1852. It was published in book form in March 1852 and within a year had sold 300,000 copies in the United States. The book was particularly popular in Britain and it was just over a year after its publication there in April 1853 that Harriet Beecher Stowe received an enthusiastic welcome in Dundee.

Despite admission to the railway platform being restricted by tickets, crowds still turned out to see her arrival. Accompanied on her journey by her husband, Professor Calvin Stowe, and her brother Rev. Charles Beecher, Mrs Stowe's train was met by Dundee's Provost Patrick Hunter Thoms, who accompanied her to a waiting carriage. Large crowds had gathered to catch a glimpse of her. A newspaper report said that she "repeatedly acknowledged the demonstrations of respect with which she was hailed and appeared very much affected by them". Stowe herself later wrote: "When we got into old Dundee it seemed all alive with welcome." The party was taken to dinner at the Provost's residence before attending a festival in honour of Mrs Stowe that evening in the Steeple Church.

The festival was due to begin at 7pm with the doors being opened at 6.30, but people began arriving long before that to catch a glimpse of the woman who had written the book that had such an impact on the anti-slavery movement on both sides of the Atlantic. Harriet Beecher Stowe arrived on the arm of Provost Thoms and took her place on the platform next to him. Stowe's own account refers to the church being "densely crowded" at this point. The *Advertiser* reported that her appearance on the platform "was a signal for the most rapturous applause, which lasted for some time, and was acknowledged by Mrs Stowe and her friends".

In attendance that night were many of the great and the good of Dundee's civic and literary scenes including scientist, writer and clergyman Dr Thomas Dick of Broughty Ferry and the well-known Dundee writer Reverend George Gilfillan, who gave a speech. Mrs. Stowe was presented with a beautifully bound volume of works by various Dundee writers.

The next morning, she had a large breakfast meeting and was formally introduced to Dr. Dick. Thomas Dick is little known or read today but his scientific, philosophical and religious works such as *The Christian Philosopher, or the Connexion of Science and Philosophy with Religion*, were popular in Britain and in the United States in this period. His publishing arrangements were such that he earned little income from them. A crown pension granted in 1847 had helped to relieve his financial situation somewhat.

Harriet Beecher Stowe was certainly familiar with Thomas Dick's work. Stowe later recalled her conversation with the man she called "good old Dr. Dick":

"[I] had pleasure in speaking to him of the interest with which his works have been read in America. Of this fact, I was told that he had received more substantial assurance in a comfortable sum of money subscribed and remitted to him by his American readers. If this be so then it is a most commendable movement."

After breakfast, she was visited by the ladies of the Dundee Anti-Slavery Society before Lord Provost Thoms took her party on a tour of the city in his carriage. As the "little woman" toured the streets of Dundee, she could not have imagined that over 150 years later that *Uncle Tom's Cabin* would still be read and discussed throughout the world, its place in history assured. It is to Dundee's credit that Harriet Beecher Stowe and her anti-slavery message were embraced so warmly at the time.

Frederick Douglass

Harriet Beecher Stowe was not the only major figure in the anti-slavery movement to visit Dundee in this period. Frederick Douglass – a black man who had been born into slavery himself – was perhaps one of the movement's most inspirational characters. Douglass was born in Maryland in 1818. Unusually, and in defiance of a ban, his master's wife had taught him to read when he was around 12 years old. The master eventually put an end to these studies, but Douglass had developed a thirst for education that never left him.

The plaque commemorating Frederick Douglass in Bell Street

In 1838, while hired out to work in Baltimore, he disguised himself as a sailor and escaped by train and boat to New York. There, he married Anna Murray, a free black woman who had aided his escape. The couple later settled in New Bedford, Massachusetts. Influenced by William Lloyd Garrison's newspaper, *The Liberator*, Douglass began to attend abolitionist meetings, gaining a reputation as an orator. In 1845, he published his first autobiography, *Narrative of the Life of Frederick Douglass, an American Slave*, which became a bestseller. Fearful that the publicity surrounding his activities might lead his master to seek to reclaim his "property", Douglass left in August that year for an extended stay in the British Isles, where he toured extensively giving anti-slavery lectures.

Frederick Douglass first appeared in Dundee at the end of January 1846, where he addressed four meetings. Three were held at the School Wynd Chapel and so popular were the first two of these that the third was ticketed. The fourth meeting was held at the Bell Street Hall. Douglass wrote from Dundee at this time: "Our meetings here have been of the most soul cheering character." A *Courier* report conveys some of the power of Douglass's talks:

"His own personal experience, the horrid scenes he had witnessed, the sufferings of the slaves, four of his own sisters and a brother being still among their number, the instruments of torture (specimens of which, consisting of a collar to prevent repose, handcuffs and anklets, with the lash, all commonly in use, were exhibited) were all described in a pathetic, earnest, and impressive manner."

At the time of Douglass's meetings in Dundee, there was a great controversy regarding the actions of the Free Church of Scotland, which had split from the Church of Scotland in the Disruption of 1843. The Free Church had accepted money from Southern churches in the United States which were closely associated with support for slavery. Douglass was one of those who was most prominent in demanding that the Free Church, in the words of the popular slogan of the time "send back the money". He told the Bell Street meeting, to great cheers, that Free Church members when they looked at their meeting houses which were "built with the price of blood" should compel their clergy to "send back the blood stained money".

Douglass was particularly fond of Scotland, writing of the country from Dundee: "almost every hill, river, mountain and lake… has been made classic by the heroic deeds of her noble sons. Scarcely a stream but has been poured into song, or a hill that is not associated with some fierce and bloody conflict between liberty and slavery."

Douglass staged a further meeting in Dundee on 9 February 1846 at Tay Square Chapel. The following day he wrote: "We held a very good meeting here last night crowded to overflowing with people whose influence cannot but be felt by the Free Church." He was particularly pleased with the continuing pressure on the Free Church, writing: "all this region is in a ferment – the very boys in the street are singing out 'Send Back the Money'". He was particularly heartened when he read in the *Courier* that the session at St Peter's (a church which is still home to a Free Church congregation today) had unanimously recommended the return of the money.

In March 1846 an "Anti-Slavery Soiree" was held in honour of Douglass and other anti-slavery campaigners at George's Chapel School Wynd, attended by Dr. Dick and the Reverend George Gilfillan among others. Despite the frequency of his visits in this period there was a great demand for tickets. Douglass used the occasion to hit back at the personal attacks made on him in the Free Church-supporting *Warder* newspaper and to praise the editor of the *Courier* for coming to his defence.

In April that same year, Douglass wrote to his mentor William Lloyd Garrison:

"Scotland is a blaze of anti-slavery agitation – the Free Church and Slavery are the all-engrossing topics…The Free Church is in a terrible stew. Its leaders thought to get the slaveholders' money and bring it home, and escape censure. They had no idea that they would be followed and exposed. Its members are leaving it, like rats escaping from a sinking ship. There is a strong determination to have the slave money sent back." The money, however, was never sent back.

In September, Douglass addressed another meeting at the Bell Street Hall in Dundee, this time accompanied by Garrison. The pair were back the following month for a further meeting. Garrison wrote of this occasion: "we had a grand attendance and a spirited meeting".

After the October 1846 meeting, it was to be a further fourteen years before Frederick Douglass addressed another meeting in Dundee. His supporters had raised the funds to purchase his freedom, meaning that he was able to return to the United States in 1847, where he established his own newspaper and continued to campaign for the abolition of slavery as well as for the rights of women.

Douglass's final meeting in Dundee was a lecture in the Corn Exchange in Bank Street on 13 February 1860, held under the auspices of Dundee Ladies Anti-Slavery Society. The chairman, former Provost Patrick Thoms, spoke of the toll that the years had taken on Douglass, saying that the cares and anxieties which he had undergone in the cause to which he had devoted his life had written some traces on his forehead and somewhat blanched his hair but his energies and his devotion to that cause remained unchanged. Great cheers greeted this and Thoms's mention of the other major change in Douglass's situation in the preceding fourteen years – that he was no longer a fugitive slave.

Douglass himself told the meeting of the progress that had been made in furthering the cause in the United States since he was last in Dundee. At that time there had only been two members of Congress who dared to say that they belonged to the anti-slavery movement, now they expected to have an anti-slavery man in the presidential chair.

Abraham Lincoln was indeed elected president later in 1860 and slavery was ultimately abolished in the United States albeit after the convulsions of the Civil War. Frederick Douglass died in 1895 and is considered today by many to be one of the most important figures in the American anti-slavery movement. There have been numerous commemorations of Douglass in the United States and as recently as 2017, the US mint issued a 25 cent coin bearing his image.

The fact that such an important historical figure visited Dundee so many times and that his message was so well received in the city is surely something that deserves to be remembered. A plaque at the Bell Street Music Centre now recalls the fact that Douglass spoke there – yet he was not the only anti-slavery campaigner or, indeed, the only fugitive slave to do so.

On 22 January 1851 a meeting at the Bell Street Hall "to denounce the atrocious American Fugitive Slave Bill" was addressed by William Wells Brown, a contemporary of Frederick Douglass who had also been born into slavery and who was an author and playwright. The same meeting heard from William and Ellen Craft, a well-known fugitive slave couple. They had escaped when Ellen used her relatively light skin colour to pose as a white male with William as her servant. The hall was said to be "filled in every corner" for the event. On the following two evenings William Wells Brown delivered lectures at the same venue "illustrated by panoramic views on 2,000 feet of canvas".

Brown and the Crafts were introduced to Dr. Thomas Dick and later visited him at his home in Broughty Ferry. Like Harriet Beecher Stowe, William Wells Brown was clearly in awe of Dr. Dick and it is worth noting Brown's recollection of their meeting, to show just how so highly regarded Dick's writings were in the United States:

"I could scarcely believe that I was in the presence of the 'Christian Philosopher'. Dr. Dick is one of the men to whom the age is indebted. I never find myself in the presence of one to whom the world owes so much as Dr. Dick, without feeling a thrilling emotion, as if I were in the land of spirits. Dr. Dick had come to our lodgings to see and congratulate Wm. and Ellen Craft upon their escape from the republican Christians of the United States; and as he pressed the hand of the 'white slave', and bid her 'welcome to British soil', I saw the silent tear stealing down the cheek of this man of genius. How I wished that the many slaveholders and pro-slavery professed Christians of America, who have read and pondered the philosophy of this man, could have been present."

There can be little doubt that campaigners such as Frederick Douglass and William Wells Brown appreciated the support they received in Dundee and the city can surely be proud of its backing for the American anti-slavery movement in the mid-nineteenth century. It is to be hoped too that the unveiling of the plaque to Frederick Douglass in Bell Street in 2016 was only the beginning of a revival of interest in this long-neglected aspect of Dundee's history.

A Place of Refuge

In 2007, a thirty-six-inch-long walking stick with a gold head and a black-lacquered wooden body ending in a brass tip was auctioned in Los Angeles. Given an estimate of between $10,000 and $15,000, it in fact realised $33,000. This was mainly because of three separate presentation engravings on the cane. The most modern of these tells of how the cane was bequeathed to nineteenth-century British Liberal politician and exponent of free trade John Bright. The original presentation engraving, meanwhile, adorns the head of the cane and describes how it was given by lawyer John A. McClernand to no less a figure than the President of the United States of America, Abraham Lincoln himself, in 1857. In between these two dedications is a small plate with a third inscription. This one reads:

> "*Presented to the Revd. Jas. Smith, D.D.* BY THE FAMILY OF THE LATE PRESIDENT LINCOLN *in memoriam of the high esteem in which he was held by him and them as their pastor and dear friend. 27th April 1868*"

The Reverend James Smith was clearly someone who meant a lot to the late president and whose friendship was valued by the Lincoln family in the period after his assassination in 1865. Indeed, such was the bond between them that the president's widow, Mary Todd Lincoln, together with her son Tad took time out to visit Dr. Smith even after he had left the United States. Because the time that they spent with him was a private matter, there was little publicity at the time. One hundred and fifty years later few know that President Lincoln's widow and son spent time in Dundee, where James Smith was the US Consul.

Smith was no stranger to Scotland, having been born in Glasgow in 1801 and educated there. After emigrating to the United States, he first settled in Tennessee, where he became the proprietor and editor of a newspaper. When the newspaper failed, Smith's career took an altogether different track and he became pastor of the First Presbyterian Church of Springfield, Illinois in 1849. This was the town where Abraham Lincoln had established a successful law practice.

The association between the Scottish clergyman and the Lincoln family began in Springfield in 1850 with the death of the Lincoln's 3-year-old son Eddie from tuberculosis. At that time, Mrs Lincoln attended the Protestant Episcopal Church, where the Reverend Charles Dresser was the minister.

Dresser was the man who had married the Lincolns in 1842, but he was out of town when Eddie died. The couple instead approached Smith, who was minister of the local Presbyterian Church, to conduct the funeral at the family home.

So impressed was Mrs. Lincoln with Smith that she began attending the Presbyterian Church and became a member there in 1852. Although Abraham Lincoln did not join the church, he did sometimes attend and rented a pew there. Smith became a trusted friend of the Lincoln family and Abraham Lincoln particularly enjoyed the philosophical discussions that the pair would have. Mary Lincoln later recalled in a letter to Smith: "you were so frequently at our house, making informal calls, meeting a few friends and very frequently in large companies".

James Smith retired from his ministry at Springfield in 1856 and returned to Scotland, where he appears to have fallen on relatively hard times. In 1861, following the election of Abraham Lincoln as president, Smith's son-in-law John Forsythe wrote to the president seeking a job for his father-in-law. Forsythe told Lincoln that Smith was "quite advanced in life and… is poor in this world's goods and therefore he needs some assistance to enable him and the old lady to support themselves in Scotland". The position of Consul at Glasgow was suggested as a suitable post. Smith himself later wrote to Mrs. Lincoln enclosing a letter to the president. Should he be appointed, Smith wrote to Mrs Lincoln, he would take his two sons with him and devote the Sabbath to "preaching to large audiences of the destitute". His letter to Lincoln said that although he would prefer to be appointed to his native Glasgow, he would be satisfied with the consulship at Dundee.

It was not James Smith who was appointed Consul at Dundee, though, but his son Hugh. When Hugh Smith resigned due to ill health, however, his father took over the position, much to the annoyance of the US Secretary of State William Seward, who was unhappy that Dr Smith's appointment had not been made through the proper channels. Seward sought to replace Smith, but the clergyman again turned to his friend Mary Lincoln, who persuaded her husband that Smith should be formally nominated.

James Smith's time as the Consul in Dundee coincided with two of the most momentous events in the history of the United States – the Civil War and, on 15 April 1865, the assassination of President Lincoln while he was attending the play "Our American Cousin" at Ford's Theatre in Washington DC. The news of the president's death was greeted with shock around the world. In Dundee, a meeting of the council on 28 April unanimously passed a resolution, stating among other things that "the Provost, Magistrates and Town Council have heard of the horrible acts of assassination in the city of Washington with sorrow and indignation, and unite in desiring humbly and respectfully, but in the kindest spirit, to represent to the government of the United States of America, and the whole people, their sincere sympathy, and the sympathy of every class of the people of this town, young and old, rich and poor, in feelings of abhorrence towards the miserable actors and their adherents, wherever and whomsoever they be".

A similar resolution expressing the town's "profound sorrow and indignation" was passed at a public meeting on 2 May, while the following day a meeting of Dundee's American citizens heard from Dr. Smith. Smith said that the meeting had been called to express sorrow at the appalling calamity which had caused the "sudden removal, by cowardly assassination, of our excellent and beloved Chief Magistrate, and at a time when that great and good man had, under God, by his fortitude, consistency, prudence, and sagacity, brought the nation safely and triumphantly through one of the most dreadful conflicts ever witnessed upon the earth". Various resolutions were passed at this meeting too – among them one expressing deep sympathy with Mrs Lincoln and the hope that "the affectionate remembrances of a great nation for him who died a martyr's death for the cause of liberty and justice may prove a solace to her in her widowhood".

Dr Smith's friendship with the Lincolns meant that his tribute to the president and sympathy to his widow were no mere lip service. He kept up a correspondence with Mary Lincoln for the rest of his life and continued to support her when many others had deserted her. It was a correspondence that Mrs Lincoln greatly appreciated. In 1866, in response to birthday greetings from Dr Smith, she wrote: "your words of friendship, breathed from a far distant land, were most acceptable to my broken and weary heart, and my gratitude, in being so kindly remembered was very great".

A constant theme of Dr. Smith's letters to Mrs Lincoln was that she should come to visit him in Dundee. In 1868, she wrote to her friend Rhoda White that her doctor had advised her to seek a change of scenery: "He thought that going abroad would alone benefit me and advised me, as soon as I could bear the change, to go to Scotland for the summer. Our old minister a very good and intellectual man resides there and has always been writing that I should visit."

By early July of 1869, the matter had gained a degree of urgency. Dr Smith's health was failing due to a heart condition and he was worried that he might not live much longer. He insisted that Mary Lincoln and her son Thomas (known as Tad), who were at that point in Frankfurt, come to visit him in Dundee. This they duly did and went on to tour Scotland in the company of Dr. Smith for the next seven weeks. It was perhaps the happiest period of Mrs Lincoln's life following the assassination of her husband. Like many an American visitor of Scottish ancestry, she was enchanted by the country. She wrote: "Beautiful, glorious Scotland has spoiled me for every other country! ... I cannot begin to enumerate all the places of interest we visited. I *am convinced*, that I shall never again be able to arouse myself to take *such another* interest in any other country I may chance to visit." She was distraught when a box containing souvenirs of Scotland had gone missing after Tad Lincoln had given it to John Smail, the clerk at Smith's office, in Dundee to post.

Despite Dr. Smith's fears regarding his health, he was to see Mary Lincoln at least one more time after the summer of 1869. She arrived in Dundee on Wednesday, 28 September 1870 and stayed until the following Monday. Like her earlier visit this was an entirely private affair. Indeed, she once asked a friend to burn a letter in which she talked of that earlier visit, so keen was she to protect her privacy. The lack of mass communications outside the printed press at this time and the lack of photographs in newspapers, together with a degree of deference from reporters, meant that it was still possible for a well-known public figure to enjoy a degree of privacy unimaginable today. It is entirely possible, therefore, that Mrs Lincoln might have visited Dr. Smith in Dundee again on other occasions than those mentioned above. Indeed, William Reid, the British Commissioner at the US consulate in Dundee during Smith's time there, said that Mrs Lincoln and her son "often visited the consulate".

James Smith died on Monday 3 July 1871, and a week later, shortly after 12 noon, he began his last journey. The hearse left the consulate in the Murraygate in a procession which included the town's magistrates and councillors and other dignitaries, a detachment of soldiers from the barracks as well as a number of naval officers, while a detachment of the Dundee Police brought up the rear. The streets were crowded with mourners and the bells of the Old Steeple tolled, while the flags on public buildings flew at half mast as a mark of respect. The cortège made its way along the Murraygate, High Street and Nethergate before turning down Union Street to Dundee West Station. From there Smith's body was taken to Glasgow for burial in Calton Churchyard. The US State Department later paid tribute to Dundee for "the respect and honour shown to the deceased Consul".

The loss of such a close friend must have been upsetting to Mary Lincoln, but an even more devastating blow was just around the corner. On 15 July, less than two weeks after Dr Smith's death, her son Tad, who had accompanied her and Smith on their tour of Scotland, died aged just 18. Tad's funeral was held in Chicago and his body was later transported by train to Springfield to be buried in the family tomb at Oak Ridge Cemetery. Mary Lincoln was too distraught to accompany the body. Unlike when her son Eddie died, she did not have Smith to turn to for consolation. She entered a deep depression and was later committed to an asylum for a period. She died in 1882.

In April 2015, a ceremony took place in Edinburgh's Old Carlton Burying Ground to mark the 150th anniversary of the US Civil War and the assassination of President Abraham Lincoln. The cemetery was chosen for the event as it is home to a monument to the Scottish soldiers killed in that war. The memorial, which dates from 1893, consists of a statue of President Lincoln with a freed slave giving thanks to him. It is the only memorial to the conflict outside the United States and was the first statue of Lincoln to be erected outside his own country.

The ceremony was organised by the Dundee-Alexandria Twinning Association, which promotes the relationship between Dundee and its sister city in Virginia. Attention was also drawn to the long relationship between Dundee and the wider United States and to the messages of sympathy sent from the city at the time of Lincoln's assassination. In 2015, Lord Provost Bob Duncan wrote a new letter which was to be exhibited at the Abraham Lincoln Presidential Museum in Springfield, Illinois emphasising the continuing links between Dundee and the United States. It seems largely to have been forgotten, however, that Scotland and Dundee in particular once provided a place of refuge for President Lincoln's grieving widow.

A Night at the Theatre

A little over two months after the death of Mary Lincoln, an American actor arrived in Dundee. Even before his arrival the *Evening Telegraph* had enthused: "The first three nights of next week are certain to be red-letter nights in the history of the Dundee stage, each rendered so by the representation of that greatest of American actors…The visit of this celebrated and, in some respects, unrivalled tragedian is an event not equalled in importance since the last advent of Henry Irving." The article went on to predict that the theatre would be taxed to accommodate everyone seeking admission and that a "splendid treat" was in store for those fortunate enough to get into the auditorium. The increase in prices for boxes at the Theatre Royal, the paper thought fully justified.

The actor who had caused such excitement was Edwin Booth. Born into an American theatrical family in 1833, he had become its most successful member. He was the founder of Booth's Theatre in New York and he toured extensively around the world. He was best known for the role of Hamlet, which he played for one hundred consecutive nights at the Winter Garden Theatre in New York. Some saw his as the greatest ever performance of the role.

There were to be different performances by Booth in Dundee on three consecutive nights. On Monday, 2 October 1882, he would perform as "Richelieu"; the next evening was to be devoted to "Hamlet", the role that had become his signature piece; and finally, his version of Bertuccio in Tom Taylor's *Fool's Revenge* would take place on the Wednesday.

Booth's performances were far more low key than theatre goers of the period would have been used to. An *Evening Telegraph* review of his performance as Richelieu brought this point home: "admirers of the robustious school, who have been accustomed to see it rendered with much vehemence of voice and gesture, would probably be disappointed by the quietness of style and general outward calmness with which Mr. Booth presented it. Judged, however, by the true standard of the art, it was a masterly personation." His performance as Hamlet, was also, the newspaper said: "performed in quieter manner than we are accustomed to". Nevertheless, the review went on to say that "the execution is far above the common one and seemed to be felt by all who witnessed it. Perhaps Mr Booth's special excellence in Hamlet lies in the clearness with which his faultless execution enables him to bring out Shakespeare's meaning." An *Advertiser* review of *Fool's Revenge* said of his performance: "Mr Booth has that rare secret of acting which makes each individual think himself the sole observer of a real scene."

Booth's style certainly did not deter the Dundee audiences, which were said to be "magnificent in numbers and enthusiastically appreciative". Hundreds had to be turned away from his performance as Hamlet. The *Evening Telegraph* noted that Booth could not "but be satisfied with the cordiality of his first

Edwin Booth

reception in Scotland, while all who accorded it must have felt that they honoured themselves in rendering their tribute of admiration to so worthy a recipient".

If Booth made an impression on Dundee, Dundee had quite literally left a mark on Booth. In the final scene of Hamlet, he was accidently stabbed in the right arm by Henry George, the over enthusiastic actor playing Laertes. Booth had little regard for some of his fellow actors as it was, even without them causing him actual bodily harm. He nicknamed the more inept of them "dogans". Writing from Edinburgh later in the month to the drama critic William Winter, he explained how he was still suffering the after-effects of the wound. He wrote: "I had been slightly stabbed by a "dogan" who stood in defence of the King in the final scene of Hamlet and owing to my own treatment of the wound, I have suffered the torments of erysipelas (in both arms) ever since and even now the itching is intolerable & I have bandaged both sides with ointment and lint." Despite both arms being "swollen and itching all the while", he had not, he told Winter, stopped acting, but had had to fence left-handed. His left arm was already, in his own words, "badly mashed" and the exertion had caused it to swell so that the next night he had "both fins in limbo". He wrote: "I presume that I am getting better – but I don't feel so I assure you."

Edwin Booth's reception in Dundee gives some indication of the level of his fame in the late nineteenth century. Like all the theatrical greats from this time, his name is still known today, but the transient nature of acting in the pre-film era means that we cannot see and evaluate his performances for ourselves and have to rely on contemporary reports. Booth, though, unlike other famous nineteenth-century actors, also has another factor that has affected his reputation. He has long suffered from being overshadowed by the infamy of his younger brother – John Wilkes Booth, the man who assassinated President Abraham Lincoln in 1865.

Edwin Booth had temporarily retired from the stage in the wake of both the assassination and his brother's death twelve days later, returning to the stage in January 1866. He once wrote of his brother:

"We regarded him as a good-hearted, harmless though wild-brained boy and used to laugh at his patriotic froth whenever secession was discussed. That he was insane on that one point no one who knew him well can doubt. When I told him that I had voted for Lincoln's re-election he expressed deep regret, and declared his belief that Lincoln would be made King of America; and this, I believe, drove him beyond the limits of reason."

During his lifetime, it seems, Edwin Booth to a great extent had managed to separate his reputation from association with his younger brother's actions by the sheer power of his talent. The association, though, appears to have reasserted itself in the years after Edwin's death when his talent was no longer accessible to new audiences.

In a strange twist of fate, sometime before Abraham Lincoln's assassination, Edwin Booth had actually rescued Lincoln's son, Robert, from serious injury or worse on a train platform in Jersey City, New Jersey. In 1909, Robert Lincoln wrote a letter to Richard Watson Gilder, editor of the *Century* magazine, in which he recalled what had happened:

> "The incident occurred while a group of passengers were late at night purchasing their sleeping car places from the conductor who stood on the station platform at the entrance of the car. The platform was about the height

of the car floor, and there was of course a narrow space between the platform and the car body. There was some crowding, and I happened to be pressed by it against the car body while waiting my turn. In this situation the train began to move, and by the motion I was twisted off my feet, and had dropped somewhat, with feet downward, into the open space, and was personally helpless, when my coat collar was vigorously seized and I was quickly pulled up and out to a secure footing on the platform. Upon turning to thank my rescuer I saw it was Edwin Booth, whose face was of course well known to me, and I expressed my gratitude to him, and in doing so, called him by name."

Twentieth Century

Over the course of the twentieth century, travel between Dundee and the United States became more routine and eventually something that could be undertaken for a holiday. Even emigration, therefore, did not necessarily mean that there was no prospect of a return visit home, as it had done for many in the previous century. At the same time, for most Dundonians, even those who never set foot in the United States, the period was one where America's cultural influence – through music and film in particular - grew ever stronger. When two of the century's greatest American musical performers, however, turned up in person in the city, their visits were surprisingly low key.

Louis Armstrong in Dundee

More than four decades after his death, Louis Armstrong remains truly world famous. In 2018, an Internet search for his name produces more than 56 million results, while visitors to his home town of New Orleans find themselves arriving at Louis Armstrong International Airport. He is still widely acknowledged as one of the greatest and most influential of all jazz musicians ever and someone who changed the face of popular music in general.

The opportunity, then, to see Louis Armstrong perform live at any point in his career is surely one that would have been welcomed by jazz aficionados and indeed lovers of popular music in general. Imagine, though, the chance to see him, not in an expansive auditorium such as the London Palladium, but in the more intimate surroundings of a local dance hall. Imagine, too, that he was not in his twilight years, but in his early thirties and at the peak of his powers.

For some lucky people in Dundee in 1933, that opportunity was a very real one and one that they readily accepted when Louis Armstrong played the Palais in South Tay Street.

Louis Armstrong, affectionately known as "Satchmo" (short for "Satchelmouth") or Pops, had come to Europe in 1933 on a tour that some maintain was inspired by a desire to escape the unwanted attentions of the Mafia in the United States. Satchmo's plan to escape the mob, however, did not involve seeking refuge in Dundee, which did not feature on his itinerary. The closest he was due to come to the city was Edinburgh where he was to appear at the Empire Theatre.

The scheduled appearance at Edinburgh planted an idea in the mind of James Duncan of the New Palais de Danse in South Tay Street, Dundee. Duncan contacted Jack Hylton, the band leader and impresario, who was acting as Armstrong's agent and suggested a detour to Dundee. It was agreed on the morning of Tuesday, 28 November that Armstrong would come to Dundee and play at the Palais on the Friday of that same week – a speed of negotiation and change of schedule that seems unthinkable for a major star today.

James Duncan's New Palais de Danse had been officially opened in 1926 by Dundee's Lord Provost William High who, together with Duncan's wife, had been first to take to the dance floor on its opening night. The "New" before "Palais" in the dancehall's title was to distinguish it from Duncan's earlier venture of the same name in the Seagate. A dance teacher from the age of 16, James Duncan later went on to open the Empress Ballroom and lease the Chalet at Broughty Ferry. He brought several innovations to the Palais including radio broadcasts of the bands.

In 1929, a new house band came to the Palais in the shape of saxophonist and clarinet player Harry Smead and his band. It was Harry Smead who together with his pianist Billy Miller travelled to Edinburgh on 30 November 1933 to meet with Louis Armstrong and reassure him that they were able to provide ample backing for him the following night. This meant that he would be able to make the trip to Dundee without the need to bring his full band. Indeed, reports seem to suggest that Armstrong came to the city alone – again something it is hard to imagine a star of his status doing today.

The same day as Smead and Miller travelled to Edinburgh, an advertisement appeared in the *Evening Telegraph* announcing the appearance of "the world's greatest trumpet player" at the New Palais the following evening commencing at 10 pm – short notice indeed for the city's jazz lovers. The admission price was four shillings – double the price of a ticket for the event at the Palais on the evening that the advert appeared – though the Bell Rock FC Dance was perhaps unlikely to live so long in the memories of those who attended as a chance to see Louis Armstrong perform. In any case, the price did not seem to deter Dundonians and a large crowd turned out on 1 December to see him. Some were undoubtedly keen jazz enthusiasts, while others were perhaps accepting the *Courier*'s challenge to "judge for themselves whether he is too much for the general public or whether he is one of the greatest dance musicians and singers the world has ever known".

Armstrong arrived by car, having driven from Edinburgh after the evening performance there. There is little record of the Palais concert itself, though a brief review of the event appeared in the *Courier* on 2 December which said that Armstrong "gave ample evidence of his amazing trumpet technique, unique vocal efforts and many personal characteristics". Among the numbers performed were "Dinah", "Tiger Rag", "You Rascal You" and "St Louis Blues".

Immediately after the performance, Armstrong got into his car and set off again for Edinburgh. His swift disappearance into that dark December night serves to emphasise the fleeting nature of his visit to Dundee, leaving only the memories of those who attended. There is no doubt, however, that Armstrong's appearance and the actions of the Palais management in securing it were appreciated. An advertisement appeared in the press thanking "the many patrons and friends for expressions of appreciation and thanks for bringing Louis Armstrong to Dundee".

Some eighty years after the event, and given that it seems unlikely that any member of the audience who saw Louis Armstrong perform at the Palais survives to tell of it, it might seem that it would be impossible to gain even a flavour of what that performance would have been like. Some film exists, however, that affords us a glimpse. This film is the earliest known footage of Armstrong in concert and was filmed at the Lyric Park Theatre in Copenhagen on October 21, 1933 – a mere six weeks before his appearance in Dundee.

Armstrong's appearance in Copenhagen was certainly not as low key as his visit to Dundee. Fans had mobbed the railway station and broken through barriers hoping to catch a glimpse of his arrival, and his appearances at the Lyric Park spanned eight nights. Also, in Denmark he was accompanied by his eight-piece touring band, the Harlem Hot Band, and not by Harry Smead's band. Nevertheless, the film is surely the closest we can come to experiencing what the Dundee appearance was like.

In the film Armstrong and his band play three songs: "I Cover the Waterfront", "Dinah" and "Tiger Rag". The last two are known to have been performed at Dundee and so it seems likely that the first would have been as well. Armstrong saunters on to the stage, full of confidence and charisma, his trumpet in one hand and his trademark handkerchief in the other. "I'm Mister Armstrong", he asserts at a time when many of his fellow black Americans would be denied even the courtesy of that title. He effortlessly powers his way through the three songs with the assistance of a voice which acts as if it were another musical instrument, and a trumpet that appears as if it were part of his body. If this astonishing performance was in any measure replicated that December night in South Tay Street in 1933, then Louis Armstrong's long forgotten visit to Dundee is surely something that deserves to be commemorated as one of the most important cultural events ever to take place in the area designated many years later as the city's "cultural quarter".

Frankie goes to the Caird Hall

On 13 July 1953, just over a month after the Coronation of Queen Elizabeth, and the conquest of Everest, Francis Albert Sinatra, one of the most popular, influential and best-selling recording artists in history, stepped out on to the stage of the Caird Hall in Dundee. He looked out on the 2,000-seat auditorium. Barely a quarter of the places were full. He addressed the scattered members of the audience, and, in particular, those in the cheaper seats at the back. "Come down where I can see you," he said and with that people began to shuffle their way to more expensive seats at the front. Despite the poor turnout, those who had taken the trouble to attend were treated to a memorable performance – at least once they had sat through an hour of Sinatra's backing band for the British tour, Billy Ternent and his Broadcasting Orchestra with vocalists Eva Beynon and Johnny Webb and the "Ternenteers".

Although he was said to be suffering from the onset of a cold, Sinatra was in fine form and he later praised the hall's acoustics. Among the songs he sang that night were the poignant "September Song", which he recorded three times in his career, and "Birth Of The Blues", which acted as a great showcase for his vocal talents. Before he launched into another song, "Nancy with the Laughing Face", he explained to the audience that it had been written for his then 13-year-old daughter. (The song had, in fact, been written by composer

Jimmy Van Heusen and actor Phil Silvers with "Bessie" as the title character. At young Nancy's birthday party, they sang it with adapted lyrics to include her name. Sinatra was said to be very moved and later recorded it.)

Sinatra also performed "You'll Never Walk Alone" in Dundee, which the audience, if they recognised the song at all, would have associated with the 1945 Rodgers and Hammerstein musical "Carousel" rather than the football terraces. It would take another decade and the recording of the Gerry and the Pacemakers version before it would be adopted by Liverpool supporters. As was his habit, Sinatra took a break in the middle of the set to chat to the audience while walking about the stage drinking a cup of tea. He said that he had been told that it was good for the vocal chords; but he drank it simply because he liked it.

An idea of what Sinatra sounded like at his Dundee performance in 1953 can be gained from a recording that was made when he appeared at Blackpool Opera House less than two weeks later. Originally available only as a bootleg, it has since been given an official release. The set list is slightly different to the Dundee one but one song that he performed in both venues is "Ol' Man River" from Jerome Kern and Oscar Hammerstein's 1927 musical *Showboat*. In the 1936 film version, it was sung by Paul Robeson, and the song would always be associated with him. Indeed, Robeson made several visits to Dundee himself and had sung it from the stage of the Caird Hall. Sinatra had performed the song in the 1946 film *Till the Clouds Roll By*, which was loosely based on the life of Jerome Kern. A Frank Sinatra version of a song written from the point of view of a black stevedore on a showboat should not, in theory, have worked but he was able to make almost any material sound as if it had been written for him alone.

After "Ol' Man River"'s dramatic conclusion, he immediately lightened the mood by launching into a parody version, aimed at his friend and rival Bing Crosby. "Ol' Man Crosby", the lyrics said, "just keeps on singing along" while his younger rivals like Sinatra, with their "throats all aching and wracked with pain", could not match his seeming effortlessness and continuing popularity. The parody included an accurate impression of the "Old Groaner", much to the amusement of the audience.

Those who attended the Caird Hall that night may have thoroughly enjoyed Sinatra's performance but it is the relatively low numbers who did so that was destined to be remembered. Sinatra himself did not express any disappointment with the turnout in an interview which appeared in the

Courier the following day. "That happens in other cities," he said. "What really matters is their response and it was wonderful. I have a very high opinion of the Scottish audiences." Privately, though, Sinatra was said to be annoyed at the poor turnout and vowed never to play the city again. He left immediately after the show for Glasgow by car and the next morning caught a plane for London.

More than sixty years after the event, the poor attendance at Frank Sinatra's concert appearance at the Caird Hall in July 1953 has become the stuff of local legend. It is often used as a stick with which to beat Dundee audiences. Here, the story goes, was one of the biggest stars in the world coming to a provincial town like Dundee, and the local population could not be bothered to turn out in any great numbers. If Sinatra, widely acknowledged as one of the great vocal talents of the twentieth century, could not secure a full house in Dundee, is it any wonder that lesser performers should choose to omit the city from their tour itineraries?

This idea that Dundee uniquely snubbed Sinatra, though, is a myth. For one thing, the fact that he played two performances at the Caird Hall on 13 July 1953, one at 6.15pm and another at 8.45pm, is often ignored. The first house attracted 586 people, while 1189 attended the second. If there had been a single performance, then the attendance might not have been close to the Caird Hall's capacity, but the shortfall would not have been worthy of remark.

The story of Sinatra telling people to come forward to the empty seats at the front of the auditorium, which happened at the first house in Dundee, was not one that was unique to the city. The day before the Dundee concert, the afternoon show at the 3,000-seater Green's Playhouse in Ayr had also only attracted around 500 people, and Sinatra had called people down from the balcony. He had also asked people to come forward during poorly-attended shows in other venues on the tour including those at the Birmingham and Bristol Hippodromes.

The truth was that in 1953, Sinatra was no longer as popular as he had once been. On a 1950 visit to Britain he had been the headline act for two weeks at the London Palladium. His British tour this time started at a somewhat less prestigious London venue – the Granada Theatre, Tooting. Seen from the perspective of the twenty first century, where Sinatra is viewed as a figure of historic importance in the entertainment industry, it is hard to imagine that there was a danger that he would just be a passing fad; but in the early 1950s, he genuinely feared that his popularity might be overtaken by that of younger stars such as Eddie Fisher and would not be as enduring as "Ol' Man Crosby"'s.

There were various reasons for Sinatra's decline in popularity at this time. His teenage audience, the so-called bobby-soxers, who had given him the nickname "Swoonatra" were growing up and developing different interests, while Sinatra himself was now nearing 40. As many artists have found since, a long-term career cannot be sustained on the passing enthusiasms of a teenage audience alone.

The younger fans that Sinatra did retain in Britain in 1953 faced another problem. They were living in a country still suffering the after-effects of post-war austerity, where some rationing was still in place. Money for apparent frivolities, such as attending a concert, was difficult to come by. After the Dundee concert, a correspondent named Catriona wrote to the local press, blaming the ticket prices at the Caird Hall, which ranged from 5 to 15 shillings, for the poor attendance. The largest part of Sinatra's following, she reasoned, were teenagers, who simply could not afford the more expensive tickets. A single reasonable price for tickets would have seen the hall packed with young people, she added.

It was not just the decline of his teenage audience that cast a cloud on Sinatra's career in this period. In 1950, his friend and publicist George Evans had died suddenly at the age of 48. Evans's skills would have proved useful in this period, when Sinatra controversially divorced his childhood sweetheart Nancy Barbato and left his young family in order to marry the glamorous film star Ava Gardner – a move that shocked many of his fans. At the same time, he suffered from throat problems which affected his voice. In 1952 Columbia Records declined to renew his contract. The quality of the material that he had recorded in the latter years of that contract, including songs such as "Mama Will Bark" and "Bim Bam Baby", left a lot to be desired in the opinion of many of his fans. Concert attendances were poor at this time in the United States – including several far worse than that in Dundee. In 1952, for example, a mere 150 people attended a concert at the Chez Paree Night Club in Chicago – a venue which had seating for 1200. In this period Sinatra was said to have made several suicide attempts.

In summer of 1953, Ava Gardner was heading to Europe to make a film called *Knights of the Round Table*. Sinatra decided to undertake a European tour to coincide with this and also to attempt to raise funds to help pay an outstanding tax bill. It was Mrs. Sinatra, however, whose star was in the ascendancy. In Naples, the audience booed Sinatra and chanted her name, and were disappointed when she did not appear with him. (Any fans in Dundee who had hoped for a glimpse of Miss Gardner when Sinatra appeared at the

Caird Hall would have also been disappointed, as she stayed in London while he toured the provinces). Poor turnouts in Scandinavia led to the European tour being curtailed.

Seen in its wider context, then, the relatively low attendance for Frank Sinatra's appearances at the Caird Hall on 13 July 1953, simply reflects where his career was at that particular period of his life. It certainly was nothing remarkable or unique and it is unlikely that he would have remembered Dundee, if he remembered it at all, with any particular disdain. On the contrary, the city may have featured in one of his happier memories of that British tour. On Wednesday, 8 July, Sinatra and his manager Hank Sanicola travelled through from Glasgow after his performance there and spent the night in Dundee. The following day they watched Sinatra's friend Ben Hogan[22] play in the British Open Golf Championship at Carnoustie.

After 1953, Sinatra never again undertook a full-scale concert tour of Britain. It seems unlikely, though, that this was because of any reaction to the relatively poor reception he had received at that time, but rather because of the success he enjoyed in later years. His concert appearances in Britain were few and far between but such was his popularity that when he did appear, he could fill a single London venue such as the Royal Albert Hall or the Royal Festival Hall for an entire week. Sinatra no longer needed to tour the provinces in search of an audience. The audience would come to him. One notable exception to this was when he returned to Scotland and performed a single concert at Ibrox Stadium, Glasgow on 10 July 1990 – just short of thirty-seven years after he appeared at the Caird Hall.

The summer of 1953 may have marked a particular low point in Sinatra's career, but the seeds of his future success had already been planted by the time he appeared at Dundee. Earlier in the year he had made a film, *From Here to Eternity*, which would see its official release the month after the Caird Hall shows and would go on to win him an academy award. The film's star, Burt Lancaster, felt that Sinatra had used his own recent experiences in his portrayal of his character, Maggio: "what he had gone through the last number of years. A sense of defeat and the whole world crashing in on him... They all came out in that performance."

As well as his film output, a revival in Sinatra's musical career was also in the offing. In March 1953, he had signed a new recording contract

---

22 Hogan went on to win the Open in a record-breaking year that also saw him triumph at the Masters and the US Open. He was unable to participate in the PGA Championship as it clashed with the event at Carnoustie.

with Capitol Records. In April, he had had his first recording session with bandleader and arranger Nelson Riddle, and the two would go on to produce many classic albums together. The first fruits of their collaboration, "Songs for Young Lovers", would be released in January 1954. "From Here to Eternity", meanwhile, would be released before Sinatra had even completed the UK tour.

When Frank Sinatra stepped out onto the Caird Hall stage and saw the level of attendance that night in July 1953, he would certainly have been disappointed but his experience on the rest of the British tour and elsewhere would have taught him that it was indeed the kind of thing that "happened in other cities" as well. He must also have suspected, knowing the quality of the material that was already "in the can" by then, that he was on the brink of a new era in his career in terms of both music and film. The paying public, it seems, just needed a chance to catch up.

7

The Sporting Life

In the last quarter of the nineteenth century, football became a craze throughout Scotland. Versions of the game had been around for hundreds of years, but it was only in the 1880s and 1890s that football as we know it today fully emerged and attracted a mass following. Part of the appeal in a largely working-class, industrial city such as Dundee was that it was not expensive to participate in or to watch the game. Indeed, this was also true of another sport that gained in popularity in the city in this period and was itself in the process of becoming the modern, regulated version of a centuries-old activity – boxing. If these sports were largely the domain of the working classes, there is another, horse racing, which has always managed to attract interest across the entire breadth of the social spectrum – although the form that interest takes is still largely decided by class and financial status. This chapter looks briefly at different aspects of all three sports in Dundee.

A Tale of Two Football Grounds

One of the most famous pieces of trivia known by football fans is the fact that the distance between Dens and Tannadice, the home grounds of Dundee and Dundee United Football Clubs, is some 0.2 miles or 300 yards – the shortest between those of any two senior clubs in Britain. The two grounds have faced each other across the street for more than a century, but this raises the question of how this situation came about – and, indeed, who was there first? The logical answer to the last question would seem to be Dens Park. Dundee FC came into being in 1893, and Dundee United (as Dundee Hibernian) were founded in 1909, and so it would seem to follow that Dundee and their ground would have been there longest. As we will see, however, things are not quite so straightforward.

In order to investigate how football first came to the vicinity of Dens Road it is necessary to get a picture of how that area would have looked in the mid-nineteenth century. At that time, the land between Clepington Road and Dens Road was mainly open farmland. A continuation of Mains Road, roughly following the line of the present-day Provost Road, was in existence, while another road forming the drive to East Clepington House and farm buildings ran parallel to it and separated Easter and Wester Clepington Farms. It was the particular nature of the farmland, though, that seems to have brought football to the area. Many of the fields were given over to grass for grazing cattle. Grass "parks" at Clepington Farm were let every year to farmers who required extra room for their cattle long before football became popular in the later decades of the nineteenth century. If not being used for its intended purpose, it is easy to see how one of these grass parks would provide a suitable venue for a football match.

As early as 1880, football was being played on one of these fields, known as Clepington Park, when it was the home of Our Boys – a club that would go on to be one of the two constituent teams that later formed Dundee FC. In the early days of association football in Dundee, from the 1870s onwards, the game was in a constant state of flux, with teams forming and re-forming, merging and being renamed and changing their home grounds before it finally settled into familiar two-team rivalry. In July 1882, a report appeared in the *Courier*, stating that East End Football Club, the team that later merged with Our Boys to form Dundee, had secured the use from the landlord, Mr. Cooper, for the ensuing season, of Clepington, the "park situated immediately in front of his house". A comparison of a modern map with one from the nineteenth century confirms that this is the site of the modern Tannadice Park.

East End's tenure of Clepington Park does appear to have extended beyond that season and the ground was later used by a variety of clubs including the fledging Violet FC. From 1891, it was the home to Johnstone Wanderers, a team that had been formed in 1885. It was during the Wanderers' time there that Clepington Park was first enclosed and the first stand erected.

In 1894, Wanderers merged with long-established local club Strathmore (founded in 1874) to form a new team, Dundonians. At a meeting held to

Close rivals: Dens (home of Dundee FC) in the foreground looking towards Tannadice (home of Dundee United)

secure the club's membership of the Forfarshire Football Association, however, objection was made to this name by the representative of the then recently formed Dundee FC, who said he had to protest against the club seeking to retain the name Dundonians. The term was one which was applicable to all local players and especially to the players of the Dundee club. It was a name, he said, that was apt to lead to confusion and to misrepresent in the minds of the public the doings and work of the two clubs chiefly concerned. The name was eventually changed to Dundee Wanderers but not before the unusual sounding fixture of Dundee v Dundonians was played.[23]

Dundee FC had been formed in 1893 by the merger of Our Boys and East End. The new team played their home matches at Our Boys' home ground of West Craigie Park for a short period before moving to East End's ground at Carolina Port. Part of the motivation for the merger is likely to have been that the new team was more likely to gain entry to the Scottish League. If this was the case, it was successful, and the team played its first league game on

---

23   Dundee won 4–2.

12 August 1893 when they held Rangers to a 3–3 draw. A year later, Dundee Wanderers also gained league membership.

The year 1894 also saw the demise of Dundee Harp, a team with its roots in Dundee's then substantial Irish population. Harp had enjoyed a degree of success since its formation in 1885 but now was suspended from the Scottish Football Association for inability to pay match guarantees to visiting clubs. Harp's most remarkable result was the one that did not quite get them into the record books. On 12 September 1885, the same day that Arbroath beat Bon Accord 36–0, to claim the largest margin of victory in senior football history, Harp beat Aberdeen Rovers 35–0. It has been claimed that the referee actually noted 37 goals but was persuaded that he had miscounted.

With the disappearance of Harp, it might have seemed that the professional teams in Dundee would settle down to be Dundee FC and Dundee Wanderers, but the latter's time in the league was a short and unhappy one. They finished second from bottom with only nine points (and two of these were awarded when the opposing team, Renton, failed to turn up for a match). They did not return to the league for the 1895/6 season and went back to playing in the Northern League.

In 1899, Dundee FC moved to their new home at Dens Park – or Dens Road Park as it was more commonly called in this period, bringing with them the dismantled stand from Carolina Port. It had often been said that their old ground was inaccessible and the new one certainly benefitted from being more centrally located. Both Dens Road and Provost Road were being widened at this time and it was said that the earth excavated from this was to be used in the creation of the pitch. The new ground was to have accommodation for at least 20,000 supporters. There would be a cycle track round the pitch and the area between the stadium and Dens Road that the club did not use was to be given over to "working men's gardens". Dens Road Park was officially opened on 18 August 1899 by Lord Provost Henry McGrady in the presence of a large number of dignitaries. The match against Edinburgh team St Bernard ended in a 1–1 draw.

Meanwhile, following the failure of Harp FC, further attempts were made to revive the idea of a team to represent Dundee's Irish population under the names of Harp and Hibernian, but these came to nothing until 1909 when a new Dundee Hibernian team was established by a group under the leadership of Irish-born Dundee cycle dealer Pat Reilly. The new outfit needed a ground and came up with a surprising choice – Clepington Park. It had been thought that an Irish team might have more success in the Lochee area, which had a large population of Irish families and their descendants, but it was later reported that negotiations for a site in that area had broken down at an advanced stage. The choice of Clepington Park was also surprising to many because of its proximity to Dundee's ground. It was perhaps most surprising of all to Dundee Wanderers FC – because they were already playing there.

Not surprisingly, Wanderers were furious at the move, feeling that Hibernian had effectively stolen their ground. In a letter to the *Evening Telegraph*, Pat Reilly protested his club's innocence while, perhaps inadvisably, passing the blame on to their new landlord: "Unsolicited by us, the offer of Clepington Park was made by the proprietor and ultimately we resolved to accept the offer. If the Wanderers feel any hardship, they need not attempt to blame us. On our part, everything was fair and above board and if the proprietor was disinclined to let the ground to the Wanderers, I presume he had good reason for doing so." The Wanderers chairman, James Baxter, responded that the "good reason" was simply that Hibernian had made an offer that the Wanderers could not hope to match.

The Wanderers did not leave Clepington Park without one last expression of their discontent. Baxter had promised that "the day the Wanderers leave Clepington Park, it will be the park they will leave and not the erections as well". The departing Wanderers lived up to their chairman's words and removed everything possible including the stand, changing rooms, goalposts and perimeter fence. The *Evening Telegraph* reported that the ground had been "completely stripped" and said that "not one inch of wood that belonged to Dundee Wanderers" had been left. On 21 May 1909, Baxter advertised "Wooden barricades, &c." for sale. An offer from Dundee Hibernian was reported to have been turned down.

The new club had their work cut out to ready the ground for the beginning of the new season but managed to stage their first game there on 18 August in a friendly encounter with their Edinburgh namesakes that ended in a 1–1 draw in front of some seven thousand supporters. By way of an official opening ceremony, Lord Provost Urquhart had kicked off. An *Evening Telegraph* reporter had complemented the Lord Provost on his footballing skills in "tipping the ball to his inside man rather instead of indulging in a mighty kick".

As if to remove all trace of the Wanderers (which, a cynic might say, was something they had tried to do themselves), Clepington Park was renamed Tannadice Park. Dundee Wanderers, meanwhile, never really recovered from being made homeless, and though they later found a venue at St Margaret's Park in Lochee, the club only survived until the end of the 1912/13 season.

The very lack of security of tenure that had allowed Dundee Hibernian to effectively oust the Wanderers from their ground, though, meant that they too could be subject to a similar move in the future. Both Dundee and Dundee Hibs were only sure of staying in their grounds for the period of their respective leases. This effectively left them in no better a position than the farmers who had once grazed their cows there. The situation changed in 1920, when Dundee bought the seven acres and two poles that comprised Dens Park for the sum of £4,900. Five years later, what was by then Dundee United bought the four-acre site of Tannadice Park for £2828 14/-. United later acquired various other pieces of land in the vicinity.

How, though, had Dundee Hibs been transformed into Dundee United? By the early 1920s, it was clear that Dundee Hibernian had attracted neither the success nor the support that its founders had anticipated. When Scottish football was resumed after the First World War, the Second Division, in which Dundee Hibernian had played, was not. The club therefore resigned from the Scottish League to join the Eastern League for Season 1919/20. They re-joined the Scottish League again in 1920 but resigned again along with other clubs to form the independent Central League after an attempt to revive the Second Division had failed. At last, in 1921, the Second Division was successfully revived and included all the Central League clubs. There was a sting in the tail, however, in that it was agreed that the bottom two teams at the end of the 1921/22 season would drop out the league altogether. Unfortunately, Dundee Hibernian were one of those sides. It looked like they would have no league to play in the 1922/3 season at all before their last-minute securing of a place in the Scottish Alliance League, effectively the reserve league for the First Division.

In November 1922, the struggling club had been bought over by a consortium of local businessmen who aimed to secure the team's reinstatement to the league which they achieved for the 1923/4 season. It was around this time that the suggestion of a change of name, in order, it was said, to widen the club's appeal, began to emerge. The *People's Journal* correspondent Unomi wrote that if the name were Dundee Rovers or Dundee City then "the barrier that keeps many from giving personal practical support to the club would be broken down, attendances would increase to a healthy level, with a consequent growth in revenue". It was a view with which the new board had sympathy and they began the process of officially changing the club's name with the Scottish League. The new name was to be Dundee City. Some saw this as a betrayal of the club's Irish heritage, while for others any association with Ireland in the period of that country's civil war was a liability. One party objected to the name on other grounds, however. Just as they had done with "Dundonians", Dundee FC once again protested that their rival's proposed name was too similar to their own. Eventually a substitute name of Dundee United was agreed and officially adopted on 26 October 1923.

Having started our story of football in the Dens Road area around 1880, it is not until late 1923 then, that we find all the elements of the modern rivalry in place, with a team named Dundee FC playing at Dens Park and another named Dundee United playing across the road at Tannadice. Even then there was one element missing that would be instantly noticeable if looking at a Dundee United team photo from this time. From their formation in 1923, until 1969, United's official team colours were black and white and their various strips over the years reflected this. It was not until a trip to the United States where they played as Dallas Tornado in a competition where overseas teams represented teams from the North American Soccer League that they played in a tangerine strip. It was decided to permanently adopt a tangerine and black strip after this to refresh the team's image. The new strips first appeared in a pre-season friendly at Goodison Park in Liverpool on 2 August 1969 which saw United defeated 4-1 by Everton.

The fortunes of both Dundee clubs have ebbed and flowed over the years. Both have suffered relegation but have also enjoyed league wins (1961/2 for Dundee, 1982/3 for Dundee United) and success in Europe (Dundee reaching the semi-final of the European Cup in 1963, United achieving the same feat twenty years later, while Dundee reached the semi-final of the Inter-Cities Fairs Cup in 1968, and United were runners-up in its later equivalent, the UEFA cup in 1987). Both have won the Scottish Cup – United in 1994 after six times as beaten finalists, and again in 2010; Dundee famously won it a century earlier in 1910, but, remarkably, have not done so since. The League Cup wins are 3–2 in Dundee's favour. Throughout all of this, however, professional football in Dundee has remained anchored to the Dens Road area. In 2017, though, it was proposed that Dundee FC might move to a new site near Camperdown Park – raising the prospect that football's (geographically, at least) closest rivalry, might at last be coming to an end.

A Day at the Races

Having first been run at Aintree Racecourse in Liverpool more than one hundred and seventy years ago, the Grand National is one of the most famous horse races in the world. It is such a fixture of the nation's cultural life that even those without much of an interest in racing will tune in to watch and many who do not gamble at any other time of the year will have a bet on its outcome.

Every time the race is run it seems to produce an interesting story, but one of the most memorable Grand Nationals ever took place on 8 April 1967. At the twenty-third fence, a loose horse called Popham Down lived up to its name, helping to cause a pile-up of many of the competitors who had made it thus far. One hitherto unfancied horse, Foinavon, was so far behind that it did not get involved in the melee, jumped the fence cleanly and went on to win the Grand National at 100/1. This produced a windfall for some residents of the Fintry housing scheme in Dundee who lived in or near the similarly named Finavon Street, Place or Terrace and had decided to have a punt on the basis of the name. A similar thing had happened in 1928 when 10-year-old outsider Tipperary Tim had been the only horse which did not fall, bringing delight to people living in the Irish district of Lochee, centred on Atholl Street, which was nicknamed "Tipperary".

A few years before Tipperary Tim romped home, and not far from where the Fintry winners of 1967 lived, Dundee briefly had its own racecourse at Longhaugh, in the area where Longhaugh Primary School is today. The flat racing course included a grandstand which was built on concrete foundations and had space for 800 people. A report in the *Evening Telegraph* struck an optimistic note as to the potential success of the venture, saying: " The impression one gets is that Dundee is to have a first rate, tidy, racecourse of its class, with plenty of elbow room, and, granted the requisite patronage, will provide capital racing, thus introducing to the district a sport that will be a novelty to thousands of people." The question was, would the course be "granted the requisite patronage"?

The inaugural two-day race meeting in April 1924 was a great success and attended by a total of 30,000 people. An *Evening Telegraph* report describes all the different means of transport that were employed in getting people to what was then a relatively out-of-the-way location: "motor cars, charabancs, horse brakes, and shanks-naigie [travelling on foot] were called into service". The number of cars in the car park and in the surrounding streets was said to be the biggest ever assembled in Dundee up to that time.

The second meeting in July saw attendances slump to 5,000 over the two days, in part caused by bad weather. Three people were arrested for illegal gambling activities. One bookmaker, John Hamilton from Edinburgh, was arrested after absconding with his takings after a horse named Preston (on which he had offered odds of 4-1) came home in first place. (Another bookie, Archibald Bennett, had been imprisoned in May for committing a similar crime at the April meeting.)

A third meeting was held at the time of Dundee October holiday. The first day, Saturday, 4 October, faced a rival sporting attraction in the shape of the match between Dundee United and St Bernard at Tannadice. Torrential rain on the Sunday meant that the going was heavy when the course re-opened the following day. The weather on the Monday was much improved, however, and between 3,000 and 4,000 people attended. A report in the *Courier* said that this was "easily the most outstanding of all the Dundee gatherings from the point of view of the quality of the racing". This third meeting had attracted entrants from further afield than had the earlier ones.

In early 1925, however, it was announced that the company running the venture, Dundee Race Meetings Limited, was in financial difficulty and it subsequently went into liquidation. The horse racing experiment in Dundee had been brought to an abrupt end. Had Longhaugh been given longer to establish itself, the city might have become a well-known flat racing venue. Instead, the racecourse is an aspect of Dundee history which would almost certainly have been completely forgotten were it not for the work of the Whitfield History Group who, in 2014, produced a booklet with the Dighty Connect project telling its story.

The Longhaugh races, however, were not Dundee's first experience with the Sport of Kings. Indeed, a race took place at Dundee almost exactly a century before the final meeting at Longhaugh. On 11 October 1824, Dundee played host to a steeplechase. This was not a steeplechase as we would know it today but the type of cross-country horse race that gave the modern race its name. The first such race is said to have taken place in Ireland in 1752 as the result of a wager between huntsmen Edmund Blake and Cornelius O'Callaghan to see which of their horses could run the four miles between (the steeples of) St John's Church in Buttevant and St Mary's Church in Doneraile.

The route of the Dundee race, however, did not actually involve any churches or steeples. It started on the summit of the Law with the finishing point in the Sidlaws at Kinpurnie Hill. Then, as now, Kinpurnie was one of the most easily distinguished of the Sidlaw Hills as it is crowned by the Kinpurnie Tower which had been built as an observatory for astronomer James Stuart-Mackenzie in 1766. The distance was around seven and a half miles as the crow flies, but the shortest practical route was said to be nearer to nine or ten miles.

Despite the weather being particularly cold and windy (an eyewitness recalled it being a "bitterly cold spring day"), a large crowd turned out to see the race start. A contemporary newspaper report speculates that there had not been so many people on the Law since General Monck's army had camped there prior to taking the town for Cromwell in the seventeenth century.

The race commenced at 12.30 pm, with a field of three. They were each owned by a local gentleman: William Maule of Panmure the MP for Forfarshire, Colonel Fotheringham of Powrie and Robert Douglas of Brigton. Douglas rode his own horse.

The previously mentioned newspaper report provides us with the nearest thing we have to a race commentary:

"A mingled sensation of admiration, astonishment and terror was instantaneously felt, when at the given signal, the horsemen dashed off down the Law with the speed of the wind. The summit of the Law is upwards of 500 feet above the level of the Tay… and its brow is rather steep and precipitous."

In those days, there was, of course, no convenient road to the top of the Law – that was not constructed until the following century. The horses instead had to make their way down the slope of the hill. One spectator remembered: "They had an awkward scramble down the steep side of the Law until they reached the fields and then away across country."

Back to our commentator: "Two of the horses took nearly a bird's flight course; Mr Douglas, a more circuitous one, availing himself of the turnpike road for some miles."

Douglas's gamble in following the road paid off and he finished first, having covered the distance in 35 minutes and coming in a mile ahead of his rivals. He had the dubious honour of having a piece of doggerel verse written about his achievement:

>"Now let us sing, long live the King
>And Douglas long live he;
>When next he rides a 'steeple chase'
>May we be there to see."

This was not his only reward, though. There was also a financial gamble involved, with the gentlemen each staking £50, meaning that he was £100 in profit – an unimaginable sum of money for most people at the time. The three gentlemen rode to Perth for dinner. It is to be hoped that Robert Douglas was paying the bill.

On the Ropes

Boxing can be a divisive sport. Where some see skill and artistry, others only see people punching each other. Perhaps only fox hunting has been a more controversial claimant to the title of sport in recent years, though the boxers are given a choice as to participation that was not open to the fox. Some choices, though, are constrained by economic necessity, and many of Dundee's finest exponents of boxing, like those from elsewhere, grew up in circumstances of poverty. The following section, however, does not deal with such local heroes as Jim Brady, Fred Tennant or even Olympic medal winner Dick McTaggart, but rather tells of the visits to Dundee of three of the most famous boxers who ever lived. First, though, a problem in researching boxing that is unique to the city.

A name to be reckoned with

Anyone who attempts to carry out research into the history of boxing in Dundee, either using the Internet or printed sources, will soon discover that many of the references to Dundee that they find will not relate to the city at all but will be referring to a surname. Several fighters over the years have had Dundee as their last name but perhaps the most well-known figure in the sport to do so is Angelo Dundee, the trainer and cornerman to Mohammad Ali and many others. The question arises – is there any connection between the surname and the Scottish city? To investigate this, we must begin with the background of Angelo Dundee himself.

Angelo Dundee was born in Philadelphia in 1921, to Italian parents. His real surname was not, in fact, Dundee but Mirena (the name had once been Miranda but the "d" had somehow disappeared over the years; Dundee also blamed his father's handwriting for the fact that some members of the family were called Mireno with an "o"). In his autobiography, *My View from the Corner*, he tells how it was his oldest brother, Joe, some twenty-one years his senior, who first took the surname Dundee:

> "... like a lot of fighters who didn't want their parents to know, Joe took another name to keep his little secret from Pop. The name he selected was Dundee, a name worn by two fighting brothers out of Baltimore, Joe and Vince, both of whom became champions."[24]

This leads us to Joe and Vince Dundee. Joe Dundee was world welterweight champion between 1927 and 1929, while Vince Dundee was world middleweight champion between 1933 and 1934. Dundee, was not, however, the brothers' actual surname either. They had been born in Sicily and their names were, in fact, Samuel and Vincenzo Lazzara. Other members of their family fought under the names Ace Dundee and Baltimore Dundee.

It had not been the Lazzara family, though, who had directly inspired Angelo Dundee's brother Joe to adopt the surname. Instead it was the man who had probably inspired the Lazzaras and whom Joe Minera had seen fight as a young man. This was an Italian-born New York featherweight champion from the early part of the twentieth century who fought some 335 professional bouts in a 22-year career and who went by the name of Johnny Dundee. Needless to say, his name was not really Johnny Dundee either. His birth name was Giuseppe Carrera. He had been persuaded to change his name by his manager Scotty Monteith, who is reported to have thought that Carrera sounded too much like carrots and that people might throw vegetables at him. In reality, it may be that it was simply an attempt to disguise Carrera's Italian origins. If this was the intention, it was completely undone by the nickname that Dundee was given in the language of the day: "The Scotch Wop".

However distasteful that nickname might be considered today, it does tell us that the name Dundee refers to Dundee in Scotland. Scotty Monteith was himself born in Scotland as denoted by his nickname (*his* real first name was William) and there is little doubt that the city was his inspiration for Johnny Dundee's name. Some accounts state that Monteith chose the name as he was a native of Dundee himself, but the records do not bear this out. They show that he was born in Motherwell in 1885. (This does not disprove

---

24 Dundee, Angelo; Sugar, Bert, *My View from the Corner,* New York etc.: McGraw-Hill; Reprint edition (2009), page 18.

the story – it simply shows that Johnny Dundee is a better name than Johnny Motherwell!)

Joe Minera's boxing career as Joe Dundee was short-lived, but as well as Angelo's name change, it inspired another brother, the boxing manager and promoter born Cristofo Mirena, to adopt the name Chris Dundee. Boxing records show that dozens of fighters have adopted the name Dundee over the years but none of them appear to pre-date Giuseppe Carrera's change to Johnny Dundee at Scotty Monteith's suggestion. It would appear, therefore, that all the Dundees associated with the noble art ultimately owe their name to Dundee, Scotland.

John L. Sullivan comes to town

John L. Sullivan was boxing's first superstar and a pivotal figure in the history of the sport. Generally recognised as the last world heavyweight champion of bare-knuckle boxing under the London Prize Ring Rules, he is also regarded as the first heavyweight champion of gloved boxing under the Marquess of Queensberry rules, though he always seems to have preferred the latter style.

John Lawrence Sullivan was born in 1858 in Boston, Massachusetts. His parents, like many other people in the city at that time, were immigrants who had arrived in the wake of the Great Famine in Ireland. He began his career at a time when boxing was still illegal in many states and when there were no formal world championships. The road to a universally recognised heavyweight championship was as long and contentious as its eventual splintering into different fragments has been in our own time. In 1882, Sullivan defeated Paddy Ryan to claim the bare-knuckle championship of America. Three years later he beat Dominick McCaffrey in a gloved contest under Marquess of Queensberry rules, and, in America at least, began to be considered the heavyweight champion of the world. In 1889, he knocked out challenger Jake Kilrain after 75 rounds of a scheduled 80-round bout. Before this, on August 8, 1887, in Boston, Sullivan had been presented with a belt which was inscribed: "Presented to the Champion of Champions, John L. Sullivan, by the Citizens of the United States." Its centrepiece featured the flags of the US, Ireland and the United Kingdom. Some see presentation of this belt as the beginnings of the world heavyweight championship.

Sullivan was more than just a great world champion; he was a great showman too and one of the first sporting superstars. His image adorned

John L Sullivan

advertising material long before many others had fully realised its potential for sports stars. He was also among the first to understand that more people wanted to see their sporting heroes in the flesh than could ever hope to see them compete in actual contests, and as a consequence of this he began to stage exhibitions and public appearances.

In November 1887, Sullivan arrived in London embarking on a British tour that was to encompass some fifty-one exhibitions. It was as part of this tour that John L. Sullivan came to be in Dundee shortly before Christmas that year. In the afternoon of 22 December, a large crowd turned out to see him at the railway station and cheered as he stepped onto the platform, accompanied by the entourage of boxers that he had brought with him, namely Kendrick, Murphy, Hopwood, Blakelock, Hickey, Hopkiss, Wallis and Williams. These were the men who would form the basis of that evening's entertainment at Cooke's Circus in the Nethergate. Also travelling with Sullivan was his own sparring partner, the heavyweight Jack Ashton. As was the case with other celebrity appearances in Dundee in this period, for many of those who turned out at the station this would be as close as they could get to their hero as they could not afford to attend the official event.

For those who did attend, the evening began with contests between the other boxers, who had been divided into pairs matched by weight. An *Evening Telegraph* reporter who was in the audience complained about the delay between these bouts and how each of them seemed to be a "made-to order kind of thing, especially at the end of third rounds, all of which ended suspiciously like each other". There was, of course, an even longer delay before the bout featuring the evening's star attraction.

Before John L. Sullivan himself appeared, an announcer made a hyperbolic introductory speech. Calling him among other things "the cleverest man in the world", he told the audience that Sullivan was there not so much for the purpose of giving boxing entertainment as to show the Dundee people what he could do and convince prejudiced people as to his claim to the championship of the world. One piece of evidence that he would not be presenting in order to back up this claim, however, was his "Champion of Champions" belt. He had brought it to Britain with the intention of displaying it at all his exhibitions, but customs officers wanted to claim £126 for bringing it into the country. "This I refused to pay," Sullivan later wrote, "as I intended to take the belt back with me to my native shores. Consequently, the British did not have the opportunity of seeing the magnificent emblem which I had to leave in the Queen's bonded warehouse until I set sail for America on the 12th day of April 1888."[25]

Sullivan was greeted enthusiastically enough by the Dundee crowd. He fought four rounds with Jack Ashton to great acclaim from those in attendance. The reports of the entertainment at Cooke's Circus, though, are somewhat contradictory. Also limbering up for a sparring match that night, it seems, were Dundee's rival newspapers the *Courier* and the *Advertiser,* who presented contrasting views of the evening's events. The *Courier* reported that there was a "large turnout of spectators including a good many influential citizens" while the *Advertiser* said that while there was a crowded gallery, "the other parts were thinly occupied". The *Advertiser* said of Sullivan and his boxing style: "He is a well built, powerful man, firm on his limbs and evidently a strong hitter but there was nothing particularly striking in his display as he defended more

---

25 Sullivan, John L., *Life and Reminiscences of a Nineteenth Century Gladiator*, (1892) London: Geo. Routledge & Sons (Limited), page 179.

than he struck." According to the *Courier:* "a noteworthy feature of Sullivan's boxing was his cool and collected manner, his evident disregard for receiving a blow about the face and the smartness and force with which he retaliated on finding an opening". The *Courier* said of Sullivan and his bout with Ashton that "judging from the manner in which he was applauded at the finish, [it] pleased immensely", while for the *Advertiser*, "the 'entertainment' was dreary and disappointing."

There may have been those in the audience who shared the opinion of the *Advertiser* reporter simply because their expectations were too high. John L. Sullivan could not have afforded to indulge in a full-scale fight every night on his lengthy British tour nor could he risk serious injury either to his sparring partner Jack Ashton or, particularly, to himself. The report in the *Evening Telegraph* the day after the Dundee event noted that Sullivan "took it pretty easy last night during the short time he was on the stage and Jack Ashton got most of the hitting and jumping about to do". Whereas at an earlier stage of his career some of Sullivan's so-called exhibition fights were, in fact, actual contests and simply advertised as exhibitions as a means of getting around the ban on boxing in particular jurisdictions, now they were exactly as billed. Anyone expecting a lengthy prizefight or a brawl was always going to be disappointed.

The *Evening Telegraph* reporter was one of those who felt somewhat cheated, going on to say that he came away with the impression that Sullivan was "a cute fellow and that his cuteness lay in the successful way he was bulldozing the British public". The writer described Sullivan as being as much a "mitten showman" as a "pugilist", revealing that John L. Sullivan's Dundee appearance took place at a point in boxing history when the transition from bare-knuckle to gloved fighting was actually underway. The *Telegraph* reporter was clearly of the opinion that that the former style was superior, saying, "the bare, hard knuckles have a convincing truthful way about them which the gloves have not and John L. Sullivan's clear appreciation of this point may account for his preference for the picturesque and paying instead of the battering and painful side of pugilism".

Any doubts about Sullivan's ability as a bare-knuckle fighter were to be put to rest in his gruelling battle and (eventual) triumph against Jake Killrain in 1889. Nonetheless, it is perhaps no exaggeration to say that the transition to gloved boxing and the adoption of the Marquess of Queensberry rules are what ultimately saved the sport from illegality and eventual extinction and, despite the *Telegraph* reporter's misgivings, John L. Sullivan was a vital part of that transition. Anybody lucky enough to have been at Cooke's Circus that night, far from being the victim of "cuteness" or "bulldozing", was actually witness to a crucial period in the history of the sport.

Sullivan himself was happy with his Scottish appearances, later recalling that he had met with "particular success" in the main cities, including Dundee. For many, there must have been disappointment in the fact that they had only seen him fighting in an exhibition style against an apparently disinterested opponent in a manner that was not regarded by aficionados as representing real pugilism. There must have been others in the crowd that night, however, who, whether they realised that boxing was on the verge of an important new era or not, continued to the end of their lives to talk of the time that they had seen the legendary John L. Sullivan in the Nethergate in Dundee.

Jack Johnson and the Dundee Masons

Though John L. Sullivan and his successors such as James J. Corbett, Bob Fitzsimmons and James J. Jeffries were each, in turn, recognised as being the heavyweight champion of the world, that world, it seems, did not include any black people. Even when black boxers were allowed to compete for other titles the world heavyweight championship was kept out of their reach. It was not until Jack Johnson defeated the Canadian fighter Tommy Burns in 1908, that the world saw its first black heavyweight champion and therefore the first man who could truly claim to be the best in the world, irrespective of the colour of his skin.

Johnson had followed Burns all the way to Australia and taunted him into accepting a contest. It was a contest that Burns had been seemingly confident of winning. "I will beat Johnson," he is reputed to have said, "or my name isn't Tommy Burns." Unfortunately for Burns his real name was actually Noah Brusso, and he was duly defeated, though, as the author Jack London put it, it was more of a slaughter than a defeat. In 1910, the former undefeated heavyweight champion James J. Jeffries, who had previously vowed never to fight a black boxer, came out of retirement to meet Johnson in the so-called "fight of the century". Johnson won that too, consolidating his position as champion.

Jack Johnson's life both before and after he won the world championship was one packed with incident, but one of the more bizarre episodes must surely involve the time he came to Dundee and the worldwide controversy that followed on from this visit. At 5.30 am on Friday, 13 October 1911, Johnson arrived at Tay Bridge Station on a train from Newcastle where he had been giving boxing demonstrations at the Pavilion Theatre. He was accompanied by his wife Etta and a man referred to in local press reports as Mr. McLaglan. The three of them made their way to the Royal Hotel in Union Street, where they had breakfast before a taxi was summoned from the rank across the road for the two men. The vehicle's hood had not been lowered and Johnson, who was wearing a heavy grey overcoat and a felt hat, crouched down in his seat. The man they called the Galveston Giant, however, cut an unmistakable figure and a crowd soon surrounded the car hoping to catch a glimpse of the world champion.

Johnson and McLaglan's destination was Meadow Street (now Meadow Lane), a street which at that time connected Meadowside to the busy Wellgate. In particular, they were heading to number 13, a Masonic Hall and home to the Forfar and Kincardine Lodge. Jack Johnson had come to Dundee to be initiated into Freemasonry.

The meeting had been due to take place at noon but was brought forward to 10 am, apparently without the knowledge of many members of the Lodge who arrived at the previously appointed time only to find that events had concluded. Nevertheless, around fifty members were reported to be in attendance. The first part of the proceedings had seen Johnson's friend McLaglan initiated into the Second Degree while the boxer waited in an anteroom before his own ceremony began at around 11 o'clock.

A speech that Johnson is supposed to have given at the end of the meeting appeared in the *Courier* the next day: "I can't go away without saying something to the boys. Right Worshipful Master and brethren, this is the most glorious time of my life. My father-in-law was a Mason and my wife desires me to be one. It has long been my great desire to be a Mason and I have now accomplished the first stage of the journey. I will always have the greatest love for Dundee and Dundee Masons. God bless every member here and his wife and family." He was greeted by much cheering and many handshakes as he made his way down the stairs.

Any hope Jack Johnson had that his visit to Dundee would remain relatively private or low key would have been lost when he left the hall. Thanks in part to a man named Duncan – the taxi driver who had taken him to his destination – word that the champion was in the city had rapidly spread and people had

Jack Johnson around the time of his trip to Dundee to join a masonic lodge

begun to gather in Meadow Street soon after he had arrived. The crowd was bolstered by the curious who had seen it from the Wellgate or Meadowside, and by the time Johnson emerged, the narrow street was packed. Johnson was carried out of the hall at shoulder height and taken to a waiting taxi amid much cheering and handshaking. People stood on the running boards of the moving taxi until it was through the crowd.

The car stopped at the Royal Hotel to pick up Mrs. Johnson, and again a crowd turned out. This time, perhaps in admission that there was no longer any realistic prospect of privacy regarding the visit, the taxi's hood was lowered and those waiting got a good view of Johnson and cheered him on his way. There was a similar scene at Tay Bridge Station. Hundreds of people lined the platforms and staff had to all but abandon their work. Luggage trolleys were knocked over as people surged forward to shake hands with the great man, and even the champion himself had to struggle through the crowd to a carriage. There was little chance of him disappearing from view though, as one newspaper report noted: "his soft felt hat and ponderous shoulders were always visible above even the tallest of the throng". A reporter asked Johnson what he thought of Dundee: "I'm sorry, I've not had much time," he replied, "but what I have seen is grand." Promising that he would be back in January for an appearance at the King's Theatre, Johnson left on the 12.17pm train for Newcastle, leaning out of the compartment window and waving his hat to the adoring crowds.

Like a good punch, Jack Johnson's visit to Dundee had been as brief as it was unexpected. Nevertheless, he had certainly left a good impression on Dundonians. The *Courier* noted that the locals were "impressed by the geniality with which he comported himself, and underneath a necessarily rugged exterior Johnson seems to have a large and warm heart". In addition, all the indications were that this was only the beginning of a long relationship between the boxer and the city. Indeed, on 21 October, the Right Worshipful Master of the Forfar and Kincardine Lodge wrote to Johnson and informed him that he would be eligible to return to Dundee to receive his Second Degree on the 27th of that month or any date thereafter and asked the boxer to reply letting him know when it would be convenient. There would be no need to wait until January. There was no indication of any controversy surrounding Johnson's initial visit to Dundee in the letter. The only reference to the earlier visit came in the form of a plea for there to be less in the way of publicity this time surrounding what was supposed to be a private meeting:

"You are probably aware that your last visit to the city caused rather a sensation and as it is desirable to avoid any demonstration. I personally should prefer that your next visit should be made known to the members only of your own lodge, all of whom are anxious to make your acquaintance, and not to all and sundry. I most particularly desire to reserve the next meeting for members only and if your visit is made public that will be impossible."

Two days after the letter was written, Johnson was the defendant in a case at Marylebone County Court brought by a former landlady, Jennie Carlton, who was attempting to recoup rent money she was owed and gain some compensation for the state in which her flat had been left and the destruction of crockery and furniture. She was awarded £7 9s with costs, which would allow her to buy a whole new tea set.

It was not the fate of Miss Carlton's tea service, however, that was concerning the Masonic fraternity in Dundee and beyond. In the weeks following Johnson's visit to the city, discontent had been brewing about the circumstances of his initiation. On 2 November, it was announced at the Grand Lodge of Scotland quarterly meeting that an investigation was to be held at the request of the Provincial Grand Lodge of Forfarshire to determine how the meeting of the Lodge was held, the notice given, the extent of any examination of Johnson's character and especially if any inquiry was made at the town of his residence. It would also ask who had been his proposer and seconder and did they know him personally? Had it been Johnson who personally asked by letter for his name to go forward and had he made all the necessary declarations?

In his rooms at the hotel Metropole, Leeds, a few days later, Jack Johnson spoke to a journalist about the situation: "I don't suppose a single member of the Lodge has complained," he said, "All I want is fair treatment and I can tell I want nothing bestowed upon me which I don't deserve." He went on to show the reporter some of the many supportive letters he had received from Freemasons including one from a Glasgow barber who promised to give him a haircut and a shave to the best of his ability when he visited the city.

Johnson's own enthusiasm for Freemasonry was undimmed: "It's the greatest thing in the world - it's wonderful," he said. "I have always wanted to be a member and I chose the Dundee Lodge because it is one of the oldest and one of the most substantial." He insisted that his membership remained intact. "I am a Freemason and as long as I live I shall be one. Only God Almighty can undo that." He confirmed his intention to go back to Dundee to receive his Second Degree.

The promised inquiry was conducted at the Forfar and Kincardine Hall on 14 November 1911. The meeting was open only to Lodge members, but a fairly detailed account of proceedings made its way into the next morning's *Courier*. The Right Worshipful Master (RWM) of the F and K Lodge stated that the meeting had been called for twelve o'clock but had later been altered to ten o'clock for Johnson's convenience. The RWM went on to explain that he went around in a taxi cab to as many members of the Lodge as he could recall and mustered an attendance of between a dozen and twenty (somewhat fewer than the fifty reported). He explained that Jack Johnson had been recommended for membership of the Lodge by Brother[26] McLaglan, who was connected with the theatrical profession and who had received the First Degree of Masonry in the F and K Lodge while on a visit to Dundee some time before Johnson's

---

26 Freemasons traditionally refer to each other as "Brother"

initiation. It was on McLaglan's recommendation that RWM Brother Blues had proposed and Past Master Brother Smith had seconded Johnson's initiation. They did not know him personally but all present at the meeting were satisfied Johnson was a proper person to be admitted into the Masonic Order.

On 9 April 1912, a crowded meeting of the Forfar and Kincardine Lodge heard RWM Brother Blues say that the Grand Lodge Committee's recommendation was that any ceremonial which had taken place in connection with Johnson was ineffective and that the Lodge should explain why it should not be suspended and why the Master and three Past Masters should not be similarly dealt with. It appears that the Lodge was not able to come up with such an explanation. On the 24 April, at a meeting of the Provincial Grand Lodge of Forfarshire, a letter from Grand Lodge Committee was read intimating that the Lodge should be suspended until November 1913, that the Right Worshipful Master should be suspended for two years and three Past Masters for one year. One member thought it unfair that sanction should be imposed on those who had nothing to do with the meeting. A meeting of Grand Lodge in August heard appeals on behalf of the Forfar and Kincardine Lodge and the individuals concerned, but the suspensions were upheld. Jack Johnson's initiation was declared null and void and his fees returned.

In studying the story of Jack Johnson's visit to Dundee, it is easy to become sidetracked into discussion or speculation regarding the particular internal workings of the Forfar and Kincardine Lodge or of Scottish Freemasonry in general a century or more ago. Looking at the situation at its most basic level, however, it is unlikely that all the members of any club or organisation would have been happy with the circumstances of a meeting like the one held to initiate Johnson, or that such a meeting would comply with any reasonable set of club rules.

Similarly, it is possible to become fixated on the role that the colour of Johnson's skin may have played in events and assume that racism explains all or part of the story. Accusations of racism have been levelled over the years at both the members of the local Lodge who were unhappy with Johnson's initiation and at the Grand Lodge Committee who conducted the inquiry. It is certainly possible, perhaps even likely, that there may have been individual members of either or both who held views that would now be considered racist – as there would have been in all walks of life in this period, even where it contradicted the professed aims of the organisation. There is no obvious evidence of racism at an institutional level, however. A newspaper report at the time of Johnson's initiation said he was "the second coloured man whose name has been placed upon the roll" at the Forfar and Kincardine Lodge and it was procedure, not race, that was at the heart of the Grand Lodge inquiry that led to the sanctions being taken. Indeed, much care was taken to make it clear that it was not Johnson's race that was being discussed. The question was directly asked at the Provincial Grand Lodge meeting in April and the answer was given that it was "not a question of colour at all", and again, at the subsequent appeal to the Grand Lodge in Edinburgh, the question of Johnson's colour was said to be "immaterial".

The key to understanding events surrounding Jack Johnson's visit to Dundee, rather, is to be found through the examination of a much more basic question, namely – why did this American, who had never set foot in Scotland before, let alone Dundee, choose to join a Masonic Lodge in the city? His own explanation was that the Forfar and Kincardine Lodge was "one of the oldest" – but there were many old Lodges in England where he had been touring the music halls. Indeed, there were specific Lodges for actors and music hall artists. It is not as if Dundee had hitherto featured on his itinerary or if he had any family or sentimental connection to the city. All the evidence seems to point to it being only because his friend McLaglan had previously been admitted to that particular Lodge that Johnson joined there.

In September 1911, McLaglan had been in Dundee as manager of an act appearing at the King's Theatre, Annie Abbott the "Little Georgia Magnet". Annie's act was summed up in a newspaper report: "one little woman sets herself up to defy the physical powers of fifteen stalwart men. The human magnet is rooted to the spot and simply can't be shifted." It was at this time that McLaglan joined the Lodge. Who, though, was the mysterious Mr. McLaglan?

Sydney Temple Leopold McLaglen (as the name was normally spelled) was born in 1884 in London. His father, Bishop Andrew McLaglen, had been born in South Africa and worked there as a missionary. Some reports say that the title of bishop was not an official one and that it was derived from the large area that his mission covered. McLaglen himself claimed to have been ordained a bishop in 1897 for the Free Protestant Episcopal Church, but by this time he was living in London. Like much about the McLaglen family, it is often difficult to separate truth and fiction. This was particularly true with the bishop's son, as the following brief sketch of his life will show.

Sydney, normally known by his middle name of Leopold or Leo, served in the Boer War, having lied about his age. In 1903, Bishop McLaglen found himself in the debtor's court, a position brought about by having lent money to his son when he went to South Africa – a debt which was never repaid.

In June 1905, Leo married Gladys Fullwood-Rose, who he had met through a newspaper advertisement, the early twentieth century version of Internet dating. The following year Gladys gave birth to a daughter, but the marriage did not last due to Leo's cruel and erratic behaviour. Within a few months of the wedding, he was spending his weekends at a hotel in Newcastle with another woman posing as his wife. He threatened suicide on various occasions and once showed his wife a gun, threatening to kill her parents with it. He wrote to his mother-in-law claiming drug addiction: "I am ashamed to mention that I continue to take the terrible morphia. I can see plainly it will ruin my life, as well as that of your poor daughter."

Shortly after the birth of their daughter, the couple split up. When she was about a month old, Leo turned up at the family home with a man he said was a solicitor. He said he was going to live in Canada and wanted to take a last look at the child. When he did so, though, he handed his daughter to the man, who ran out of the house with her. Gladys McLaglen had to take to the courts to regain custody of her daughter.

In the next few years Leopold McLaglen re-invented himself as an instructor in Jiu Jitsu, styling himself as the Jiu Jitsu Champion of the World. His level of proficiency at the intricacies of the martial art is disputed. Some say that he was much more of a showman than anything else and this seems to be borne out by his activities at this time when he toured America calling himself "Leopold the Mighty" or the "Irish Giant". He claimed, too, to have fought Jack Johnson – something which is said to have annoyed his brother Victor McLaglen, later famous as a successful Hollywood actor and someone who had actually fought Jack Johnson.

It was around this time that Leo met a woman called Prudence Ward, whose married name was Rolfson and who used the stage name Marie Rolfson. She took on the name and act of another performer – Annie Abbott the "Little Georgia Magnet" – the act that had brought him to Dundee in the first place. The two toured the world together and Prudence added another name to her collection – McLaglen – though it is doubtful that they were ever actually married.

As we have seen, McLaglen had joined the Freemasons when he was in Dundee. His family was of Scottish descent and their original name was McLachlan. McLaglen's Scottish roots perhaps help to explain why he wanted to join a Masonic Lodge in the city. When he encountered Jack Johnson in Newcastle on the music hall circuit, he would have been able to use the connection to his brother Victor as a means of introduction, if the two had not met before. When Johnson expressed an interest in joining the Masons, McLaglen undoubtedly would have offered to facilitate this.

The British Army, meanwhile, seems to have believed in Leo's abilities in the field of martial arts, and he was commissioned as a lieutenant. In 1914 he was in Shanghai lecturing on Jiu Jitsu and later he was in New Zealand instructing soldiers in a new form of bayonet fighting incorporating Jiu Jitsu moves. In 1916, he was promoted to captain in the Middlesex Regiment. He published books on both Jiu Jitsu and bayonet fighting including *Jiu-Jitsu: A Manual of the Science* and *Bayonet Fighting for War*. After the war, he continued to travel, lecturing on Jiu Jitsu all over the world, training soldiers and police forces in particular.

In the early 1930s, Leo tried to make it in Hollywood with little success – a fact that he attributed to his brother's interference rather than his own lack of ability. In 1931, he took Victor to court, alleging slander and defamation of character, claiming £20,000 in damages. He claimed that Victor had said that there was "only room for one McLaglen in Hollywood". Victor, he said, had hired detectives to follow him, and slandered him, closing the "doors of opportunity" against him. Needless to say, the action was not successful.

In October 1937, Leo was arrested for "subornation of perjury and soliciting a commission of a crime". He vehemently protested his innocence blaming a "frame-up". He was released on bail but was later charged with attempting to extort $20,000 from Philip Chancellor, a millionaire watch manufacturer. His defence included claims that he had been employed as a secret agent, with the approval of the British authorities. He was found guilty and sentenced to five years in prison. He did not serve the sentence, though, having instead opted to leave the United States immediately and promise not to return for five years – an option that was supposedly offered due to the intervention of Victor McLaglen, who undoubtedly wanted to see his brother out of the country.

Leopold McLaglen died in Devon in 1951. He is an enigma of man – some reports of his life show him as a talented individual; others denounce him as a fantasist. In either case, it is easy to see how the officials of the Forfar and Kincardine Lodge would have found him a very persuasive character. He clearly had the showmanship to win over audiences and the teaching skills to persuade others to do what he asked. In a class-ridden era, he would also have had the type of accent and persona that was associated with the Establishment. He was, after all, an officer and a gentleman and the Dundee Freemasons would have seen no reason to doubt his word. Add to this mix the worldwide celebrity of Jack Johnson and you have the recipe that resulted in the Forfar and Kincardine Lodge officials abandoning their normal procedures that morning in 1911.

By the time Jack Johnson finally returned to Dundee at the beginning of 1916, his name had been adopted as a nickname for the large German shells that rained down on the British troops on a daily basis in the ongoing Great War. He was back in the city not to advance in Freemasonry but rather to appear on the stage of the King's Theatre in the Cowgate in a revue called *Seconds Out*. A large crowd turned out to watch his white sports car arrive at the theatre, and the shows were well attended. The advertisement in the *Courier* on the 4 January proclaimed that there had been hundreds turned away the previous night and advised people to book early. If Johnson looked at this advertisement with satisfaction, what his thoughts would have been if he had happened to glance further up the same column and see the notice for a meeting of the reinstated Forfar and Kincardine Lodge remains open to speculation.

The reviews for the show were good. A reviewer from the *Evening Telegraph* said that Johnson made a "very interesting appearance". It had been advertised that Johnson would sing, but on the night that the *Telegraph* reporter visited he was unable to sing due to a cold and delivered a talk on boxing instead. He also gave an exhibition with a sparring partner and involved a number of "budding pugilists" from the audience.

The review continued:

"The local men seemed dead earnest about making a good show, little men though they were, but Jack Johnson took their most vigorous efforts in a very kindly way, and acting purely on the defensive, he gave them the satisfaction of being able to say that they had "boxed" with Jack Johnson. And, after all, that is something to say, for the name of the great fighter will go down in the annals of the ring for all time."

There does not appear to be a mention in any of the reviews of *Seconds Out*, or of Johnson's previous visit to Dundee, nor does any reporter who interviewed him appear to have asked him about the episode of his attempted initiation into Freemasonry in the city only a few years earlier. The reports restrict themselves to his boxing career and the revue itself. Coming in for particular praise with regard to the latter was Mrs. Jack Johnson, who took to the stage with her husband. She played her role as Lady Thurlow "very neatly" according to the *Telegraph*, while the *Courier* praised her performance of "the Oyster Dance", which was described as being "full of graceful movement". It was also noted that "amid much excellent dancing in the revue it undoubtedly takes the leading place".

This was not, however, the Mrs. Johnson who had accompanied her husband to Dundee on his previous visit. In September 1912, shortly after his membership of the Forfar and Kincardine Lodge was finally rescinded, Johnson's then wife, Etta, had committed suicide. She had long suffered from depression, a situation exacerbated by Johnson's constant infidelity and abusive behaviour. On one occasion he had beaten her so badly that she was hospitalised. Within a month of her funeral he was seen in public with an 18-year-old prostitute from Milwaukee named Lucille Cameron. Before the end of the year they were married, albeit after Johnson was convicted of "transporting a woman across state lines for immoral purposes", forcing the couple to live in exile, though he eventually served a ten-month sentence. Lucille had, at least, actually married him. There had been many previous "Mrs Johnsons" who had travelled with the boxer – many of them prostitutes – who had not. The new marriage, almost inevitably, ended in divorce due to Johnson's infidelity.

Had the Dundee Freemasons known anything about these aspects of his character and conduct, rather than simply accepting the word of Leopold McLaglen, it is unlikely that they would have accepted Johnson's nomination in the first place, and indeed, if McLaglen's own character had been fully investigated, perhaps his own suitability for membership would have been questioned. Nevertheless, in Johnson's case, many have felt over the years that his conviction by an all-white jury was racially motivated and intended as a punishment for his unapologetic nature and his liaisons with white women. In 2018, he was granted a posthumous pardon by President Donald Trump, a move welcomed by members of Johnson's former Lodge in Dundee.

Jack Johnson died in a car crash near Franklinton, North Carolina on 10 June 1946. It is said that he had just been refused service in a diner on account of the colour of his skin. His life had been defined by his colour and it even appeared to play a role in his death. The debacle that followed his attempt to join a Masonic Lodge in Dundee, though, appears to owe its origins not to Johnson's race or even particularly to the internal workings of Freemasonry, but rather to the Lodge officials being dazzled by Jack Johnson's celebrity and their willingness to listen to the persuasive tongue of Sydney Temple Leopold McLaglen.

Sugar Ray and Dundee's other champion of the ring

In September 1964, a man walked into a Dundee pub. This most ordinary sounding of events was still being talked about over half a century later, with some doubting that it even happened. This was because it was no ordinary customer who had entered the Ellenbank Bar at the corner of Alexander Street and North Ellen Street that evening, but the man that some consider to be the greatest pound-for-pound boxer ever. Sugar Ray Robinson had held the world welterweight title from 1946–1951 before going on to hold the middleweight title before he retired in 1952. His professional record at that point included 128 victories (84 of them knockouts) including a 91-fight unbeaten streak.

Robinson's extravagant lifestyle and the relative failure of his attempts to establish an alternative career as a singer and dancer saw him driven back into the ring by 1955. By the time of his trip to Dundee in 1964, he was in his forties and long past his best as a fighter. He was on an eighteen-month boxing tour of Europe which had taken him to Paisley Ice Rink on 3 September to fight British Middleweight Champion Mick Leahy in a scrappy contest which Leahy won on points. As a newsreel commentary of the time stated, Robinson had actually been fighting two opponents that night – the second being age. Another British boxer, Terry Downes, who also defeated Robinson in this period, summed up the situation best. "I didn't beat Sugar Ray," he said, "I beat his ghost."

Robinson was in the Ellenbank Bar at the invitation of the landlord, George Kidd, who had bought the pub the previous year. Kidd introduced Robinson to several well-known personalities from Dundee's boxing scene that evening. Kidd was himself one of the city's most successful ever champions of the ring, but he was not a boxer. He was, in fact, a world champion wrestler.

George Kidd was born in Hill Street, Dundee in 1925. He attended Clepington Primary and Stobswell Secondary Schools. On his first visit to a local boxing club as a boy, Kidd was on the receiving end of a punishing beating when he grabbed his opponent's legs and dragged him to the ground. This was not only the end of his boxing career but perhaps the very beginnings of his remarkable career in wrestling.

Kidd enlisted in the Royal Navy in 1943, serving in the Fleet Air Arm as a mechanic, and it was there that he began wrestling. At the time of his demob, though, George Kidd cut an unlikely figure for one who was to take up a career as a professional wrestler, being five-feet-six inches tall and weighing nine and a half stones. Nonetheless, he approached George de Relwsykow, a wrestling promoter and was given a chance. On 8 January 1946, Kidd appeared in front of over 2,000 people as part of an evening of wrestling at the Caird Hall. A *Courier* reporter wrote at the time: "[the] opening bout featured a local lad, George Kidd in a lightweight contest against Len Ring (London). George proved himself a fast and clever wrestler and was having a good share of the fight before being KO'd early in the third round." The reporter's use of the word "clever" was perceptive. In the years to come he would often, by use of his sheer intelligence, outthink opponents who seemed, on paper, likely to defeat him. Losing a bout, however, was not something that George Kidd was to make a habit of in the future. His rise in the professional wrestling world was rapid. By the end of 1947, he had defeated fellow Dundonian Tony Lawrence to take the Scottish lightweight title.

In 1948, his progression continued when he secured the British title, defeating Jack Dempsey, and the following year he won the European title in Paris. In 1949, he defeated the man generally recognised as the reigning world champion, Rudy Quarez of Mexico. "George Kidd Wins World Title" proclaimed a *Courier* headline, but not everybody agreed. The American Wrestling Alliance, for example, refused to recognise Kidd's title, preferring the claim of the Frenchman Rene Ben Chemoul. Kidd, could, of course, have simply ignored them and held a rival title but he wanted to be the undisputed champion – so he duly defeated Chemoul as well.

George Kidd took his wrestling seriously and studied the sport and its various manoeuvres and holds as well as investigating other means of self-defence and methods of achieving fitness. Where other fighters simply concentrated on building bulky muscles, Kidd practised yoga to keep his muscles supple and his mind sharp; where others adopted outlandish gimmicks and nicknames, he concentrated on his wrestling. He put a great deal of effort into finding ways to escape holds, so successfully that he was sometimes compared to Houdini.

When wrestling became a major television phenomenon, Kidd did not appear as often as some of his fellow professionals, perhaps fearing the impact that over exposure on television might have had on wrestling as a sport. By the 1960s, he was well aware of the impact of TV, having become a well-known personality in the Grampian TV region as presenter of Wednesday People and The George Kidd Show. Grampian viewers voted him Personality of the Year in 1965. In the same year he became Dundee's "First Citizen".

George Kidd retired from wrestling in 1976, still the undisputed and undefeated world lightweight wrestling champion. He had just defended his title for a remarkable forty ninth time, seeing off a challenge from Steve Logan. His career had lasted thirty years and had involved more than 1,000 bouts which included very few defeats. He had fought many of the top names in wrestling – such as Mick McManus and Jackie Pallo – in an era when the sport was arguably at its height. In 1963, he had appeared at a command performance for the Duke of Edinburgh in the Royal Albert Hall.

Kidd spent his retirement living in Broughty Ferry and died in 1998. In 2015, he became the first inductee into the Official Scottish Professional Wrestling Hall of Fame. A permanent memorial was unveiled at the Caird Hall to mark his achievements in 2016. It takes a special kind of person to be so successful over so long a period in their chosen field, and George Kidd is still fondly remembered in Dundee today.

8

Ordinary Dundonians?

On the afternoon of 23 July 1878, a man was buried in the Eastern Cemetery, Dundee. Alexander Ross had died at his home at Dallfield Walk three days earlier. He was 83 years old – a quite remarkable age for that time. It might have been thought, therefore, that so many of his friends and relatives would have predeceased him (he had outlived his three wives, for example) that attendance at his funeral would be relatively poor; but, in fact, crowds turned out to see his funeral procession, which included a hundred of the troops then stationed at Dudhope Castle. The reason for the interest in the death of this seemingly ordinary old man among so many who did not know him was that he was the last man in the Dundee district to have fought at the Battle of Waterloo.

Ross had enlisted in the 42nd Regiment (the Black Watch) in 1812. He had fought in the Battle of Orthes in 1814 in which the British were victorious. They had then followed the retreating French to Toulouse. There, Ross's company stormed a gun battery and took it. It was later lost and retaken again all in the same day. Ross was captured by the French but eventually released and allowed to return home when it appeared that the conflict was over.

He returned to active service in 1815, though, landing at Antwerp and marching to Brussels where, on the night of the 15th June at half past eleven at night, the troops were ordered to quit the city. The same night they marched twenty-two miles, taking part in the chaotic Battle of Quatre Bras before coming to the fateful field of Waterloo. He was on the battlefield for the whole day but emerged unscathed. Ross was discharged in 1820 and was awarded a small pension.

Alexander Ross's name is not widely remembered in Dundee, but like many seemingly ordinary Dundonians, he would have had quite an extraordinary tale to tell. This chapter rediscovers some of these people.

Distant Cousins?

Vic Ruse was in many ways an ordinary Dundee man of his time. Born in 1918, Vic was a railway man and, like many of his generation, spent most of his working life in that one industry. As was common at the time, he got married in his twenties. In 1944, at the age of 26, he married 22-year-old Agnes Martin, who was then doing her bit for the war effort working in a munitions factory. Together Vic and Agnes had three children and, like most people in Dundee then, they lived in a rented house.

Vic had, nonetheless, achieved two things which ranked highly among the dreams and ambitions of the average schoolboy of the period. For one thing he was a train driver, having first worked, as was traditional, as a railway fireman. He was also a footballer (a centre forward just to perfect that schoolboy dream).

Before the Second World War he played for junior club Arnot FC. He had a rare ability to take advantage of any goal scoring opportunity. On one memorable occasion in 1939, Arnot were 4–2 down against Downfield with three minutes to go. They went on to win 5–4, with Vic having scored four of their goals. Hat-tricks were not unusual for him. Little wonder, then, that when three teams, Anchorage, Carnoustie and Stobswell, attempted to secure his transfer in 1941, their offers were turned down. Anchorage were successful in securing his services the following year, though, and he later moved to Carnoustie, where his success continued. The club presented him with a canteen of cutlery in 1944 on the occasion of his marriage.

Later that year, Vic played a couple of games for Raith Rovers, helping them to beat Arbroath 5–3 with yet another hat-trick, and it was thought that he might sign for them on a permanent basis but instead he signed for Dundee FC. His career there was erratic: he was loaned out to other teams and even played in goal for the Dundee "A" team on one occasion. The normal Scottish League was suspended due to the war at this time anyway, and Dundee played in the North Eastern League. Perhaps, given more stable circumstances, Vic's career would have reached greater heights.

After the war Vic turned out for Forfar Athletic, Brechin City, Arbroath and even commuted to play for Forres Mechanics at one stage. He also played for Kenilworth, a Dundee team, and for the Scotland team of the newly nationalised British Railways. In his later years he became a well-respected referee among the local teams in Dundee.

Vic died in 1978 at the relatively young age of 60 and was much missed by his family and friends. His life had been just about as far removed from the glitz and glamour of Hollywood as it is possible to imagine and yet there was a very real link between Vic and Tinseltown – in fact, there was a family link. Vic had two cousins who had, to say the least, done very well for themselves there. They were Olivia de Havilland and Joan Fontaine – two of the top stars of the golden age of cinema.

How could the cousins' lives have gone in such radically different directions: Olivia and Joan living in Paris and California and attending the Academy awards, and Vic living in the St Mary's housing scheme and running about muddy football pitches in Dundee? The answer lies back in the Ruse family history.

Vic's grandfather, Alfred Ruse, started out his working life as an ironmonger's assistant and worked his way up to the position of manager. Clearly an ambitious man, he appears to have afforded his children every opportunity to pursue their own dreams. Alfred produced a talented family, some of whom would travel far and wide from their relatively humble origins. His eldest son – also Alfred, but known as Fred – was Vic's father. Fred was born in Sandgate, Kent in 1870 and always had an interest in music. When he was 17 he was an assistant in a newsagent's, working from 5am to 9 pm each day and earning a half crown a week. When he asked for a night off to play piano at a concert, his boss refused and Fred resigned on the spot. It was to be a turning point in his life. For the next eighteen years, he travelled the country, playing piano for a group of touring actors and becoming the first member of the family to gain a foothold in the world of entertainment. It was as a result of his chosen profession that Fred met and married Vic's mother, an actress named Moya Osborne. The couple wed in Glasgow in 1895.

Moya's family had a background in the entertainment business. Her parents (Vic's grandparents) were also actors going by the stage names of Leslie G. Kean and Miss Osborne Kean. Moya herself had been on the stage since she was a very young child when she was billed as "the great child actress – La Petite Moya Kean". The names Osborne and Kean came from her father's full name: Leslie George Kean Godolphin Osborne. Godolphin Osborne was the family name of the Dukes of Leeds, so it may be that there is more than Hollywood aristocracy in Vic's family.

Fred and Moya eventually found their way to Carnoustie, where Vic was born, and then to Dundee. Initially, Fred played in cinema orchestras, providing accompaniment for silent films but with the coming of talking pictures, this work dried up and he took up music teaching in both Dundee and St Andrews, where he was also part of a Scottish country dance band. His spare time was devoted to running a children's concert party called the Sunbeams. In his later years Fred lived in Constitution Road. He died in 1958 at the age of 88.

Fred had lived a long and eventful life, but one opportunity he had not taken up when he was younger was the offer of a post assisting his brother Ernest who had become a professor of languages at Waseda University in Tokyo. Ernest was also the co-author of a book, *Practical Anglo-Japanese Conversation*. When Fred declined, his younger sister Lilian (and Vic's aunt), another of ironmonger Alfred's talented brood, had gone in his place.

Lilian Augusta Ruse was born in Reading in 1886. She was a gifted singer and studied acting at the Royal Academy of Dramatic Arts in London. Lilian was said to be a snob, however, who was embarrassed by her background and who hated her surname, which she insisted on spelling as Rusé, with an accent on the last letter. She would soon put a vast distance, both socially and geographically, between herself and her relatively humble origins.

It was around 1912 that Lilian set sail for Japan. While there, she met another Westerner who was teaching at Waseda, and he too was an author. He had written the definitive book on the Japanese game called "Go" but he was most famous for his works on patent law. His name was Walter Augustus de Havilland, and soon after meeting Lilian Ruse, he had proposed to her.

Lilian was at first wary, but Walter was persistent. On her return trip to England via the Panama Canal, she discovered that he had followed her on board. When he again proposed, she suggested they toss a coin for it. She lost. Walter and Lilian were married in New York City on 30 November 1914. They returned to Japan, where Olivia Mary de Havilland was born on 1 July 1916, and her sister, Joan de Beauvoir de Havilland, on 22 October 1917. Despite the birth of their two daughters, the marriage was not a success. De Havilland was said to be a cold man and a serial womaniser who disapproved of Lilian pursuing her musical ambitions by singing and playing piano for the entertainment of their fellow Western exiles in Tokyo.

In 1919, when Walter's womanising came a little too close to home in the shape of the de Havillands' maid, Lilian left him, taking the two children with her. She sailed for California and lived for a while in San Francisco, but later moved to San Jose. It was there that she met the man who was to become her second husband, George Fontaine. After their marriage, Fontaine inflicted a strict and often cruel regime on the young Olivia and Joan. Lilian, nonetheless, allowed the girls to follow their dreams of acting – or perhaps she was simply living out her own unfulfilled dreams through them. Their eventual success, however, must have been beyond her wildest dreams.

Olivia was to become one of the stars of the classic Hollywood epic *Gone with the Wind*, and in a career spanning more than five decades won two Academy awards for Best Actress for her roles in the films *To Each His Own* (1946) and *The Heiress* (1949). Joan also enjoyed a long career and won the Best Actress award for her performance in Hitchcock's *Rebecca* (1941), when she beat Olivia to the honour. She had supposedly adopted the stage name "Fontaine" when a fortune teller had told her that a stage name ending in "e" would bring her luck, and her stepfather's surname was the first that came into her head.

For all the sisters' success in Hollywood, their personal lives were not without their problems. They had six failed marriages between them, and tragically, Olivia's son Benjamin died in 1991 after a long illness. In Hollywood gossip terms, it was the decades-long feud between the sisters themselves which gained the most attention. The roots of this went back to their childhood, but the first public indication was at the 1942 Academy awards when they both received nominations. Joan wrote that after winning the award and being ordered by Olivia to "get up there" that "all the resentments and jealousies of an uncomfortably shared childhood returned; the hair-pulling, the savage wrestling matches, the time Olivia fractured my collar bone, all came rushing back in kaleidoscopic imagery. My paralysis was total… I felt age four, being confronted by my older sister."[27] At the 1947 ceremony, when Olivia won, she was seen to snub Joan's congratulations.

Other disputes and perceived slights bubbled away over the ensuing years, but according to biographer Charles Higham, it was not until 1975 and a

---

27 Fontaine, Joan, *No Bed of Roses*, 1978 New York: Berkley Books, page 148.

dispute over their mother's memorial service that all ties between the sisters were broken[28]. Even in their nineties the feud showed no sign of abating. A commemoration for the centenary of the birth of their contemporary Bette Davis in 2008 saw Joan agree to attend when it appeared Olivia would not, then withdraw when she learned her sister would, after all, be attending. In a 2009 interview Olivia was asked about her relationship with Joan, and said: "That is one subject on which I never speak. Never," she replied.

It seems unlikely that the sisters were ever reconciled before Joan died in 2013. The day after her death Olivia released a statement saying that she was "shocked and saddened" by the news.

Ultimately, the sisters' upbringing and the Hollywood treadmill had both taken their toll on what should have been one of the closest relationships of their lives. Despite all their fame and fortune, perhaps they sometimes wished for an ordinary life in an ordinary town, like that of their cousin in Dundee, Vic Ruse.

Across the Herring Pond: The forgotten voyage of Robert McCallum

One day in June 1895, around five thousand people gathered at the area known as The Battery on the southern tip of Manhattan Island in New York. The crowd had come to see a nineteen-foot sloop named the *Richard K Fox* set sail. Aboard, under sails bearing the legend "Police Gazette", were the vessel's only two occupants: a 19-year-old boy from Dundee named Robert McCallum and a little Scottish terrier, Jack.

Robert McCallum was undertaking a challenge set by the aforementioned Fox, the Irish-born publisher of the National Police Gazette. It was certainly quite a prospect – the boat was bound for Queenstown in Ireland on the other side of the Atlantic. Sums ranging from $1,000 to $5,000 were mentioned in press reports should McCallum be successful. He would also be the youngest person ever to complete such a crossing. The *Gazette* reported: "The task which the brave and hardy young Scotsman has set himself is one that will require all his nerve, coolness and courage, and one that, if successful, will show what a man can do when he tries. If he reaches Europe in his cockle-shell the youngest

---

28 Higham, Charles, *Olivia and Joan* (1984), London: New English Library, page 205.

navigator will have succeeded in crossing the briny in the smallest boat which ever rode the billows of the Atlantic."

Who, then, was this intrepid sailor? Robert Curtley McCallum was born on 15 February 1874 at 70 Murraygate Dundee. His parents and older siblings had all been born in Aberdeen. It was not just his Dundonian birth, however, that marked young Robert out as being different from the rest of the family. When he was growing up, he got into what his mother called "piles of scrapes". She used to refer to her son as "the big headed loon" believing that some abnormal development had led him to attempt things which other children would not consider.

When he was around 14 years of age, Robert went to work in a local mill. It might have been thought that the drudgery of working life would calm him down but after a short time he disappeared from Dundee. He was traced to Paisley but soon vanished again. This time it turned out that he had gone to sea aboard an English coaster named the *Isabella Walker*. It was not until the ship was frozen up that he wrote home. It seems that the sea was in young Robert's blood; he was, perhaps, seeking to follow in the footsteps of his merchant seaman father. He was said to have studied the art of navigation from the age of 10.

Robert McCallum certainly enjoyed an eventful life at sea. He was shipwrecked twice, once on Goodwin Sands off the Deal coast in Kent, England when only he and the captain were rescued. He also spent time in Australia and New Zealand before returning home. It was not long, however, before he was off again, this time joining a voyage to Brazil. The next his family heard of him was when his Atlantic attempt made the newspapers.

McCallum expected to complete the voyage in forty-five days but carried sixty days' worth of rations, mostly consisting of canned goods and thirty gallons of water. He also carried oil to pour on the troubled waters he would undoubtedly encounter. He intended to take what he called the middle passage in order to be in touch with passing transatlantic steamers, which he hoped could pass on news of his progress. No news was received, though. The weeks and then months began to pass. It was not until November that MacCallum's fate was reported in the Dundee press.

He later gave his own account of what happened on the voyage. Having left New York on 13 June he had steered a course east-south-east, and the next morning lost sight of land. That evening the weather took a turn for the worse and he had to "heave to" putting out his sea anchor and a bag of oil. He spent the night with the waves breaking over the boat. He recalled: "This kind of thing continued until the 16th. I was soaked in water to the skin. The boat, too, had made about six inches of water and I did not like it." This was not the only source of danger: "On the 18th I had a narrow escape from being run down by an American barquentine, which suddenly came out of the fog not 50 yards from me. The crew looked utterly astonished at me, not knowing what to make of my little craft."

On 21 June, MacCallum found himself in the Gulf Stream and covered 115 miles in the next 30 hours, but owing to what he called the "treacherous and confused sea" the boat overturned and he was left clinging to its side. He eventually manged to right the vessel and steered a course out of the stream.

From the 23 to 26 June, he found himself in a relatively calm situation, though the sun during the day was intensely hot. He spent much of the time sleeping and also succeeded in catching some fish. He must have thought that things were looking up at this point but was dealt a terrible blow when he found that one of his casks of water had gone bad and had begun to smell. He feared that the same thing might happen to the other. The remaining days of June passed peacefully enough and by the 1 July he had covered some 840 miles.

On 2 July, however, a gale blew up. McCallum later recalled the resulting ordeal:

"The seas kept continually breaking over the boat, and altogether I had a bad time of it. I suffered terribly. My clothes were soaked through and through and I dare not open any part of the little craft to get anything to eat – neither could I get at the pump, although she had 18 inches of water aboard. Things became so bad that I had to run her before the gale. This proved a terrible experience as the little craft frequently stood up on end and was buffeted about in every direction by the huge waves and I was momentarily expecting her to be smashed up."

McCallum ran before the storm for 120 miles before the winds calmed on 5 July. After twenty-six days at sea, he had not made the progress he hoped for and became "very dejected". On 22 July, another storm blew up and McCallum decided to attempt to sit this one out. He tied down the mainsail and tethered himself to the boat. He lowered his sea anchor and put out some bags of oil: "I did all that it was possible for a man to do to make her live out the gale. The seas were as high as mountains and the fury of the wind as it howled and screeched through the rigging was awful to listen to. Wave after wave swept across the boat and only that I had lashed myself on I would have been washed overboard."

At midnight, the wind veered to the north-east and the boat was turned on its side. MacCallum began to feel that his situation was hopeless. Nevertheless, he somehow managed to crawl to the wire rigging and put his feet against the mast. He held on to the rigging and remained in this position for the next six hours or so. He later remembered: "God only knows what my sufferings were during that time. I felt my reason was leaving me. In the morning I was almost frozen to death and utterly exhausted."

Just at that time, a wave hit the boat on the starboard side and suddenly righted it. McCallum recalled: "It was only the howling of the dog that brought me to my senses, as I was then in a state of stupor. I managed to crawl into the cabin and partook of a glass of brandy, all I had left. The boat had over two feet of water in her and everything I had in the cabin, such as matches, clothes, oil, water etc. were all destroyed. This was a sad state of things as I was then over 1,600 miles from New York and more than 400 miles from the Newfoundland coast."

The weather became calm on the 23 July, and after McCallum pumped the water out of the boat, he settled down to a breakfast composed of some of the few biscuits he had left, dipped in salt water. He set a course for the island of St. Pierre but had only travelled some 25 miles when he spotted a ship which turned out to be the *Stalwart* of Yarmouth, Nova Scotia. He shouted out to the captain, asking for water. The reply was not the one that he had hoped for: "You young beggar, you ought to be drowned," cried the captain. McCallum thought that this was "chilling and inhuman" considering his exhausted state. "Well, if you think so, I will be drowned," he shouted back and set off on his way. The *Stalwart* came after him and the captain said that he would give him water but predicted that he would never reach land. McCallum manoeuvred his boat alongside the ship, but it was lifted by a high wave and dashed against the side of the *Stalwart*. The port side had been smashed and the water began to pour in. The crew threw him a rope and he was hauled aboard with his dog Jack in his arms. The *Richard K Fox* could not be saved and was cast adrift.

The *Stalwart* was bound for Buenos Aries and arrived there on 19 September, thirty-five days after picking up McCallum. He stayed at the sailors' Home there before setting out to cross the Atlantic again, this time aboard the liner *Arabian Prince* which was bound for Limerick. He was reunited with his parents in early December.

For most people, Robert McCallum's efforts to cross the Atlantic would have been adventure enough for a lifetime but almost immediately he began to prepare for another attempt. D. Brown Livie, a Dundee boat builder of some repute who had carried out work for the Admiralty would build the vessel. This boat's nineteen-feet-long keel would be made of metal and the boat would weigh around half a ton. There would be a galvanised tank at one end to hold forty to fifty gallons of water and an air-tight locker for food and provisions at the other.

In an interview with the *Courier*, McCallum expressed his pride in being from Dundee and Scotland. "There is some pluck in Dundee yet," he said. It would be an honour for Scotland, he went on to say, were his venture to be successful. This time his journey would start in Dundee. He would proceed to Leith before taking the canal to Glasgow and heading to Ireland before proceeding across "the herring pond" to New York. His previous experience, he said, would stand him in good stead.

Livie began to build the boat in early February 1896 and it was intended that McCallum would begin his voyage in May. The boat would be exhibited in central Dundee to raise funds for the venture. McCallum also appeared in music halls in Aberdeen and Dundee where he gave "a thrilling account of recent experiences while attempting to cross the Atlantic in an open boat". Views illuminated by limelight showed McCallum, his boat and his new dog, an Irish terrier named Rona who was to accompany him on the journey. (Although he survived the voyage, it is not clear what had happened to poor Jack.)

On 9 May, McCallum's boat went on display at the Greenmarket and two days later he set sail from the Earl Grey Dock. A crowd of several hundred people had gathered to see him off, though this was not actually the start of his trip. His immediate destination was not New York, but rather Perth, further up the Tay, where he intended to exhibit his boat in a tent on the South Inch in order to raise funds before going to Aberdeen for the same purpose. McCallum left Dundee again on 16 May with the intention of going to St Andrews, Kirkcaldy, Burntisland and Grangemouth before heading for Leith and following the route he had previously suggested.

There was much astonishment in Dundee late on 19 June, therefore, when McCallum's boat turned up at Camperdown Dock. There was even more astonishment when it turned out that the man aboard was not Robert McCallum but a local man named Andrew Adams. Adams had to be helped from the boat as he was stiff and sore from his voyage. His journey had not involved crossing the Atlantic, however, but merely travelling from Burntisland. He had arrived at the mouth of the Tay on the Thursday but had missed the tide and had been much battered by the wind and rain. Where, though, was Robert McCallum?

Adams explained that McCallum had decided to abandon the venture, at least for the time being, due to lack of funds. His previous attempt had left him penniless. He had taken the boat to all the places he had intended but had not raised the money he had anticipated to fit out the boat. He then found out he had to pay £8 on account for the boat, which he had expected was going to be a gift. Given his situation, he had joined the steamer *Sapphire* as a sailor. A reporter caught up with McCallum on Tyneside and he made it clear that it was only the financial situation that had prevented him attempting to cross the Atlantic again and that it was a great disappointment to him.

Even as McCallum was speaking, two Norwegian-born Americans, Frank Samuelsen and George Harbo were rowing their way across the Atlantic in a boat called the *Fox*, named, as McCallum's boat had been, after Richard K Fox of the *National Police Gazette*. Samuelsen and Harbo successfully completed the crossing in 55 days. Their record still stands. It took 114 years for their time to be beaten but that took a team of four rowers. The rumoured prize money from the *Police Gazette*, however, appears to have been just that – a rumour. It seems that it had not even been offered but was just something that had been invented by the press. The report of the men's success in the *Police Gazette* itself said only that, "Mr. Richard K. Fox... after whom the little craft was named, will present Harbo and Samuelson with gold medals to commemorate the accomplishment of their marvellous trip." In this, at least, McCallum had beaten them to it. He had already been presented with a medal at an event held in his honour in Dundee. The inscription referred to "his plucky attempt to cross the Atlantic in an open boat."

If it is true that history is written by the victors, then it is equally the case that it is generally only those who are successful in any particular field of human endeavour that are remembered. If Robert McCallum had managed to cross the Atlantic, he would have been one of Dundee's most famous sons and his story would have graced every local history book. When he was presented with the medal he expressed the hope that his success would bring honour to his native city. Although he never completed the crossing, perhaps it is time, that the "big headed loon" and his "plucky attempt" are remembered in Dundee.

Edward McHugh: Your Gospel Singer

"Ladies and gentlemen, I have a grave announcement to make. Incredible as it may seem, strange beings who landed in New Jersey tonight are the vanguard of an invading army from Mars." Anybody who doubts the power of radio in 1930s America need look no further than the events of 30 October 1938 when the broadcast of this fake news bulletin as part of Orson Welles's version of *The War of the Worlds* caused widespread panic among listeners who believed it to be authentic. If radio could spread fear, however, it could also provide hope and comfort for Americans in the face of the economic hardship at home and uncertainty abroad. The nationwide broadcast on a daily basis of a selection of familiar hymns sung by a man with a beautiful, soothing voice brought solace to many in the era of the Great Depression and made a household name of the man who was billed as "Your Gospel Singer". Interrupted by messages from its soap-powder sponsors, this was a peculiarly American type of programme, yet the "Gospel Singer" was no Bible Belt preacher, but a man from Dundee.

Edward McHugh was born in Tait's Lane, Dundee in 1893 into a working-class family. His father, Michael, died just before Edward's second birthday, leaving his mother, Sarah, to bring up her family alone. On leaving school, Edward was apprenticed as a baker but his destiny did not lie in this trade nor even in his home town. On 11 May 1912, two weeks before his nineteenth birthday, together with his mother and three brothers, McHugh boarded the steamship *Grampian* in Glasgow and headed for a new life in Canada.

McHugh made his public singing debut later that year at the Montreal Hunt Club, singing "God Save the King". This brought him to the attention of a most unusual talent-spotter in the shape of the Governor General of Canada, the Duke of Connaught and Strathearn (and uncle of the king of whom McHugh had been singing). As a result of the Governor General's interest, McHugh was sent to the Royal College of Music in London with a view to pursuing a career as an opera singer. He is also known to have studied in Paris. His singing, however, always tended towards a more popular style. "True musicians find fault," he once told an interviewer, "but I'm not singing for the critics."

There are scant details of McHugh's life over the next few years, but it seems likely that he tried to pursue his musical career at home. In 1921, however, he walked into the travel agents MacKay Bros and Co. in Whitehall Crescent, Dundee and arranged to leave the country for a second time – this time booking a trip from Liverpool to New York. On this occasion, his occupation on the passenger list is given as "singer".

Among his first jobs on arrival was a tour of East Coast High Schools with a production based on Robert Burns' "The Cotter's Saturday Night". This was followed by years of hard graft singing at venues throughout the country and taking jobs where he could find them in places such as railroad yards and department stores. In 1927, another lucky break came his way when he was hired by the WBZ radio station in Boston to do a short programme singing hymns. Within days more than two thousand fan letters had arrived, some addressed simply to "the Gospel Singer".

McHugh's popularity continued to grow and he came to the attention of one of the country's major networks, NBC. From 1933 his show went nationwide. He would broadcast a fifteen-minute show to the entire nation on an almost daily basis for the next ten years. It was the start of a hectic period for McHugh (or MacHugh as his name was now consistently spelled). Each morning he would be singing for his show at the Radio City theatre and often in the evening he would be jetting off to fulfil a concert engagement. He received fan mail and requests from all over the United States. The influence of his show is demonstrated by an occasion when he mentioned on his show a seven-year-old boy who had been blinded in an accident; soon afterwards the boy was deluged with messages of support from MacHugh's listeners. In 1939, it was said that an envelope addressed simply "Edward MacHugh, United States" would reach him.

MacHugh published two popular books of hymns and poems during this period and did much to bring new favourites to the fore. Old and obscure tunes were given a new lease of life simply by being featured on his show. When MacHugh adopted "An Evening Prayer" as his theme song, it caused a revival in churches across the country of this hymn written by C. Maude Battersby in 1911. It was later recorded by many artists including Jim Reeves and Elvis Presley.

It was perhaps fortunate for MacHugh's enraptured listeners that they were not party to what went on in rehearsals. The NBC presenter George Ansbro remembered how the gospel singer would entertain friends with light-hearted stories which often featured "off-colour" language. MacHugh always had the loudspeakers in the studio visitors room switched off before and after the show so that tours passing through would hear only the "Gospel Singer" they knew and loved.

It was fortunate too that the listeners could not hear what happened at the conclusion of one particular show in 1935 when MacHugh was arrested and charged with entering the country illegally. The situation was resolved, however, and MacHugh became a US citizen in 1951. That occasion provided one of his most unusual public performances when he, among hundreds of other new citizens, sang the "Star Spangled Banner" at a naturalisation ceremony in central High School, Bridgeport Connecticut. It had been a long journey from his rendition of "God Save the King" in Canada in 1912.

MacHugh married his wife Jean in 1936 and in the same year he started a poultry farm at Westport, Connecticut where he raised seven kinds of prize hens and six species of pheasants, geese and turkeys. This had been a long-term ambition of his. He once told the Pittsburgh Press: "You know, some day I'm going to have a huge bird farm where I'll raise birds just for the fun of it and the joy I get out of watching them live. They are fascinating creatures and much more intelligent than some people think."

MacHugh's national daily radio show ended in 1943 and he retired two years later. In 1956, he and his wife moved to Fort Lauderdale in Florida where he died the next year following an operation for cancer of the liver. He was 63 years old. Such is the transient nature of radio broadcasting and musical tastes, that despite having been so popular in his own era, Edward MacHugh is virtually unheard of today. He did make recordings, but these are difficult to come by even as 78 rpm discs. Anyone lucky enough to hear McHugh's rich baritone voice in any format today, though, will surely, even from the distance of several decades, appreciate the warmth that so appealed to Americans in the hard years of the Depression. If they listen closely, they will also hear something else – the vaguest hint of a Dundee accent.

The Testimony of Pie Jock

One of the most fascinating books ever written about Dundee is *Dundee Worthies – Reminiscences, Games, Amusements* written by George M. Martin and published in 1934. At first sight, it appears to be a straightforward exercise in nostalgia for the readership of the time. It would be unfair, however, to suggest that this is the only purpose of the book. While it for the most part consists of a collection of character sketches and anecdotes relating to some well-known, if rather eccentric, Dundee figures of the past, many of the characters and events featured in the book would have been within the living memory of only a relatively small number of people by 1934. Martin himself states in the introduction that, having interviewed "many hundreds" of elderly people only "a very few could describe the peculiarities, appearance or speech of these worthies". Part of his intention, it appears, was to preserve the memory of these once well-known personalities and features of daily life in Dundee. Indeed, he goes on to say: "It will be obvious to the reader that many of these reminiscences would be lost with the passing of this generation."

One of the characters who is most vividly portrayed in the book is John Fergusson, who was known throughout Dundee as Pie Jock. He is described as being "light, short and crooked, and bent to one side; his clothes were threadbare, having rents stitched, and holes patched, and a light cloth cap, drawn down over his eyes, covered his towsey locks". Around his neck, secured by a leather strap, he wore a specially constructed oven. The oven had two compartments: the lower one contained a charcoal fire to heat the pies in the upper one. Jock wandered the streets with this contraption shouting, "Pies, Hot Pies!" and selling his wares. He died in 1863, before George Martin himself was born, and yet it appears that his name was still known in the city at the time that *Dundee Worthies* was published. By recording his story, Martin succeeded in keeping Pie Jock's memory alive, and he has been featured in several other Dundee related books over the years. David Phillips, for example, in his biography of William McGonagall, *No Poet's Corner in the Abbey*, featured a fictional encounter between the poet and the pieman.[29]

The fact that knowledge of Pie Jock was fading by the time that *Dundee Worthies* was written might suggest that there would be nothing left to add to the story of this particular "worthy", but a search of the records that are now available means that it is possible to piece together more of his story. Of particular interest is an interview with Jock himself conducted by the Dundee writer James Myles in 1850. The interview reveals a man far from being the simpleton that he was commonly perceived to be: "Daft Jock" to some – but rather someone who made the best of the circumstances in which he found himself.

John Fergusson was born in 1794, not in Dundee but in the Parish of Glenisla, near Alyth, Perthshire. He recalled for James Myles the chain of

---

29 Phillips, David, *No Poet's Corner in the Abbey*, (1971), Dundee: David Winter and Son Limited, page 87. The two men lived not far from each other and may well have met, though McGonagall did not "discover he was a poet" until after Jock's death.

events that brought him to Dundee: "My father was a small farmer, who got embarrassed in circumstances when I was very young, and was obliged to leave his farm, after all his stock and furniture were sold by the laird. He came to Dundee and earned his bread by carrying coals to John Baxter, who was then a coal merchant in the Chapelshade."

Young John got little or no education and was forced to go earn his keep as soon as he was able, beginning work in Buik's ropeworks. Like many another young lad growing up in what was then a busy seaport, he dreamed of going away to sea. He told Myles: "I used to go down to the harbour every night – look at the ships and listen to the sailors. At last, without my father's knowledge, I got on board the *Antelope* as an apprentice. Our first voyage was to Newcastle and as I got a severe beating with a rope's end from the skipper, my love for the sea was somewhat cooled when I returned to Dundee, yet I did not desert my post. Our next voyage was to St Petersburg, where we took in a cargo for Rotterdam, and on our passage to that city, we were totally wrecked on one of the islands in the Zuyder Zee."

The crew survived. John Fergusson was left with only the trousers, shirt and stockings he was wearing. They made their way to Amsterdam and got home on a Dundee vessel. After this, he returned to work in the ropeworks for a few years before joining the army. He enlisted in an artillery regiment and, after seven years' service, was discharged, by his own account, about six weeks after the Battle of Waterloo. He returned to Dundee and to his father, who was still working as a porter in the coal yard.

A correspondent to the *People's Journal* in 1869, recalled Jock in the early 1820s. At this time, he worked as a heckler[30] for John McLeish at Meadowside:

"I first became acquainted with the subject of this sketch, whom my playmates, with juvenile discrimination, had designated 'Daft Jock'. John might have been safely admitted into an Anti-Labour Society without any other certificate than that of personal appearance. He only took as much of Adam's curse [work] as to ward off absolute starvation, consequently his moves were frequent. About 1822, he came to work with my father in his capacity of hackler, when, young

---

30 A heckler (or hackler) was a textile worker who teased or combed out flax or hemp fibres. The alternative meaning of "heckler" meaning to interrupt a speaker or performer is sometimes said to have originated in the Dundee mills where one worker would read out the day's news. The hecklers, who tended to be among the most radical elements in the workforce, would interrupt with comments and questions.

as I was, I took much pleasure in studying the varied phases of his strange character. 'Jock' was very talkative, and the subjects on which he delighted to descant were all embodied in his own person, consequently he disliked adult society, preferring to practice on the incredulity of childhood. 'Jock' professed to have been a soldier. This, however, we never believed, although we listened with apparent wonder and delight to his rehearsal of desperate deeds done by him in Spain and other far-away parts of the world."

This passage demonstrates the view of Pie Jock as a work-shy individual of limited intelligence that persisted down the years. This might be a fair representation but then again it may simply be that many people's memories of him, including those consulted by George Martin, date from when they were children. For many children Pie Jock was a figure of fun and someone they would taunt in the street. The young man and his friends might never have believed in Jock as a soldier and his exploits during that time, but this does not mean to say that he believed his own stories either. Rather, he might have been seeking simply to entertain the youngsters. James Myles thought that Jock was someone who was "the very opposite of constitutionally heroic" and so was interested to ask him if he was ever engaged in battle during his time in the army. Fergusson's reply was far removed from the tales of derring-do with which he had regaled the children: "Oh dear, no," he said. "Thank God I never killed anybody."

Jock fell into a period of ill health which seems to have ended his time in paid employment. Ever resourceful, he bought a few shillings' worth of stock and began travelling the country selling hardware. He recalled that he "did pretty well for some time" at this trade. The *People's Journal* correspondent who had first met Jock as a heckler next encountered him in his guise as a hardware salesman. He recalled: "an unaccountable noise was heard on the stair, as if a canine quadruped had been ascending with some tin-plate manufacture attached to his posterior appendage. I cautiously approached the door, and on opening it, who stood before me but the veritable 'Jock,' clad from head to foot with flagons, pans, coffee pots, and jugs – no bad personation of an iron-clad warrior of a former age."

Things could be dangerous for an itinerant salesman in the first half of the nineteenth century, though. One day, Jock came into Dundee and spent all his money on new stock. He then set out on his route to Arbroath but was attacked at Monifieth by a notorious gang of thieves known as "Wallace's Gang". They left him with nothing but an empty basket. Not to be defeated, Jock described his next move in the interview with James Myles: "I borrowed a shilling from my father, bought 'tape and stringin" and lived for a few years by selling these two articles alone. I had large profits. If I sold a shilling's worth I has seventeen pence clear."

When his health improved, Jock began to deliver bread to the bakers in town for five shillings a week and spent the next three years doing this until a baker in the Murraygate[31] got a portable oven made for him. The oven was said to resemble a barrel organ in its size and shape. "It was slung round my neck by a large belt," he remembered, "and contained a neat fire department with accommodation for a few dozen of the penny and two-penny pies." It goes without saying that this was the cause of the soubriquet, "Pie Jock". "I never mind," he told Myles, "names dinna brak banes."

In *Dundee Worthies*[32], George Martin tells how much of a treat a hot pie would have been for people in the first half of the nineteenth century: "Pies were not so rife then as they are now, and 'siller' was not so rife either, the wages of a vast number of working people not exceeding 6s. or 7s. a week. 'There were not many fine things in those days,' said an elderly lady to me, whom I interviewed with the view of obtaining reminiscences of the pie-vendor, 'and a tuppenny pie from Pie Jock on a Saturday night was regarded as a great luxury'."

Jock at one time had a sweetheart who lived in Heans Lane, which was just off Small's Wynd. When he visited his customers there, the object of his affections would be favoured with a pie free of charge. One night, though, Jock was sold out by the time he reached her and the expected pie was not delivered. Clearly put out by this, the young lady asked where her pie was adding: "You're no my lad unless I get my pie." Jock's affections were clearly not for sale, however and he replied: "If you're only my lass for my pies guid nicht. My lass min be my lass, pie or no pie."

Jock recalled that he made a good living out of the pies, most of the time: "At times I did extremely well, especially on a Saturday night. In the winter time, I have often on a Saturday night sold 30 shillings worth of pies, which yielded me a profit of five shillings but then, on other nights through the course

---

31   Martin says that Jock worked for Mr Peebles in the Perth Road and he may well have done so in later years.
32   Martin, George M., *Dundee Worthies – Reminiscences, Games, Amusements* (1934), Dundee: David Winter and Son, pages 13-15.

of the week I made little or nothing. I have frequently on a cold stormy winter night wandered on the streets with my oven and pies from half past seven to half past twelve at night and only drawn one shilling which yielded me twopence for my five hours hard work."

Nevertheless, it might have been thought that he would have remained in the pie business as long as he was able, but he suddenly quit. Martin speculates that this was because of increased competition and the decline in the demand for pies, which caused the baker to dispense with Jock's services. The real reason appears to have been forgotten by the time *Dundee Worthies* was published. Martin writes that Jock never married but, as he himself put it: "unfortunately I fell in love with a woman in Lochee".

In September 1843, he married that Lochee woman, Helen Glennie. This was to change Jock's fate, as he recalled: "My wife insisted on me to drop the pies as she did not like to hear the boys and girls calling me "Pie Jock" so I began to manufacture healing ointment and writing ink but I made poorly out with them. They did not pay so well as the pies and still the youngsters called me by the old name and my wife was seized by mortification and died."

It is little wonder that Helen Glennie did not like the abuse her husband received. George Martin tells how Fergusson was often annoyed by boys who would jostle him or pull at his basket shouting, "Pie Jock!" and sometimes singing:

"Pie Jock beats them a',
For he's been up and round the moon
Wi' John o' Arnha"[33]

Martin goes onto say that, "the harmless creature was often so provoked that he would suddenly turn round upon his assailants and chase them, meanwhile also threatening to beat them with his stick". This would have undoubtedly encouraged rather than deterred the children. Unsurprisingly, Fergusson preferred the smaller towns away from Dundee to sell his wares. He told Myles: "the laddies there do not know me, and they do not meddle and cry 'Pie Jock'. I like the laddies of Broughty Ferry, they are quiet and decent."

---

33 John Findlay was a Montrose Town Officer in the early nineteenth century. He was known for telling boastful and exaggerated stories about himself and his adventures. George Beattie wrote a comic poem about him called John o'Arnha which featured Findlay in some even more unlikely situations. 'Arnha' is thought to relate to Arnhall, near Edzell.

After the death of his wife, Jock did not return to his former trade as he did not feel he had the strength to carry the oven and pies through the streets. Instead he began to sell "speeches" and peppermint water as well as continuing in the ink and ointment trade. The latter business could sometimes be lucrative as he explained: "The ointment, ye see, is first rate. You would wonder how easy it is to make folk believe that they can cure anything. It costs me little or nothing and sometimes I sell three boxes in a day."

Most of Jock's income in this period came from selling what he called "speeches" – presumably the broadside leaflets that were the tabloids of their day. These single sheets carried news, speeches or songs, though Jock seems to have specialised in obituaries. Once again, for a man who was supposedly of limited intelligence, he had his profit margins well calculated: "I buy them, ye see, at three halfpence the dozen, and if I sell a single dozen in a day, I make 4 ½ d of profit. Now, I can live on 2s a week and 2s 6 d does me nicely. When there's anything startling in the 'speech' line I often sell six dozen in the day but there are many bad days I can get none to hawk and taking the good with the bad, I do not average more than 3 s 6 d a week."

Some subjects for the "speeches" proved more profitable than others. The fatal stabbing of a young man named John Crombie outside the Howff in March 1850, led to the sale of many dozens of leaflets, some sold as far away as Kirkcaldy. The death of Sir Robert Peel, on the other hand, in July that same year resulted in relatively few sales.

The public appetite for such material was readily catered for in this period by the *Police Gazette*, which was published every Friday by Messrs Douglas and Brown in the Scouringburn and contained reports of the cases that had been tried during the week in the police court. It sold for one halfpenny and Jock became its principal vendor. George Martin recounts his sales technique in *Dundee Worthies*:

"Jock would remain on the High Street all Saturday night up to the latest hour, peregrinating through the seething crowds, and crying: 'P'lice Gazeet; this week! Great crimes th' day, an' a' Irish!' On the following Saturday his cry would perhaps be different, such as 'P'lice Gazeet, this week; great crimes; the Scotch as bad's the Irish'."

One man remembered another way that Jock would adapt his customary cry of "Great crimes! great crimes!":

"When he knew the name of any particular delinquent, out it came. 'So-and-so's in this week' and should he err again, it was a grand catch for Jock. 'Aye, here he is - in this week again'. On one occasion there was nothing particular to notice; but Jock could not allow the excitement to die down, so he bawls out, 'Come awa', they're a' in thegither this week'."

The names of some of the miscreants allowed Jock to display a degree of wit: "There never was the like o' this ane. There's Willie Lamb took up for shootin' doos oot at Pitalpin. The Bailie lat Will aff on account o't no being proved, but he had nae doots o' the lamb's wolfish deed."

The *Police Gazette* had a huge circulation but ceased publication after falling foul of the authorities. Jock went back to selling his usual wares, supplemented by matches, blacking, and blue dye. He lived out the rest of his days in a room at Ritchie's Lane, which runs between Hawkhill and Perth Road. He lived to the age of 70, quite an achievement for a poor man in this era. A neighbour, Peter Gray, described the sad circumstances surrounding his death: "For some days previous to his death he was very ill. On Wednesday, at his urgent request, and seeing he was in a very dangerous state, I went to the offices of the Parochial Board of Dundee (from which he had been in the receipt of one shilling a week) and stated that he was evidently in a dying state and that his destitute condition required immediate medical and other aid. I got the shilling and the person I saw in the office stated that the Inspector was out, but that the moment he came, attention would be given to the matter. In case of any neglect, I called back in about half an hour and again pressed upon them the urgency of the case, offering if they would give me a 'line' to go for the doctor myself, when I was told that the Sub-Inspector was now in, so that I need give myself no further trouble. With this assurance I went home. No doctor nor Inspector called, and the poor old man was found dead the next morning."

John Fergusson seems to have been a victim of many of the prejudices of the time in which he lived. James Myles, who conducted the interview quoted from above, gives the impression that the printed version consisted pretty much of Jock's own words. He says: "I give it in phraseology almost as plain as it was conveyed in." A modern reading of that phraseology might see a man whose life was blighted by poverty, ill health and ill treatment but yet who could still find ways to make a living and who understood the financial calculations necessary to get by. Myles, though, while he saw fit to "claim for poor John a respectable moral standing", appears to have viewed Fergusson's predicament as part of the natural order: "I have adduced him as an illustration of the truth that some men are naturally adapted for the humblest walks of life." There could only be one conclusion, Myles thought, on reading the interview: "The reader will, without doubt, guess that John, to speak in the language of the phrenologists, is a little deficient in the frontal regions of the brain, or if it is average in size it is inferior in texture and quality, as his mental status is by general consent placed among the genus called in the west of Scotland 'haverils' and in the east 'doited fouk'." The supposed science of phrenology suggested that certain areas of the brain had specific functions and that measurements of the human skull could determine the strength of those functions. Though easily dismissed as nonsense today, it was widely believed in his time and it may be that much of the opinion of John Fergusson as a "haveril" or simpleton stems from his appearance.

James Myles was a poet, author and bookshop owner, a reformer and Chartist sympathiser. He was a witty and intelligent man who died at the tragically young age of 32. That he even thought to write about and interview a humble street hawker in 1850 is truly remarkable and so we should not be too judgemental about the fact that he could only see John Fergusson through the prism of the ideas that held sway in his time. As we try to guess what Pie Jock was like as a person on the basis of the existing evidence about him presented here, we should be aware that we too cannot but help viewing things in light of the ideas that prevail in our own time.

One thing is certain, though. Thousands of people have been born, lived and died in Dundee since that July morning in 1863, when Pie Jock was found dead in his bed by his neighbours. Many of these have achieved great success in life and important positions in the city and beyond – yet their names are not recorded in local history books. Perhaps this is simply because there is still something that appeals about the image of the diminutive figure wandering the streets with the smoking pie oven strapped round his neck. It may be, though, that John Fergusson is the person responsible for starting Dundee's love affair with the humble "peh", which surely makes him as important a figure as any in its history.

Local hero? The story of David Webster

On 6 March 1874, news reached her home port of Greenock that the *Arracan*, a 1040-ton vessel which was carrying coal from Shields to Bombay, had been lost at sea after the cargo had caught fire. Following three explosions, the whole crew of nineteen had escaped the burning ship, however, departing in three boats. The captain and eight crew members had taken to a longboat, the first officer and four men had escaped in a gig, while the second mate and four others had left in a pinnace. These last two boats had attempted to stay together but soon became separated. Each of the three escape vessels had around fourteen days' worth of supplies.

Captain Leslie and his men were picked up after ten days at sea by a passing ship and arrived at Aden on 4 March. The gig and its crew landed at Cochin on 17 March. Days and then weeks began to pass, however, with no news of the pinnace and its crew of five. These must have been worrying times for the families and friends of the missing men, who must surely have begun to fear the worst. The relatively slow speed of communications in this period, though, must have given them some hope. It was perfectly possible that their loved ones had already been rescued and that the news had just not yet reached home.

Among these worried relatives was the family of the second mate of the *Arracan*, 24-year-old David Webster. The Websters lived at Loftus House, Broughty Ferry. David's father, Robert, was a successful grocer and was later involved in the wine and spirit trade in both Dundee and Broughty Ferry. He was also at various times a police commissioner, member of Dundee's Harbour Board, a Bailie, a magistrate and President of the Grocers' Benevolent Society. Status and relative wealth were no protection against personal tragedy in the Victorian era, though, and by the time that Robert Webster and his wife Elizabeth celebrated their Golden Wedding anniversary in 1892 (itself a remarkable achievement for the time), the couple had outlived nine of their thirteen children. David Webster was not among the nine, however, and on 27 April 1874, Robert Webster received a letter from his son from Calcutta dated the third of that month. He and the other crew members on the pinnace had been picked up by the *City of Manchester* under Captain Hardie on 20 March. They had been adrift in the open boat for thirty-three days and were 600 miles from the nearest land.

The surgeon on the *City of Manchester* described the state that the men were in when they came aboard: "They were in a very exhausted condition and could not stand on their feet, eyes staring from their sockets and perfect skeletons, their bodies covered with sores, their noses frayed with the strong sun, and altogether the most wretched and piteous sight ever I had the misfortune to behold. Their constant cry when lifted on board and laid down on mattresses covered with blankets, was, 'Water! Water!'"

David Webster arrived back in Dundee at the end of May, to the relief of

David Webster of the *Arracan*,

his family and friends. The tale he had to tell of the ordeal he had suffered, however, was worse than any of them could possibly have imagined. With him on the pinnace had been three sailors: Thomas Layford, William Davies and Francis Stobbie, and also a boy, John William Horner. After twenty-one days at sea, their food and water had run out and the men had offered a desperate and horrific solution to their plight: cannibalism. Webster remembered: "About five o'clock on the afternoon of the 10th, the men wanted to cast lots, but this I would not sanction. The men then cast lots among themselves and the lot fell upon the boy. They then woke me up and said they were going to take his life but I would not allow it. They were then quiet for some time till after dark, when they tried to take my life."

This time it was Horner who came to Webster's rescue by waking him up. Seeing that he was in possession of a gun, the men backed off. During the course of the next day, however, Webster awoke from a sleep to find them struggling to take the gun from him. Two hours after this, they again attempted to kill Horner, when Webster leapt up and stopped them, threatening to kill the first man who harmed the boy and throw him overboard. William Davies had his arm around the boy's neck at this point but on hearing Webster's threat began to plead for his life. Webster spared Davies, who remained quiet for the rest of the day but had clearly lost all reason.

Webster described what happened next: "Next day he attempted to sink the boat and refused to bail it out; when I again got him down, and only allowed him to get up when he promised to be still. Things went on in this way for the next two days, when he again refused to bail the boat, tried to sink her, and said he would have the boy's life before twelve hours. I then presented my gun at him and pulled the trigger..."

Nothing happened. The gun had failed. No sooner had Webster managed to get it working again than a bird flew over the boat. He fired and killed it. One of the men dived into the sea after it. The bird was eagerly ripped to pieces and devoured, according to Webster, feathers, bones and all. After this feast, the crew remained quiet for the next five days. They subsisted on the barnacles that attached themselves to the bottom of the boat and on jellyfish.

Webster's account continues: "the men became delirious and asked to be killed. One of them, Thomas Layford, of London, lay down exhausted and Davies struck him three blows on the head with an iron belaying pin, cutting his head badly. The blood was caught in a tin and drank between Davies, Layford and Francis Stobbie of Birmingham. After this I threw the belaying pin overboard along with some others and bandaged up his head."

The same day, Davies and Layford fought for an hour before collapsing exhausted. They shook hands but then started all over again an hour or two later. Webster lay keeping watch with Horner beside him through all of this insanity until their ordeal was brought to an end by the appearance of the *City of Manchester*. When they got on board, Thomas Layford dropped to his knees and thanked God for their deliverance.

There could be little doubt, it seemed, that David Webster's actions had been heroic. In July, an intimation was issued by the Board of Trade: "The Queen has conferred the Albert Medal of the second class on Mr David Webster, the late second mate of the barque *Arracan* of Greenock, residing at Broughty Ferry, Dundee." The Albert Medal had been instituted in 1866 in memory of the Queen's consort, Prince Albert, and was awarded to recognise the saving of life at sea.

There were leading articles in praise of Webster's bravery in the major London papers. The *Times* said: "To the nerve and coolness of Webster, the preservation of his own life and the lives of the four men whom he found under his command is due, and never was the Albert Medal more deservedly bestowed." The paper regretted, with some justification, that an award had not also been made to the cabin boy, Horner. The *Telegraph*, while appreciating that the Albert Medal was the highest civilian award available, felt that "something more in this instance might be given", suggesting a lieutenant's commission in the navy, a harbour-mastership, commission in the coastguard or a role at a dockyard or arsenal be given to Webster. His heroism, the paper said, was "worthy of the glorious old days when names such as those of Drake, Raleigh and Frobisher made England famous".

Not everybody, though, was quite so effusive in their praise for Webster. Nathaniel Leslie, the captain of the *Arracan*, gave the *Aberdeen Free Press* his side of the story. He had sharp criticisms of Webster and contrasted his behaviour with that of first mate Ferguson, who he thought should be given the Albert Medal for steering his men to safety, while, "a leather medal with a hole in the middle suspended with a hemp string might be substituted for the Albert Medal in Webster's case."

"From first to last," Captain Leslie said of Webster, "he has been a stubborn young man – for he is a beardless young man of 22 or 23 and not the veteran he has been spoken of being. Being little satisfied of the appearance of things after they were in the boats, the master offered to take Webster and the men who were with him into his own boat, but Webster refused, although there was sufficient room on board the captain's boat. And why, in the name of common sense, not to say competent seamanship, should his boat have had to toss about for thirty-one days when the first mate found no difficulty at all in steering to the place appointed." Leslie went on to say how Webster had been second mate on several vessels within the space of a year prior to joining the *Arracan*, clearly implying that – either because of his personality or lack of competence – he had difficulty holding down a position.

The paper also carried a statement from the first mate which told of the difficulties of keeping the escape boats together and again emphasised Webster's "stubborn" nature:

> "The second mate and all of his crew would go to sleep. Then I had to go running after them. On the 23rd [there was] a strong breeze and a heavy sea. I told him to heave to and ease his boat, but he would not do it. The next I saw he had stove [holed] his boat and had his sail down altogether. I went to see what was the matter and he was heaving everything out of the boat. I told him

not to or he would not be able to carry sail. However, he paid no attention to what I said so after the leak had been stopped I told him to heave her to… but he would not do it. I told him not to get away too far or we would be losing one another. However, I saw no more of him in the morning."

Webster was quick to hit back, writing a long letter to the *Courier* in which he stated that whereas the captain and the mate's boats were fully equipped with navigational instruments, he only had a quadrant and that this was why he did not have the same success in navigating his boat. He and his crew had certainly been asked by the captain to come on board his boat but Leslie had, at the same time, strongly advised him to keep in company with the mate as their boats could sail faster and he did not expect them to encounter bad weather. The first mate's statement that they would all go to sleep was "so absurd that it hardly requires contradiction" and a regular watch was kept all the time. Nor was the mate correct when he said that Webster had left him: "Instead of this, I went under his stern and asked him to give me a rope for the night but did not get it. I then asked him to show his light…When darkness came on we could not see his light." They had called out several times but received no answer. Webster had then "steered a course as near as I could guess by the stars and the rising of the sun". Finally, Webster stated: "until I was to be presented with the Albert Medal, I as well as my father, was in friendly correspondence with Captain Leslie".

Webster also enclosed a letter to his father from Captain Hardie of the *City of Manchester*, the ship which had rescued him and his crew. Hardie told how the rescued men had pointed at Webster and said that is the man who saved us. The captain was in no doubt that it was Webster who had prevented them all from cannibalism or madness. "I am sorry," Hardie wrote, "that his captain should be envious of the honour conferred on your son." This was a sentiment echoed in many of the letters to the press on the subject.

The debate raged on in the newspapers for several days with both Captain Leslie and David Webster taking to print again until Webster declared that he would not be taking any more notice of Captain Leslie's letters as both he and the public were "heartily sick of the controversy". The Dundee Marine Board, however, had taken these matters seriously. Webster's medal had been sent to Dundee by the Board of Trade and arrangements made for its presentation but, the day before this was due to happen, Captain Leslie's account of events had appeared in the press. Despite apparently not having the authority to do so, (its job was merely to present the medal that had already been awarded) the Marine Board sent the medal back to London and asked the Board of Trade to reconsider the award in the light of Leslie's letter.

When the reply came, it stated that having read Webster's response to the statement of Captain Leslie, the Board of Trade saw no reason to withhold the medal and it was duly sent back to Dundee to be presented to Webster. There was really no other decision that could have been reached. As a leading article in the *Courier* pointed out, Webster had not been awarded the medal because of "either his seamanship or his obedience to his superiors" and there was nothing in anything that Captain Leslie had said that disproved that if it was not for Webster, the boy Horner would have been killed and eaten. Horner's own bravery was finally recognised in November 1874 when the South Shields Marine Board on behalf of the Board of Trade presented him with "an aluminium binocular glass" for his gallant conduct in the open boat after the loss of the *Arracan*.

There is a sad postscript to the story of David Webster. In October 1897, he was first mate aboard the *Glenfinlas* of Liverpool when it left Newcastle, New South Wales, Australia bound for Manila. The ship never reached its destination and eventually all hope for her crew was abandoned. This time there was to be no miraculous return for the Broughty Ferry hero. His name and deeds slipped from the local consciousness as the years passed but surely deserve to be remembered.

Departure: The Lochee man who helped to change our way of death

On 18 October 1936, a 58-year-old woman named Minnie Anderson died at the Dundee Royal Infirmary. Two days later, her death notice appeared in the *Courier* and it was clear that the funeral arrangements would be very low key. The intimation ended with the words: "Funeral private. No flowers." Even today, it is likely that most people would read such a notice as suggesting that they should not attend unless asked to do so by the family. When the day of Minnie Anderson's funeral came around, however, the pews were crowded for the short and simple ceremony conducted by Rev. Hemming of St Paul's Episcopal Cathedral. Most of the congregation, though, according to a newspaper report, "consisted of persons unconnected with the deceased". The numbers were increased, the report said, by a party of members of an organisation called Dundee Women Citizens who attended because they happened to be visiting the premises at the time. The reason for all this interest is that Minnie Anderson's funeral was the first to take place in Dundee's new crematorium.

The crematorium had been formally opened by Lord Salvesen the previous week. Salvesen said at the ceremony that cremation was the most hygienic way of disposing of mortal remains and even called for it to be made compulsory. He envisioned cemeteries becoming a thing of the past, with the ground turned over to leisure use. Lord Provost Phinn, who also spoke, seemed more concerned with the value of the land. The site the Howff burial ground occupied, he said, was most valuable yet at one time it was an out of the way spot and it was thought possible that it would never encroach upon the centre of the city.

Phinn's concerns about urban expansion certainly had historical precedent. The reason that Mary, Queen of Scots had granted the Howff, the site of the former Greyfriar's monastery gardens, to Dundee as a burial ground in 1564 was because the previous one was the churchyard of St Clement in the very centre of the town (around the site of the City Square today). The Queen was aware that this was unhygienic and compared it with the situation in France where she grew up "within the realm of France and uther foreign parts there is na deid buryit in gret touns". As Phinn said, though, expansion of Dundee had led to the Howff itself being in the city centre.

This process was to continue in the future. Demand for city centre land was to lead to the removal of the "New Howff" at Constitution Road and its replacement with a multi-storey carpark in the 1960s. Even the new cemeteries which opened later in the nineteenth century at Balgay Hill and the Eastern at Arbroath Road are now in areas more built up than those who planned them could ever have imagined.

Lord Salvesen's concerns about hygiene would also have had resonance in Dundee. Before the newer cemeteries had opened, The Howff and the Logie Burying Ground at Lochee Road had become so overcrowded with burials that human bones were often brought to the surface when graves were dug. At Logie, there was often difficulty getting coffins into the ground so densely packed were the previous internments. There was real concern for public health at both sites. It is perhaps little wonder that some began to consider cremation as an alternative around this time.

In 1936, such was the fascination with the cremation process that the new crematorium building was opened to visitors for two hours every Sunday afternoon from October until the end of March 1937, attracting 3,000 visitors on one occasion. The crowds touring the premises, however, are likely to have been unaware of the important role in the cremation movement of a man from Lochee.

William Eassie was born at Lochee in 1832, the son of another William Eassie and his wife, Jean Boyd. Eassie senior, who had himself been born in Lochee in 1806, was a carpenter and wheelwright. Father and son would probably have lived out their lives in Lochee were it not for the pace of industrial change in this period. The coming of the railways took Eassie and his family to England where he worked on the East Lancashire Railway before establishing a timber business in Gloucester supplying railway sleepers to the Gloucester and Dean Forest Railway. The business expanded quickly, and by 1853, he employed some 200 men.

When the railway boom subsided, Eassie began to diversify, getting involved in the construction of houses and railway wagons. He built greenhouses for the Royal Agricultural Society's Show in Gloucester, and doors, windows and even complete buildings for export to Australia during the gold rush there. By Victorian standards, Eassie was a generous employer, treating his workers and their wives to a Christmas tea party, establishing a Mutual Benefit Club and allowing a half-day holiday on Saturdays. In 1854, he was elected to Gloucester Corporation as a Liberal.

The Crimean War brought more opportunity for Eassie. The British and French governments ordered prefabricated huts, of a type that Eassie had sent to Australia, to house the troops. In 1855, partially due to the campaigning of Florence Nightingale, the renowned engineer Isambard Kingdom Brunel was asked to design a hospital that could be manufactured at home and transported quickly and easily to the Crimea. Brunel wrote to Eassie in February 1855 asking for his help. The result of this was that Brunel designed the hospital buildings which were prefabricated at the Gloucester works and sent to the Dardanelles in Turkey for construction as the Renkioi military hospital.

William Eassie junior was sent there to help supervise the construction work. Some reports suggest that he had trained as an engineer under Brunel and it may be that this is how Brunel knew of his father's business. On the other hand, it might be that their association began at this time. In any case, there is little doubt that Brunel respected 23-year-old Eassie. He specifically asked that Eassie's initial role was expanded so that he became second engineer of the whole project and was given a captain's commission. Several of Eassie's obituaries describe him as a "favourite assistant" of the great man.

While in Crimea, young Eassie met Edmund Parkes and the surgeon Thomas Spencer Wells. All three went on archaeological digs, reputedly carrying out work on the site of the ancient city of Troy, long before the famous excavations carried out by Dr. Schliemann. How meticulous Eassie's work there was must be called into question. His obituary in the *British Medical Journal* says he went to excavate Troy with "a band of navvies". Nevertheless, it was the discovery of ashes in burial sites there that led him to consider the benefits of cremation.

In the 1870s, after the death of his father, William Eassie junior began to practise as a consulting sanitary engineer. In 1872 he published a book, *Healthy Houses*, which promoted the cause of sanitary reform. He was one of the founders of the Cremation Society of Great Britain in 1874 and became its honorary secretary. In 1875, he published *Cremation of the dead: its history and bearings upon public health*, which became the standard work on the subject, discussing its history in different cultures and its sanitary nature as well as the drawbacks of burial which he viewed as causing pollution. He also discussed what he saw as the lack of any prohibition of cremation in Christian scripture and the technicalities of cremating apparatus. Eassie's book and his work with the society slowly began to change people's minds on the subject.

In 1879, Eassie negotiated with the London Necropolis Company the purchase of a one-acre site at Woking for a crematorium, supervising the construction of its cremator. As engineer to the Cremation Society, Eassie attended many of the earliest cremations including that of Jeannette Pickersgill at Woking in 1885, the first legal cremation in Britain. Only two other cremations took place in the country that year, whereas in the twenty-first century around seventy-five percent of the dead are cremated. The fact that cremation is now so commonplace makes it easy to forget the extent to which Eassie and his associates were pioneers.

Largely forgotten in his birthplace, there is no memorial to William Eassie in his native Lochee but there is a tablet in the chapel of Woking Crematorium. He died at his home in London in 1888... and was buried![34]

---

34 Why would such a firm advocate of cremation have his remains consigned to the earth? The answer appears to be a religious one. Eassie was buried in St Mary's Roman Catholic cemetery at Kensal Green. His baptism was registered in the Church of Scotland but he may have become a Catholic later in life, perhaps when he married. At the time of his death the Catholic Church did not allow cremation – though this was later amended. While the Church still prefers "the pious custom of burial", it does not forbid cremation, "unless this is chosen for reasons which are contrary to Christian teaching". Some Christian denominations and other religions such as Islam and Judaism still do not allow cremation.